Red Dragon, Yellow Horse
The I Ching in Ritual & Meditation

The Red Dragon of Heaven descends from the light of the sky.
The Yellow Horse of Earth comes forth from the darkness of the Underworld.
Uniting in ecstasy, clashing in war, from their play arise all life and death.

This book is primarily concerned with the Book of Changes and its links to Taoism, the magickal practices of the Chinese Wu, and related schools of thought. My ambition has been to open up the I Ching so that it can be approached on several levels, all of which are important aspects of the overall whole.

Whereas most books on the I Ching focus on the system's oracles as a means to divination, my work builds on that important base to include the potential for magickal rites and meditations, blending traditional ideas with contemporary experimentation. In this way, it allows for a greater personal appreciation and assimilation of the primal elemental forces that underpin the Trigrams and Hexagrams. In doing so, it not only describes the basic tools appropriate for Chinese-style magick, but also explains the symbolism and esoteric theory behind their use.

Parallels that I have drawn between Taoism and other worldviews such as shamanism, Ninjutsu, Shinto, Thelema, and Tantra help to broaden and explain fundamental occult concepts. Hexagram correspondences bring together interpretations of the figures with related symbols, gods, ritual instruments, and appropriate magickal workings in a way never before attempted in a work on the I Ching.

—Richard Herne

About the Author

Richard Herne (Great Britain) has been actively involved in the study of many Eastern and Western magico-spiritual philosophies for twenty years. He teaches Thelemic pagan philosophy and is an official representative for the National Centre for English Cultural Tradition based at the University of Sheffield.

To Write to the Author

If you wish to contact the author or would like more information about this book, please write to the author in care of Llewellyn Worldwide and we will forward your request. Both the author and publisher appreciate hearing from you and learning of your enjoyment of this book and how it has helped you. Llewellyn Worldwide cannot guarantee that every letter written to the author can be answered, but all will be forwarded. Please write to:

Richard Herne
℅ Llewellyn Worldwide
P.O. Box 64383, Dept. 1-56718-207-0
St. Paul, MN 55164-0383, U.S.A.
Please enclose a self-addressed stamped envelope for reply,
or $1.00 to cover costs. If outside U.S.A., enclose
international postal reply coupon.

Many of Llewellyn's authors have websites with additional information and resources. For more information, please visit our website at
http://www.llewellyn.com

The I Ching in Ritual
& Meditation

Magick,
Shamanism
&
Taoism

Richard Herne

2001
Llewellyn Publications
St. Paul, Minnesota 55164-0383, U.S.A.

First Edition
First Printing, 2001

Book design by Donna Burch
Cover illustration © 2001 Mark Busacca
Cover design by Lisa Novak
Editing by Andrea Neff

The quoted material on page 33 originally appeared in Aleister Crowley's book *The Holy Books of Thelema*, York Beach, ME: Samuel Weiser, 1983, pp. 60–61. The quoted material on page 83 originally appeared in Aleister Crowley's book *Liber Aleph*, York Beach, ME: Samuel Weiser, 1991, p. 57. Used by permission.

The original black-and-white illustrations in this book appear courtesy of artist Tanith Hicks. Permission to use this artwork is gratefully acknowledged.

Illustrations of mudras (pages 91–95, 144, and 155–156) by Carrie Westfall.

The original Chinese character illustrations in part 4 were drawn by the author.

Library of Congress Cataloging-in-Publication Data

Herne, Richard, 1969–
   Magick, Shamanism & Taoism : the I ching in ritual & meditation / Richard Herne.
     p. cm.
   Includes bibliographical references and index.
   ISBN 1-56718-207-0
   1. Yi jing. 2. Taoism. I. Title.
PL2464.Z7 H47 2000
299'.512582—dc21   00-052029

Llewellyn Publications
A Division of Llewellyn Worldwide, Ltd.
P.O. Box 64383, Dept. 1-56718-207-0
St. Paul, MN 55164-0383, U.S.A.
www.llewellyn.com

Printed in the United States of America

Acknowledgments

My great thanks go out to all the friends and many other kind people of the Island and elsewhere, too numerous to mention all by name, who have given me their encouragement for this book. Special acknowledgment, though, must go to Tony and Fiona Trowbridge (yes, it's here at last!), and Frater D. in the north of Alba (Keep up the great work, and I hope this helps your quest!).

As always, my deepest love and gratitude are reserved for Tanith, for so many reasons that it would be impossible to list all of them. Thank you for your artwork, your magickal masks, and your continual support. Without your assistance and much valued trust in my work, this book might never have been written.

Contents

List of Figures and Mudras ix

Preface xi

PART ONE
History and Philosophy

Chinese Magick and Taoism 3

The Philosophy of the Way 27

PART TWO
The Temple and the Magickal Tools

Introduction 37

The Temple 39

The Ritual Sword 43

The Robe 47

Equipment for Making Talismans 49

The Bell 53

The Magick Mirror 55

The Drum 59

The Spirit Wand 61

The Fan 65

The Ritual Light 69

Incense 73

Mudra 77

PART THREE
Practical Magickal Work

Introduction 83

Banishing and Purification: Assuming the Form of Fudo . . . 89

Stone Warriors 97

Consecration of the Ritual Tools 101

Investigating the Hexagrams 103

Pathworkings 107

Chi-Kung and the Cosmic Winds 109

The Magick of Talismans 115

Mu-Jen 123

The Gate of Dreams 129

In O Musubi 137

Invoking the Dragon Force 141

Working with the Astral Body 147

The Mountain Invocation 155

K'un Meditation 159

Ch'ien Meditation 163

The Trigram Wheel 165

PART FOUR
The I Ching Hexagrams

Hexagram Table 171

Introduction 173

The Sixty-Four Hexagrams 175

Appendices

A: The Eight Taoist Immortals 305

B: I Ching, Tarot, and the Qabalah 315

C: Pronunciation of Chinese 319

D: A List of Gods, Goddesses, and Spirits 321

Chronology of the Chinese Dynasties 329

Glossary 331

Selected Bibliography and Further Reading 337

Index 341

List of Figures and Mudras

1. Lao-Tzu riding upon a water buffalo into the West
   (from a Sung dynasty incense burner) 10

2. Chang Tao-ling, founding father of religious Taoism
   (based on traditional Chinese paintings) 19

3. The Tai-Chi, representing the primal unity of Yin and Yang . . . 28

4. The fang-sheng 42

5. The ritual sword 45

6. Two types of ritual fans 67

7. Examples of Chinese lanterns 71

8. Fudo, god of wisdom and fire 90

Mudra 1. The Fists of Anger 91

Mudra 2. The Triangle of Fire 92

Mudra 3. Sword in the Scabbard 92

Mudra 4. Sword drawn from Scabbard;
   Scabbard placed on head 93

Mudra 5. Sword in the Scabbard 94

Mudra 6. Sword drawn from Scabbard, ready for use 94

Mudra 7. Sword in the Scabbard 95

9. Chinese characters for shih kan t'ang 98

10. The Seal of Lao-tzu 116

Contents

11. Chinese characters for *sheng* and *ch'i* 125

12. Chinese characters for Tsi-ku and *chao* 134

13. An example design for a Dragon Talisman 143

14. The dragon, symbol of the continuous creative
    movement of the Tao 143

Mudra 8. The Diamond Thunderbolt. Front view and back view 144

Mudra 9. Outer Bond 155

Mudra 10. Inner Bond 156

15. The sword of Lu T'ung-pin 306

16. The bottle gourd of Li T'ieh-kuai 307

17. The fish drum of Chang-kuo Lao 308

18. The castanets of Ts'ao Kuo-chiu 309

19. The flute of Han Hsiang-tzu 310

20. The fan of Chung-li Ch'uan 311

21. The basket of flowers of Lan Ts'ai-ho 312

22. The lotus of Ho Hsien-ku 313

Preface

The Red Dragon of Heaven descends from the light of the sky. The Yellow Horse of Earth comes forth from the darkness of the Underworld. Uniting in ecstasy, clashing in war, from their play arise all life and death.

 First and foremost, this book is concerned with both theoretical and practical magick and meditation. It is not intended to be just another translation of the I Ching, intended only for the purposes of divination.

My aim, instead, has been to create something that may help readers view the I Ching on a much more expansive and experiential level. I hope that they will see that it is more than just an oracular system or tool for analytical psychology, important though such aspects undoubtedly are.

The I Ching is comparable to the well-known Qabalistic Tree of Life. Like the other, it comprises a "cosmic map" that seeks to define categories for all the possible permutations of elements and circumstances that exist in the universal cycle of creation and destruction. As the Qabalah is inextricably linked to magickal practices and the magicians who perform them, so, too, for the I Ching. Sadly, however, scholars in the West have often viewed this association with open hostility, or else they have just ignored it. Yet, without an acknowledgement of this vital link, it is impossible to appreciate the very cultural roots to which the I Ching owes its existence, and from which it continues to draw energy and meaning.[1]

Since the Opium Wars in the nineteenth century opened the interior of China to an influx of European missionaries and literati, especially in the period after the Treaty of Tianjin of 1858 C.E., the I Ching has been subjected to a great deal of analysis. In the West, this has come primarily from three main sources: Christian or Christian-influenced scholars, who have sought to find within its pages an element of "ancient Chinese Christian-style thought," and whose comments often reflect such an obsession; academics who have a general interest in the anthropological history of the I Ching's development; and psychologists concerned with finding comparative concepts to various Jungian ideas. All these groups have certainly added to the available literature on Chinese philosophies, and have helped to open the I Ching and its Taoist links to investigation by the Western public. However, in many cases there seems to have been a desire to cleanse the Hexagrams of their "embarrassing" associations, such as ancient shamanism and magick. This has sometimes resulted in somewhat sterile presentations and translations that do not adequately reflect the primal elemental forces that form the bedrock of the I Ching's existence.

To be fair to Carl Jung, he was committed to presenting I Ching divination as an antidote to mindless Newtonian, materialistic, and mechanistic views of the cosmos. However, in seeking to rid the Hexagrams of a Western scientific notion of "causality," and hold them up as examples of "synchronicity" instead, I believe that he did not fully clarify the following essential points.

1. Divination, whether using the I Ching or any other system, is based on an understanding that the seeker's present circumstances are directly influenced by past action, either originating from that person or from other people. Such a combination of Then and Now formulates an image of that which is likely to be in the future if the course of the seeker's movement either remains unchanged or is adjusted according to any advice that the divination gives.

2. The fundamental principles of Taoist thought, and hence of the I Ching, are based on an acknowledgement of the motivating force of the Tao that operates in and through the entirety of the cosmos and all of its myriad beings. To the sage, in an esoteric sense, synchronicity and causality are but two sides of the same coin; they are not necessarily separate and incompatible ideas. The links between seemingly unrelated yet synchronous physical events—such as the "random" selection of a Hexagram and the circumstances to which the divination refers—is certainly not discernible to the rational mind; in ordinary situations, the cause of the one is not necessarily the cause of the other. However, in an ideal situation where the seekers are following out the course of their Tao without interference, it is that subtle yet supreme actuating principle that both speaks through oracles such as the I Ching and motivates the Tao-jen's other physical actions. In that case, synchronicity and causality are one and the same.[2]

Yet, in practice, all such arguments are relatively academic. The fact is that divination, when properly performed, is a potent investigative tool. In the end, does it really matter why it works?

I began my own personal and self-motivated investigations into the occult and paganism at the very young age of ten, much against my family's wishes. Five years later I embraced Aleister Crowley's system of Thelema as my own, and, since then, I have never looked back. As part of this ongoing personal quest, I have been keen to seek out parallels to various Western magickal theories and practices in the spiritual systems of the East. As a result, I have delighted in ploughing the fertile grounds of philosophies such as Taoism and Tantra, and the I Ching has been a constant companion to me. Past training and study in shukokai karate and the Shaolin styles of kung fu have also given me much inspiration. The current book has therefore been written with the influences of this somewhat broad background very much in mind, and is consequently a little different from other titles that deal with the I Ching. I make no apologies for pointing out the similarities between certain cultural views where necessary, or for their active fusion in the development of new techniques in tune with the Will/Tao.

Finally, on a technical note, although I habitually use the pronouns and possessive pronouns "he" and "his," and so forth, throughout this book, I have done so purely for ease of writing and not because I'm a misogynist. In no way do I wish to imply that women are not the equals of men when it comes to magico-spiritual matters; as a matter of fact, they're very often better!

WILL
———
LOVE

---

1. Negative comments on the role of magick in the development of the I Ching and its parent system of Taoism can be readily found in the works of two of the West's most prominent Sinologists, namely James Legge and Richard Wilhelm.

2. For Jung's own view on the matter, see his foreword to Richard Wilhelm's translation of the I Ching, *I Ching or Book or Changes* (London: Arkana, 1989).

PART ONE

History and Philosophy

Chinese Magick and Taoism

The influence of occult ideas on Chinese civilization has a notable and venerable history, stretching back many thousands of years and with a force that continues to affect present-day thoughts and actions across the globe. Many people in the Western world are aware of such subjects as the Tao, Yin and Yang, the I Ching, and so on; the ever-increasing popularity of the Book of Changes, as a system of divination, attests to a perennial fascination with Eastern spirituality. However, the history of metaphysics in China, and the extent to which related philosophical viewpoints have actually operated within Chinese society, remain a closed book to many.

In order to attempt to understand the nature of such theories and the techniques derived from them, in a truly holistic manner, it is beneficial to study the actual culture in which they were created or developed. This may seem like self-evident advice, but it never ceases to amaze me just how many people who are interested in matters such as Taoism and the I Ching know little about China as a whole, and care even less for it. The development of all magickal systems, which have a lasting effect on people's attitudes to life, takes place within the context of human interaction and mutual learning. Such systems do not stand apart from the lives of their adherents, but continuously affect them on all levels of being, both esoteric and mundane.

Consequently, if you wish to discover as much as you can about Chinese magick, it is also a good idea to learn as much as possible about the links between the magico-spiritual and social history of the Chinese people. Such an area of study is obviously beyond the scope of this book, which is primarily concerned with working theory and practical experimentation. However, the following sections give a snapshot of this important area of research, and my hope is that it will stimulate a sympathetic desire in its readers to seek out more information in their own time.

Shamanism and Wu

When thinking of the magickal practices of China, the most common image that springs to mind is of the Taoist magicians and priests who have incorporated many such elements into their philosophy. However, it is not generally understood that the system of Taoism (Chin. *Tao chia*) arose from a bedrock already laid down by the actions of shamanistic practitioners and the animistic magicians known as Wu. Developed Taoist thought came into being as a direct result of such ancient background influences, and not in spite of them; this is an important point which should always be remembered if the history and philosophy of Taoism are to be at all understood.

Ancient Chinese shamanism held many ideas in common with other types of the practice, as found in such tribes as the Turanians of Central Asia and the Turkic and Tungusic inhabitants of Siberia. For instance, the shamans' most important and defining role was to act as the spiritual intermediaries for their local communities; by interacting with the gods and spirits while in a state of profound ecstasy, they were able to secure advantages for their people by the favor of those spirit-powers. If such a goal also required a shaman to go to war with a preternatural foe, depart on a dangerous mission into unsafe regions of the spirit-worlds, or fight with another shaman from an opposing tribe, then such acts would also be done on behalf of the community, no matter what the risk to body and soul.

Such ancient communion with the gods, and its consequent long-term effect on Chinese spiritual mentality, are attested to by the etymological history of an important Chinese word, *hsien*, commonly translated as "an Immortal." This word, in Chinese characters, literally means "a man and a mountain," and is thought to have reference to the practice of religious pilgrimages to sacred peaks carried out by Taoist devotees—acts that are thought to help speed up the process of human spiritual evolution. Yet, some scholars such as Arthur Cotterell have pointed out that *hsien* was originally written by characters that implied acts of drunken (i.e., ecstatic) dancing.[1] Sacred mountains, too, are forms of the axis mundi or World Pillar. So, the original "man on the mountain" was not a hermit or pilgrim, but a shaman whose arduous ascent to the summit was a physical imitation of a parallel climb in the spirit up the omphalic column to Heaven. The physical dangers encountered in the ascent were also comparable to the psychic ordeals that would be met with in the spirit-journey.

The strenuous activity of dance was an integral part of shamanistic trance-inducement and personal empowerment. It was also used in ceremonies designed to directly influence natural phenomena by sympathetic magickal methods, such as the production of vital rain by the deliberate encouragement of perspiration on the skin of the occult dancer. Interestingly, a Chinese word for supernatural/magickal power or spiritual force, *ling*, was in ancient times formed by word-characters that referred directly to the ecstatic trance-dances of shamans and their power to draw rain from the heavens on behalf of their agricultural communities.

By identification with the spirits of hunted animals, the shaman (Chin. *shen kun*, "a divine staff") was also able to increase the potential catch of such creatures. A pottery bowl dating from the fifth–fourth millennium B.C.E. shows a circular human mask with two fish attached to the head. This implement seems to have had a ritualistic or magickal function. Such an intention may have been to influence physical fish, by the use of the shaman's own piscine animal-spirit allies, so that they could be caught more easily and in greater numbers.[2]

Bearing an identical purpose to the "mountain at the center of Earth," one of the most abiding of sacred images to shamanistic practitioners, which may be seen in various forms across the globe, is that of the World Tree. This well-known symbol represents the shaman's universe, with all the dimensions of consciousness available to his traveling spirit, including the physical world, gathered about its vast and spreading form. By ascending the Tree into the heights of Heaven, or descending to its very roots in the dark bowels of the Underworld, the shaman is able to come into direct contact with spiritual entities. From these he may sometimes obtain occult powers that are vital to his own continued well-being and that of his tribe as a whole. By journeying through the various zones of the Tree, control can be gained over magickal beings who dwell therein and who are deemed to have important influence over differing aspects of the natural world. Such quests for power very often result in the acquisition of animal-spirit allies, whose tasks are then to act as sources of additional magickal energy that the shaman may draw upon when necessary, and to be his guides and defenders when he roams out of his physical body. The concept of the World Tree was so important to the early Chinese that it was depicted on some of their ancient cosmological and geographical maps. In Chinese mythology, the World Tree stood halfway between the sun's sacred place in the East, and the moon's in the West. Linking Heaven and Earth, it provided the passageway for journeying spirits and human adepts alike.

The magicians known as Wu also flourished in China prior to the formal establishment of the Taoist schools of thought. Like the shamans, they also continue to practice their arts to the present day. The word *wu* means "a magician, witch; magickal practices, etc.," and is properly applied to individuals whose occult acts contain marked ingredients of shamanistic and animistic origin. However, the term has also been somewhat wrongly applied by some scholars to any type of practicing occultist or Taoist magician. The writer Kenneth Grant has also suggested another interpretation, by defining the Wu as "white magicians," as opposed to the Ku who are practitioners of "black magick."[3] This, however, is unsatisfactory as it bears little resemblance to the actual role of Wu in Chinese society, where acts that may be considered by some Western commentators to be "black magick," may be viewed by the Wu themselves as essential for self-defense or the meting out of justice. Intellectually defined parameters are rarely precise in actual practice!

The Wu were originally responsible for conducting the ceremonies that brought the living into contact with their deceased ancestors. The need to obtain the approval and blessing of the dead for the acts of their descendants was, and remains, of critical importance to the harmony and well-being of Chinese society. Without the cooperation of the ancestor spirits, day-to-day affairs could not be guaranteed to go ahead without unnecessary difficulties. Enraged forebears could become dangerous *kuei*—ghosts that seek revenge for errors made by their families and try to do any amount of harm before being pacified, or banished by exorcism.[4] The act of *ming-ch'i* (Chin: "spirit items"), the ancient custom of burying objects with the dead, was designed to avert this sort of trouble by making useful items available to the deceased in the afterlife, as well as being an effort to protect bodies from attack by hostile supernatural forces. Sometimes, funerary talismans were carved from jade, often in the form of cicadas, and were placed in the mouths of corpses. In such cases, the goal was not only protection, but also to help the spirits of the dead be happily reborn into a new state of consciousness in the Otherworld, or to achieve successful reincarnation into a new physical body.

At times of ritual contact with the ancestors and other important spiritual entities, the Wuist magicians would allow their bodies to become the mediumistic vehicle for those discarnate beings. Sometimes, they would then cut their own tongues and press them onto paper. The resulting bloody impressions were subsequently divined as messages from the spirits. Considered to be magickally powerful, these shapes then gave rise to many later designs for magickal talismans.

An initiation ceremony carried out in certain Taoist schools may also have its distant origins in a similar spiritistic act. Among other requirements, prospective candidates were expected to ascend a symbolically significant "spirit ladder," the rungs of which were formed from blunt sword blades. In ancient times, this may have been a shamanistic act that used sharp-edged blades instead. The ascent up such a spirit ladder would have been intended to imitate the act of soul-flight to the celestial abodes of the gods, which was habitually carried out by the shamans in their trances. The emblem of a ladder to Heaven appears in the records of visions experienced by many tribal shamans. As one would expect, the sharp blades would have resulted in the magician's bare feet becoming badly lacerated. His blood, seething with potent magickal energy, would not have been wasted, and may have dripped down onto paper spread beneath the ladder. In the same manner as the "tongue talismans," the "random" shapes formed by the blood would have been viewed as powerful spells and portents revealed by the will of the gods, through the medium of the magician's physical suffering.[5]

The image of the spirit ladder also appears in many other cultures in both the Far and Middle East. In Japan, for instance, the Creation legend known as the *Kojiki* relates that the sun goddess Amaterasu, and her brother, the moon god Tsuki-yumi, were able to ascend the Ladder of Heaven into the Firmament, and hence shed their lights for the benefit of the newly formed Earth.[6] In ancient Egypt, the god Osiris, assisted by Heru-Ur (Elder Horus) and Set, was said to have gained access to the realm of Nuit, goddess of the arcing vault of Space, by means of a magickal ladder. As *The Egyptian Book of the Dead* declares, the spirits of the newly deceased also hoped to use this method, so that they, too, might shine as divine stars in the body of the Black Goddess. This explains the discovery of talismans in the shape of ladders in some Egyptian tombs.[7] Of course, there is also the very revealing Judaic story of Jacob's Ladder, a tale that has pronounced pre-Jewish shamanistic origins.

The Wu, who in practice are often indistinguishable from shamans, can be male or female. Some attempts have been made to show that it was mainly the province of women to act as spiritual representatives for early Chinese communities, and they do appear to have had prominence in funeral rites. However, the available evidence has not exclusively proved their total dominance in the role. Early dynastic rulers appointed many such people as court oracles, rainmakers, vital intermediaries between mankind and the spirits, and so on. The rulers themselves were also expected to play an important ritual part in keeping the essential spiritual balance between Heaven and Earth, thereby ensuring both the continuing fertility of the land and general harmony in the community. When unexpected drought or pestilence afflicted the country, and disorder reigned in human affairs, then the ruler was deemed to have failed in his task; Heaven had pronounced judgment on his lack of ability, and rebellion by the populace was often swift to follow. The Taoist master Chuang-tzu declared:

"Want of harmony between the Yin and Yang; unseasonableness of cold and heat, affecting all things injuriously; oppression and disorder among the feudal princes, their presuming to plunder and attack one another, to the injury of the people . . . these are the troubles of the Son of Heaven and his ministers."[8]

This particular concept of kingship is an ancient one, having a certain echo in the West in such cultures as that of the early Maya of Central America, where the sovereign was expected to physically suffer by ritually shedding his own blood for the good of his people. This was not intended to result in his death. The basic idea states that the right to rule exists only so long as the balance between the natural and seasonal periods of creation and destruction is kept level. Should the balance tip over, resulting in long-term and unusual hardships, then out the leader must go for the good of all, or in some other way he is expected to atone personally for his country's problems. In this way, harmony is restored to the land.

Interestingly, the Chinese word *Ti*, which is present in a number of god-names and was used by earthly Chinese sovereigns because it means "a ruler," was initially meant to refer to a ritual sacrifice. The word's ideograph seems to represent votive meat that has been placed upon a pyre. This is a reference to the fact that it was the emperor's job to take command of the regular sacrificial ceremonies, but it could also be seen as a double-entendre, implying that the one who gave the offering could also become one himself if he wasn't careful!

Lao-Tzu, the Tao-Teh Ching & Taoism

The first known record, in literature, of the Way of the Tao is ascribed to the famous and semi-legendary philosopher Lao-tzu. His date of birth is tentatively given as 604 B.C.E., but this seems to be a date of choice rather than a provable fact. Some scholars believe that he should be placed in the late fourth century B.C.E. Chinese legend states that he gestated in his mother's womb for seventy-two years, and when he was finally born, he had white hair and was a master of the magickal arts. This period of time is symbolically very significant, as it expresses the idea that Lao-tzu had gained full knowledge of the interacting and codependent forces of Yin and Yang, which have their origin in the ever-pregnant Womb of the Tao from which all manifested things have ultimately sprung. Nine is a number associated with Yang, while eight reflects the force of

Yin: 9 x 8 = 72. This idea of great occult mastery is further emphasized by Lao-tzu's white hair, which is a traditional indicator of sagaciousness; a similar tale is told of Zal, the great cultural hero of the Persians. By virtue of his unity with the Tao, Lao-tzu acquired the ability to magickally manipulate the energies of Heaven and Earth, according to the needs of his Way.

The name *Lao-tzu* is simply a title that means "Old Master," such as one might naturally give to an ancient and revered sage. However, he is also known by the names Li Erh and Lao Tan. According to certain sources, the Confucians also gave him the rather unflattering and insulting nickname "The Madman of Chou"—i.e., of the Chou dynasty which reigned at the supposed time of Lao-tzu's earthly life.[9] He is said to have worked as the chief archivist of the Chou official records at Loyang, the ancient capital of the Chou rulers. Little else is known of his life—tales that claim he socialized with Confucius seem to be fictional—until his legendary exodus from China, date unknown.

According to the *Shi Chi*, the historical records compiled by the historian Ssu-ma Ch'ien around 100 B.C.E., Lao-tzu was presciently aware of the impending decay of the Chou state, and sought to leave the country before disaster struck. At length, he came to the Han-ku Pass. Here there dwelt a border guard by the name of Yin Hsi. He was already aware of the sage's reputation for great wisdom, and so asked him to leave a book of instruction on the Way of the Tao and how human beings should live in accordance with it. Lao-tzu proceeded to do this, and it resulted in the eighty-one verses of the *Tao-teh Ching*, "The Classical Book of the Way and its Power."

Having left this book with the guard, the great sage then departed for the distant West, riding upon a water buffalo (see figure 1). Some tales say that he eventually crossed over the border into Tibet, others that he turned up in India. Either way, physically speaking, he was never seen or heard from again by the Chinese. Some scholars consider that his symbolic journey westward merely indicates that he died—the West being seen as the quarter most associated with the dead—and that the lack of a known tomb or place of death for the man simply indicates the idea that ancestor rites were insignificant to the ancient Taoist priests. Yet, it may also be the case that the story refers to the idea that Lao-tzu did not expire in the conventional sense, but obtained immortality by his Taoist skills and became a *Hsien*, an enlightened and, usually, ever-living being. The West is said to be a sacred zone of the Hsien, who have a special connection to the ancient goddess of magick, Hsi-wang-mu, "the Queen Mother" of the Western Paradise. She traditionally owns the sacred Peach of Immortality, which is a

Figure 1. Lao-Tzu riding upon a water buffalo into the West (from a Sung dynasty incense burner).

secret reference to the female genitalia and the mysteries of longevity inherent in Taoist sexual practices.

Hsien are said to come in a variety of categories and guises, not all human: *T'ien Hsien* (celestial and godlike beings who live permanently among the deities); *Shen Hsien* (immortals of a nonhuman nature, such as animal-spirits or other magickal beings who are incarnated on Earth for a limited time and then return to the spiritual state); *Shih Chieh Hsien* (immortals who possess no ties to a physical body); *Jen Hsien* (immortals who were once human and then attained a form of privileged eternal life in Heaven); and *Ti Hsien* (earthly Taoist adepts who achieve physical immortality and who remain in the human world in order to teach their wisdom to others; a famous example of this type is Li T'ieh-kuai, one of the Eight Taoist Immortals who are described in greater detail in appendix A).

In Japan, these magickally advanced beings are known as *Sennin*, and many tales are told of their fantastic powers and occult prowess. They have also been occasionally linked to some of the ninja groups. Some Chinese also say that some Hsien have attained longevity, but not full physical immortality. These reclusive occult masters

10

then elect to take on the role of secretly teaching to chosen students the deepest mysteries of the Tao, away from the prying eyes of the merely curious, and revealing themselves only to those most worthy of their knowledge.

Although the *Tao-teh Ching* was the first text to set down the philosophical principles of Tao chia, contrary to popular opinion such ideas did not originate with Lao-tzu. It is likely that they were in existence for some centuries prior to the time of the sage's life, and were built upon the foundation of shamanistic and Wuist theories and practices. References within the *Tao-teh Ching* itself state that Lao-tzu was merely setting down, in writing, wisdom that was already ancient by his time:

"The skillful masters of the Tao in old times, with a subtle and exquisite penetration, comprehended its mysteries . . ."[10]

However, such principles really only began to come into their own, and have a marked effect on the development of Chinese society, after the era of the "Old Master." The Chan Kuo period of the Warring States (480–222 B.C.E.) saw the collapse of the lands ruled by the Chou kings. Principalities fought against each other incessantly, and into this political turbulence stepped various philosophical and spiritual factions who wished to impart some stability to an increasingly bad situation. Each had its own particular views on how best to achieve this end. Five main groups argued their various positions: Legalists (Chin. *Fa chia*), who believed in extreme authority, and encouraged the enactment of some very harsh laws; Mo-ists (*Mo chia*) who espoused poverty as being the greatest moral virtue; Naturalists (*Yin-Yang chia*) who, like the Taoists, saw Nature as being based on the fundamental duality of Yin and Yang; Confucians (*Ju chia*), who believed in the importance of filial piety, social hierarchy, and the necessity of a feudal state; and Taoists. Of these, only the last two ultimately survived as organized and distinct systems of thought, though the others were also absorbed into general Chinese consciousness to a greater or lesser extent.

Their social sense being directly determined by their magickal practices and mystical experiences, Taoists consequently believed that a straitjacket of laws imposed by the state onto people was not the way to sort out the country's ills. Instead, it was considered to be merely a reflection of humanity's increasing movement away from the natural and spiritual way of life. In the Taoist view, humankind needed to return to the fundamental teachings of the Tao, and free itself from the stress of artificial social structures. If people were in tune with the Way, minding their own business and individually following out their true Paths as the Tao moved them, then there would be no need for human laws, politics, benevolence, or charity. Each person would naturally, and automatically, respect and support the rights of others without having to be told to do so or because altruistic acts were considered to be meritorious. To the Taoists, laws could also be self-defeating, as they often created the very problems that they were supposed to prevent; in short, the more legislation, the worse the state of the nation.

However, in practical terms, Taoists recognized that such an ideal was not an instant solution, and that the majority of people were sadly in need of a legal structure to guide them. Yet, they believed that this should be limited to an absolute minimum, and should not do anything to infringe individual freedom or reduce genuine self-expression; otherwise, only misery could result. Social constructs such as family and society were also believed to be important only so far as they reflected and supported the uniqueness of their constituent members, rather than being used as excuses to create arbitrary class and domestic hierarchies for their own sake that had to be stuck to rigidly and that represented the only "right" way to live.

This was in direct opposition to the nonmystical and feudal Confucians, for whom all such Taoist ideas were the height of irresponsibility. They strenuously resisted all "deviation from propriety," and it was their viewpoint that ultimately prevailed with the governing powers—not surprisingly, given that the inevitable outcome of a Taoist victory would have been the lessening of the rulers' powers!

Inability to influence the warring chiefs led the Taoists, on the whole, to reject public affairs. Although some of them are famous for having adopted the lifestyles of recluses, living in caves on the slopes of sacred mountains, such a choice had just as much to do with exasperation over the state of politics as with a need to gain an uninterrupted and closer attachment to the Tao. This, and their desire to study Nature firsthand, on both a mystical and physical level, led the Confucians to call them "those irresponsible hermits!"

In time, Taoist magico-religious principles were further expounded by sages such as Chuang-tzu (350–275 B.C.E.), whose proper name is really Chuang Chou. He was considered to be a worthy spiritual descendant of Lao-tzu, and his wisdom was esteemed throughout the land—so much so that he was even offered the job of prime minister of the state of Chou, which he rejected on the grounds that his Taoist principles would have been inevitably compromised by the strictness of Confucian bureaucratic life. He is well-known as the author of many important Taoist texts, and is renowned for an episode that asks many questions regarding the nature of "reality": While asleep one day, he dreamed that he was a butterfly. On awakening, he announced to his waiting students that he was uncertain whether he was a man who had been dreaming that he was a butterfly, or really a butterfly who was now dreaming that he was a man.[11]

As previously mentioned, the Taoist magicians and priests incorporated many elements from the practices of the shamans and Wu into their own burgeoning magico-spiritual system. An important example of this can be seen in the way that trance-dances were enthusiastically embraced as ways to attain altered states of consciousness. One instance of this is the ritual of the *Yu-Pu,* "the Walk of Yu." Here, the priest goes through a series of well-defined steps that seek to mimic a magickal dance used by an ancient demigod and hero called Yu. This deity was said to have tamed the Primal Flood, and could turn himself into a bear at will. By using this ritual, the Taoist invokes the power of Yu, and, as a consequence, astrally shape-shifts into the bear form—all in the great tradition of shamanism. In practical terms, this rite is also used to control snakes and catch errant spirits.

However, in spite of their close links, Taoist philosophers and the Wu did not always see eye to eye. Rivalry sometimes existed, and at times some of the early Taoists sought to present themselves as being superior to their shamanistic cousins. In an anecdote related by Chuang-tzu, a certain adept of the Tao is depicted as regularly outwitting and confusing the clairvoyant talents of a Wu with his own power of thought control and an ability to manipulate the currents of Yin and Yang within his body. The tale looks like a vain attempt by some of the Taoists to distance themselves from their own roots.

At the time of Chuang-tzu, the use of *chi-kung,* breathing techniques akin to the yogic *pranayama,* was also becoming widespread among the Taoists. Initially, this process was intended to be used as an additional aid to other meditative and magickal techniques that were designed to bring the adept into a closer union with the Tao. Also, the increased generation of ch'i was—and remains—an important component of healing practices. At a later date, chi-kung was also incorporated into some of the martial arts, in order to increase the personal power and strength of warriors. However, as the techniques have the potential to increase the length of human life, it was found that some practitioners were beginning to focus on this goal to the exclusion of all else. Chuang-tzu scoffed at those who attempted to extend their lives with no thought of any other kind to personal evolution:

"Blowing and breathing with open mouth; inhaling and exhaling the breath; expelling the old breath and taking in new; passing their time like the dormant bear, and stretching and twisting the neck like a bird; all this simply shows the desire for longevity."[12]

Some commentators have suggested, on the basis of the above passage, that Chuang-tzu was wholly against the idea of physical longevity. In my opinion, this is not the correct view, as a study of his other writings will show that he was quite happy to accept the possibility of extended life; however, he believed that it should not be sought after but allowed to occur naturally, if considered necessary for a person's Path. He felt that it should come about as a result of mystical oneness with the omnipresent Tao, rather than through deliberate acts designed to achieve long life and nothing else.

To some groups, Taoism became increasingly synonymous with the desire for immortality, and they often took little notice of other important philosophical principles. Their quest led them to develop chi-kung still further, and to alchemical experimentation with often deadly plants and minerals.

In 221 B.C.E., the ruler of the Ch'in state, Ch'in Shih-huang-ti, completed his annexation of all other neighboring lands, which he had begun in 230 B.C.E. He became the first emperor of a unified China, which is named after his dynasty. The Emperor is renowned for having ordered the construction of the Great Wall, and is particularly well-known for his famous funereal Terracotta Army. A supreme tactician, he not only roundly defeated all his enemies, but also drastically reorganized Chinese bureaucracy. What is not so well-known is that the man was renowned by his contemporaries for his immense brutality toward his subjects. He was also consumed by an obsessive fear of his own death. In order to avoid that final journey to his ancestors, Ch'in Shih-huang-ti went to great lengths to attract, and hold, many Taoist magicians. He demanded that they create for him an Elixir of Life. Of course, facing the threat of their own premature deaths if they refused, not many were to reject such a "request." They were given the resources to experiment, and this period saw a consequent proliferation in new alchemical ideas. The Emperor also sent out expeditions into the eastern seas to search for Peng-lai, one of a series of legendary islands that were said, like the Western Paradise of Hsi-wang-mu, to house the immortals and to hold the secrets of eternal life. One ship was even said to have had a crew comprised entirely of children! None of these explorers ever returned home; either they were all shipwrecked and drowned, or else some may have taken the opportunity to escape from the Emperor's clutches. Chinese legends state that some of these fugitives went on to colonize the islands of Japan, though there is no proof to support this idea.

In 212 B.C.E., the Taoists and other scholars finally decided that they had suffered quite enough at the hands of the Emperor. They fled from the capital in secret, and began a campaign of verbal defiance against his regime. Four hundred and sixty of these rebels were subsequently rounded up and executed, while others who also did not manage to evade the hunt were banished to hostile border areas.

Yet, for all this display of imperial power, Shih-huang-ti remained as distant from the Tao, and his desire, as ever. He died at the relatively young age of forty-eight during a tour of his eastern lands. For a man so bent on holding off death by preternatural means, which he so desperately sought by the enslavement and torture of those wiser than himself, the final manner of his death seems like very ironic justice. He is said to have had a dream in which he fought a sea-god. Advisors suggested that this was a sign that he should kill a great creature of the deep, and that this act would finally secure his luck, achieve his aim for immortality, and, to cap it all off, raise him to the rank of a god. Dutifully, he then killed a whale with a crossbow. Within a month, he became mysteriously ill and died. Did the advisors know more about the message of that dream than they chose to tell their hated Emperor?

The I Ching

By the time of the First Emperor's reign, the I Ching—"The Classical Book of Transformations," better known as "The Book of Changes"—was already considered to be an important magickal and mystical text that enshrined many Taoist and pre-Taoist principles and esoteric lore. In 213 B.C.E., the Grand Councilor to Shih-huang-ti, a man by the name of Li Ssu, called for the infamous Burning of the Books. The goal was to extinguish all texts other than those that dealt with official Ch'in records, medicine, agriculture, official court ceremonies, and divination. Of the latter type, the I Ching was considered to be a vital source book, though by no means the only one.

The history and development of the I Ching is worthy of many separate volumes, but a few words here will help to introduce those who are new to the subject. Chinese legends say that the first elements of the system arose during the time of Fu-hsi. This primal and antediluvian deity is often depicted in art as part man, part snake; in some pictures he is shown coupled with his twin sister, Nu-kua, in a helix pattern reminiscent of the Caduceus symbol and the awakened Kundalini of Tantric Yoga. Fu-hsi is credited with bringing the arts and crafts of civilization to humankind, including the knowledge of the Trigrams—the nuclear Eight Diagrams (Chin. *Pa Kua*) of the I

Ching system. These mystical, linear figures are said to have been derived from markings on the back of a "dragon-horse" (alternative legends say a tortoise or turtle) that rose from the waters of the Yellow River. They comprise a binary system of eight permutations of unbroken Yang lines (_____) and broken Yin lines (__ __). Each of the Diagrams is formed from three such lines placed in a short column arrangement, and together they represent various planetary and elemental aspects of the cosmos (such as Heaven, Earth, Fire/Sun, Water/Moon, etc.). The various combinations of broken and unbroken lines show the strength of the Yin and Yang forces at work. At a later date, these Eight Diagrams were then expanded into the full contingent of the Sixty-Four Hexagrams by multiplying them by themselves (i.e., 8 x 8); this represents the complex spiritual interaction in the universe of the different cosmic aspects, and their associated reactions in the phenomenal worlds. So, when used in divination, the Hexagrams indicate which of these interactions best captures the nature and direction of both the querent and the querent's question at the time the reading is carried out.

Archaeological evidence shows that the system of divination used by the I Ching is based on the ancient use of oracle bones and tortoise shells. Here, questions requiring answers from the spirits would be scratched onto the bones (usually the scapulae of oxen), or the plastrons of turtles (the parts of the shells that cover the animals' breasts). These were then subjected to great heat, possibly from a source applied directly to the objects. This would then cause cracks to appear on the surfaces, and these were looked upon as being the desired divine responses, and were interpreted by the Wu accordingly. Large numbers of these oracles have been found during excavations, and in addition to increasing our knowledge concerning the importance of divination in ancient Chinese culture, they also offer valuable information on the evolution of the Chinese writing system itself.

From this foundation came the use of yarrow stalks as divinatory tools. This plant was not the common *Achillea millefolium*—commonly called milfoil—that we know in the West, but true Chinese yarrow, *Achillea sibirica*. As with the tortoise-shell and bones, this plant was regarded as being particularly sacred, and was thought to be naturally invested with great spirit-force. The author of *The Sirius Mystery*, Robert Temple, has theorized that the specific use of yarrow originally came about because its shape resembles the archaic Chinese word-character for *pu*, "to divine," which was habitually written upon the oracle bones.[13] One of the shamanistic roles was to carry out the necessary divinations, an intimate association reflected in the Chinese word-character for the casting of yarrow-stalks that is based upon that for the word Wu.

The esteem in which the ancient Chinese held divination can be clearly seen in the culture of the Shang dynasty (c. 1600–1027 B.C.E.). Official recognition and respect for the wisdom of the oracles touched all levels of society. This went to such an extent that the eleventh Shang ruler was even able to persuade his people to move the state capital to a new location in the north of the country because the spirits advised it via the tortoise-shell. Another ruler, just prior to the official beginning of the Shang dynasty, even used the bones to elect the best person to be his successor after his death.

An early title for the I Ching was the *Chou I,* "the Changes of Chou." This referred to its development and use by the rulers of the Chou dynasty. The famous King Wen, father of the first official Chou emperor, was imprisoned by the last of the Shang rulers with whom he was at war. During his time of incarceration, he developed the basic symbolic and pictorial correspondences for each of the Hexagrams as we know them today. He also reassigned the Trigrams to new compass points.[14] His son, Tan, the Duke of Chou, continued this work by adding some of the oracular commentaries which, among other things, give many references to the Shang-Chou War.

An ancient stone stele that dates to the time of King Wen further indicates the venerable history of the I Ching and its indivisible connection to the Chou rulers. This monument lies in the ruins of the Chou town of Youli, in Henan Province, and it depicts the full range of the Sixty-Four Hexagrams.

Taoism was not the only philosophy to look upon the I Ching with reverence. Confucianism also adopted the Book of Changes into its ethos. However, in the latter case, the I Ching's inherent mysticism was lessened, and the main emphasis of the oracles came to reside in their implied political etiquette. To Confucians, *tao* meant the "proper" conduct of people within a structured feudal society, rather than the expression of each individual's true nature. All people were expected to know their place within the class hierarchy. Rites such as offerings to the ancestors, which are counseled by the Book of Changes, were valued for their tradition and their consequent power of social cohesion, though not necessarily for any magico-spiritual or mystical experiences that could be derived from them. For Confucians, the I Ching reinforced their views by displaying both the "correct" and "inappropriate" modes of behavior between individuals of different social rank, such as son and father, daughter and mother, subject and emperor, and so on. Such interpretations of filial duty were to ultimately shroud the Book of Changes in a Confucian aura that has been rather overemphasized, to the detriment of the I Ching's other important associations.

Another alternative name for the Book of Changes was *Kun Chien*, "Earth and Heaven." This referred to the dual forces of Yin and Yang, as expressed through the divine creativity of Mother Earth and Father Heaven. Their ceaseless interplay gives birth to every facet of Nature, as symbolized by the Hexagrams.

From its very beginnings, the I Ching was considered to depict the various spiritual workings and occult permutations of the cosmic forces of Yin and Yang. These powers bring about the essential transformations in the universe, and lie behind the magician's own ability to cause magickal changes.[15] Consequently, in a manner akin to the runic systems of the Germanic and Scandinavian peoples, the "cosmic map" displayed by the Book of Changes is viewed not merely as a means to divine the flow of the Tao in Nature, but the linear symbols and their associated Chinese word-characters are also thought to have an integral power to actually manipulate the fabric of existence—i.e., to cause the very mutations that they signify. To divine, and to actively affect, are simply two sides of the same coin; each symbol is a means to access elemental and planetary realms of creative magickal influence. The Pa Kua represent the inner divine power that is manifested in the outer world(s); referring to this same idea, the I Ching commentary known as the Great Treatise states that when the Trigrams are active, there is a consequent echo in the cosmos. Manifestation proceeds from the within to the without. The active occult use of the characters has been particularly prevalent in talismans and other powerful occult diagrams. The complete Pa Kua design, arranged as an octagon, is also considered to be a potent device against misfortune and the mischief caused by unruly spirits. The section on talismans gives more detailed information on the way in which Chinese word-characters and symbols are viewed in magickal practices.

The Development of Chinese Magick

Formal Taoist magickal schools first arose during the Han period; this was an age that saw a general proliferation of many different types of occult ideas and their attendant art forms. The founding father of religious Taoism, as an organized system of magician-priests, was the deified Chang Tao-ling (see figure 2). He was a magician from the province of Szechwan, and around the year 150 C.E., he established a school that came to be known as the Heavenly Master Sect (Chin. *T'ien Shih*, named after Chang himself who bore the title). This was otherwise known as the Way of the Five Bushels of Rice, because of the fact that each prospective student was required to pro-

Figure 2. Chang Tao-ling, founding father of religious Taoism
(based on traditional Chinese paintings).

vide the group with just such an amount of food, prior to initiation. (According to some accounts, this was also the price demanded by the Heavenly Master from those who came to him for his healing powers. Hence, his opponents sometimes called him "the Rice Thief.")

This sect emphasized the use of talismans, spirit evocation and exorcism, the esoteric use of sex, and other magickal and shamanistic practices. It also established the idea that personal spiritual evolution could be greatly enhanced by formal membership in the organized Taoist religion. Forgiveness for earthly acts that transgressed Heavenly law, and greater spiritual movement away from the artificial aspects of life and toward the Tao, would be offered by the gods to those who had been formally initiated into the Taoist religion. Chang's community was based on the mutual dependency of its members, and, for a time, it even governed its own lands on an autonomous basis.

The magician is said to have begun his occult career very much in the manner of the holy Taoist hermit. He chose a sacred mountain as his reclusive abode, and, in his solitude, committed himself to the cultivation of mystical and magickal experiences. Chinese tales say that in the course of his endeavors he gained contact with the spirit of the Old Master, Lao-tzu, who taught him how to prepare a potion of longevity called the Dragon-Tiger Elixir. This was apparently named after the mountain on which Chang had his retreat, but it is also a seeming double-entendre relating to an alchemical essence of a sexual nature, which combined the seminal fluids of the male/dragon with those of the female/tiger.[16] Another visitation from a different spirit-being then made Chang aware of the existence of some ancient magickal texts that held powerful occult knowledge; these were said to be hidden somewhere on the slopes of Po-sung Mountain. The magician was successful in unearthing these tomes, and by following out their instructions, he gained numerous new abilities, such as the projection of his consciousness beyond his physical body, clairaudience, and so on. A goddess further instructed him, and by her advice he also became able to exercise great control over the ranks of spiritual entities, the forces of the Five Elements, etc. Such knowledge he then passed on, in turn, to other sincere students who sought in him a means to their own enlightenment.

Chang Tao-ling's system encouraged the testing of student's skills, courage, and self-confidence by the imposition of various difficult ordeals. The Heavenly Master, himself, is said to have finally risen above his own personal trials by virtue of his superior experience and wisdom. Taoist legend states that he left his neophytes, at the age of 123, by ascending into the celestial abode of the gods as an enlightened immortal, apparently leaving only his clothes behind! As a result of this transcendence, he is now invoked by earthly devotees as a god of Taoist magick and exorcism. His physical descendants, however, continued to govern the T'ien Shih sect, and this has remained the case right up to the present day with the current Grand Master, the sixty-third man to bear the title of Heavenly Master, who lives in Taiwan.

A major aspect of Chang's magick, and that of the Chinese as a whole, lay in the realm of talismans and charms. Of all the various designs that he passed on to his students, his most widely known legacy is probably the so-called Seal of Lao-tzu, described in greater detail in the section on talismanic magick in part 3 of this book.

After the time of Chang Tao-ling, the inherent magickal principles of Taoism were further developed by an expansion of more sects and schools, which were often linked to particular family groups. Members of the Ko clan, for instance, were renowned for their magickal powers. Ko Hsuan, to whom the authorship of the Taoist text *Ch'ing-ching Ching* ("The Classical Book of Purity and Stillness") has been credited, was said to have had the ability to walk on water, and remain comfortably under its surface for hours without suffering hurt.[17] His clan had taken on board all the classic techniques of Chinese magick and shamanism. At a later date, it also went on to influence the practices of various other schools such as the notorious Shang-Ch'ing ("Highest Clarity") sect, otherwise called the Mao Shan school after their sacred mountain home, which arose in the fourth century C.E.

Many such groups were to be created over time, each with its own set of priorities. For instance, some schools emphasized the importance of stillness and passive meditation, and so are generally designated by the term "Quietist." Others, however, saw greater advantage in active ritual work and spell casting. The new techniques for meditation that were presented by Buddhism, as it became established in China in the first century C.E., also offered the Taoists fresh opportunities for experimentation; the ideas of this new and foreign religion had a great impact, as well, on the organization of Taoist monasteries. The Buddhists, in their turn, also freely borrowed elements from Taoism, particularly with regard to shamanistic trance practices and the breathing methods of chi-kung.

During the periods of the later T'ang and Sung dynasties, many of the talismanic designs and esoteric theories that we associate with Taoism today were created. Scholars and initiates during the Sung era, especially, were very keen to acquire lost wisdom from China's ancient past and incorporate it into the thinking of their own time. This is noticeably apparent in a maturation of the concept of the Tai-Chi and its vital place in the creation of the phenomenal cosmos.[18]

Magicians of all schools and types generally experienced social benefits under the regime of the later Yuan dynasty. Paradoxically, however, these rulers are also held responsible for destroying copies of the *Tao-tsang*, the official Taoist canon; extant versions of this book date from the fifteenth century C.E. The Yuan, better known as the Mongols, had invaded China in the thirteenth century C.E. and finally gained control of it in 1271 C.E., under the leadership of the infamous Kublai Khan. From the account of Marco Polo's travels through China, we know that shamanistic magicians were greatly honored in Kublai's court; Polo declared that at one feast he witnessed magicians, whom he called *bakshi*, levitating drinking cups for the entertainment of the khan and his guests.[19] The overall importance of occult practitioners to the Yuan is indicated in the levels of social hierarchy established by Kublai Khan; Taoists came a high fourth, being outranked only by the most important court officials, rulers of the provinces, and Tibetan lamas.

For all the subsequent notoriety of the Mongols, the Yuan dynasty lasted a mere eighty-eight years before it was finally overthrown and replaced by native Chinese, who then went on to form the well-known Ming dynasty. Violent reaction to the ousted Mongols caused an initial period of repression and persecution of shamans, Taoist magicians, and Tibetan religious practitioners. Confucians, seeing an opportunity for revenge against some of their ancient opponents, encouraged the Ming rulers to punish these other groups because they had been tolerated and supported by Kublai Khan and his descendants.

Thankfully, this situation was not to last for long, and over time the influence of such magico-religious philosophies began to creep back into mainstream attitudes once more. For instance, as part of the official examinations, prospective mandarins (state officials) had to show a degree of understanding of various Taoist principles, such as the art of *feng shui*.

Unfortunately, such state acceptance was not always beneficial. Shamanism, so long the vital backbone of China's spiritual and social culture, foundered under the later Manchu emperors, the last of the country's imperial rulers. Many Chinese hated the Manchu because they were a non-Han people, related to the Mongols, and, like them, they had also invaded China and displaced the native rulers. However, the Manchu did share a common and ancient heritage of shamanism with the Chinese. In many respects, the practice had retained an even greater importance in the traditional culture and identity of the newcomers. So, over time, shamans were encouraged by the Manchu to become thoroughly integrated into the official affairs of court life, their traditional binding role in tribalism being identified with the primary task of the emperor in the country as a whole. This was accompanied, in the eighteenth century C.E., by the formation of a type of official State Shamanism that was laid down in writing, dogmatized, and "civilized" by the presiding Confucian bureaucrats. The result was a spiritually void religion, alienated from its true empowering roots. Many shamans who were enticed into its fold saw their psychic powers slip away and die.

After this, the essential shamanic tradition remained in an unsullied state only in the most remote areas of the steppe-lands of northeastern China—ironically, this was within the borders of the original Manchu homeland; there, life had been relatively untouched by the shenanigans of the central Chinese court. This sad state of affairs worsened even further under the later Communists, who included shamans, Wu, Taoists, Buddhists, and others in their condemnations of "counter-revolutionaries."

Fortunately, there are some signs that this situation is now, finally, in reverse to a small degree, though there is still a long way to go.

Korea & Japan

The influence of Chinese occultism is not restricted to the culture of the Middle Kingdom itself. The indigenous tribal practices of the Koreans, for instance, also adopted many elements from Chinese shamanism. In that country, the spirit-masters became known as *mudang,* or *mansin,* and their ceremonies were called *kut.* Unfortunately, as in China, a catalogue of troubles and intolerance from bigots burdens the history of these practices. The ancient migration of Confucian ideas into Korea resulted in pressure being brought against mudang; this caused the legal prohibition on men becoming shamanistic practitioners, it being deemed an unworthy and degenerate occupation for the masculine gender. For this reason, most mudang are now traditionally women. Sadly, they are still viewed with embarrassment by the Korean authorities, who consider them to be a "primitive block" to modern "progress."

However, in spite of such opposition, other aspects of magickal practice still retain popular support. The I Ching is used extensively for divination, and Chinese word-character talismans abound. The importance of feng shui geomancy is also acknowledged; so much so that during World War II, when the Imperial Japanese forces invaded Korea, the occupiers sought to additionally disrupt native capacities for occult resistance by sinking iron rods into the ground along lines of feng shui energy. These veins of power (Chin. *lung mei*) are traditionally associated with dragons. Oriental lore states that iron is the metal most feared by dragon-spirits, and such poles were customarily dropped into dragon-inhabited lakes and rivers in order to fend off the creatures' unwanted attentions. Strangely, only in recent years have the Koreans found the time to finally remove these offending items.

From the dawning of its civilization, the nation of Japan has been influenced by the philosophical and religious ideas emanating from China. The classical example of Japanese spirituality, Shinto, is derived, to a large degree, from ancient Chinese ideas of animism, shamanism, and Taoism, as well as from elements borrowed from the indigenous Ainu people. The very word *Shinto* comes from the Chinese *shen* and *tao,* meaning "The Way of the Gods"; the actual Japanese version of this term is *Kami-no-Michi.*

Shinto looks upon the entirety of the natural world, including so-called inanimate objects such as rocks and trees, as being full of *kami*—gods, spirits, or essences that are spirit-like. By entering into communion with those kami, humans are able to have a subtle influence on all the aspects of the world that are governed by the spirits, and obtain their assistance in their endeavors. Personal contact with the metaphysical substrata of Nature, and the avoidance of actions that offend it, bring the Shinto adept into the state of *nagare*, or oneness with the harmonious and ever-changing flow of the universe. This is identical to the Taoist's acceptance and assimilation of the limitless Way. Sadly, this respect for Nature is not always reflected in the general Japanese population any more than it is in the profligate attitudes of the West.

At a relatively early stage, Taoist travelers brought to Japan the concept of Yang and Yin, which in Japanese are named In and Yo. Where the Chinese color this Tai-Chi symbol black and white, the Japanese depict it in red and yellow (in Korea, it is blue and red). Japan also adopted Chinese magickal lore concerning deities associated with the cardinal compass points, sacred colors for the Quarters, the theory of the Five Elements (Chin. *wu hsing*; J. *gogyo setsu*), and so on. Such spiritual traffic continued for many years, resulting in the wide acceptance and use of traditional Chinese magickal practices, particularly those connected with the use of mudra and word-character talismans.

An interesting result of this cross-cultural exchange is the creation of the sect of Shugendo. The practitioners of this school, who are known as Yamabushi ("mountain warriors"), absorbed various magico-religious ideas and techniques from sources as diverse as native Shinto, Tantric Buddhism, and Taoism. In the latter case, this is said to have been learned from priests who fled to Japan during a period of anarchy in China after the fall of the T'ang dynasty. The Yamabushi, who are particularly devoted to the god Fudo, are famed for their incredible magickal powers, such as the ability to exorcise *onryo*—malevolent ghosts, identical to the Chinese kuei—control fires, and other marvelous feats. Their capacity to withstand ascetic discomfort is also legendary; their initiation ceremony involves five main components that correspond with the sacred Five Elements: perilous suspension over cliff faces; protracted fasting; deprivation of drinking fluids; sumo wrestling; and exhaustive trance-dance.

It is to Shugendo and Taoism that we must also turn in order to understand the origins of the mysterious and infamous ninja. Far from being the popular image of near-invincible deadly assassins, available for hire to all, these secretive figures began their existence as warrior-priests. Circumstances obliged them to develop their finely tuned fighting skills in order to protect their chosen spiritual and social way of life from attack by the samurai. Daisuke Nishina began the tradition of the ninja, particularly those who lived in the prefecture of Iga—now called Mie Prefecture. He was a Yamabushi who had trained in all the arts of the Shugendo priests. In his wanderings through Iga, he came across a Chinese Taoist warrior-priest who was known, in Japanese, as Kain Doshi. Training under the eye of this sage, Daisuke learned more about the Way of the Tao. When he eventually said farewell to his master, he went on to develop a tradition called Ninjutsu, or Ninpo, which combined all the varied elements of his previous training.

The exoteric social structure of Ninjutsu, as it existed in medieval Japan, was based on clan loyalty and mutual dependency among individuals with similar philosophical views, as opposed to unthinking prostration to a central and nontribal government divorced from the people. Complementary to this, the esoteric magico-spiritual goal of the ninja was called *shin-shin, shin-gan*, "the mind of a god, the eyes of a god." The ninja achieved this by *musha shugyo*, the Warrior's Quest. Although this has sometimes involved an actual physical journey in search of wisdom, the real adventure takes place within the ninja's own psyche. To all intents and purposes, this is identical to the spiritual journeys of Taoists who set out to discover their Way, their own Paths, and then live them to the full.

The world of the magician continues to exercise great influence in the East. In those areas inhabited by the Chinese that avoided the early effect of Communism, such as Hong Kong, Macao, and Taiwan, the old ways of life remain relatively strong. Taoist and other types of Chinese magickal organizations have also sprung up in Western lands through emigration. In Hong Kong and Macao there exist important Taoist temples that still operate with strength and popular support, and a large number of individual occult practitioners can also be found: mediums, Da Siu Yan, Wu, Tao-jen, feng shui masters, I Ching diviners, and many more. It remains to be seen what effect, if any, the reunification of these areas with mainland China will have on their thriving magickal lives.

---

1. See Arthur Cotterell, *The First Emperor of China* (London: Macmillan, 1981), 131.
2. See William Watson, *The Genius of China* (London: Times Newspapers Ltd., 1973), 47, plate 14.
3. See Kenneth Grant, *Hecate's Fountain* (London: Skoob Books, 1992), 14.
4. Certain Chinese magicians have traditionally dealt with this problem by capturing the kuei in spirit traps, and then have used them as personal servants in the same manner as the familiar spirits of Western magick.

5. It may be, however, that in some instances the ladder of swords was not intended to cut the magician's feet, but was once again used to draw blood from his tongue. In her book *The Book of Chinese Beliefs* (London: Arrow Books Ltd., 1985), 86–88, Frena Bloomfield describes a modern ceremony that was observed in Taiwan in honor of Chih Wang Yeh, a deified adept of spiritism. In this rite, possessed mediums also used a sword-ladder, but showed their personal power by climbing up the sharp blades without injury to the soles of their feet. However, one medium deliberately cut his tongue on one of the "rungs" and allowed this precious fluid to drip down and consecrate charms placed on the ground.

6. *Kojiki* means "record of ancient matters," and was the first book to set down in writing all the Creation stories of the Shinto religion. It was collated in the eighth century C.E., by order of Empress Gemmei (or Gemyo), from the many tales scattered across Japan.

7. See R. O. Faulkner, *The Ancient Egyptian Book of the Dead* (London: British Museum Publications, 1989), chapters 149 and 153.

8. See James Legge, *The Texts of Taoism* (New York: Dover, 1962), 2:195.

9. Chuang-tzu, however, applies this epithet to another Taoist by the name of Chieh-yu. See Legge, *The Texts of Taoism*, 1:170.

10. Ibid., 1:58, verse 15.

11. Ibid., 197.

12. Ibid., 364.

13. See Robert Temple, *Conversations with Eternity* (London: Rider, 1984), 146.

14. For more information on this matter, see the introduction to part 4.

15. See the remarks of Chuang-tzu; Legge, *The Texts of Taoism*, 2:216. It is not certain that the sage is wholly responsible for all statements made in this part of the Texts, which includes a specific reference to the I Ching. Yet, if for the moment we accept that he did write them, then the mention of the Book of Changes at such a point in history gives an opposing argument to the idea that, prior to the Han dynasty, only Confucius had made specific literary references to the Book of Change's existence. See Palmer, Kwok, and O'Brien, *The Contemporary I Ching* (London: Rider, 1989), 18–20.

16. These are signified, respectively, by the Trigrams of Li, "the Sun," and K'an, "the Moon."

17. Aleister Crowley claimed to have been Ko Hsuan in an earlier incarnation. He produced his own version of the Ch'ing-ching Ching in the form of verse. See Aleister Crowley, *The Confessions of Aleister Crowley* (London: Arkana, 1989), 839, and *Tao Te Ching* (York Beach: Weiser, 1995), 103–108.

18. See "Yin and Yang: The Eternal Dance" in the following section, *The Philosophy of the Way*.

19. Certain current scholars, such as Frances Wood, believe with some justification that Polo never actually went to China as he claimed, but simply rehashed the observations and accounts of Persian travelers as his own adventure. See Frances Wood, *Did Marco Polo Go to China?* (London: Secker & Warburg, 1995).

The Philosophy of the Way

"The Tao in its regular course does nothing,
and so there is nothing which it does not do."
Lao-tzu, *Tao-teh Ching*.[1]

Taoism is a vast subject requiring many separate volumes to describe all of its varied aspects and sects. Such a task is obviously beyond the scope of this present work, but two of the philosophy's main foundation blocks, namely the dual interdependency of Yin and Yang and the much vaunted but little understood concept of wu-wei, deserve particular attention here. Familiarity with their ideas is vital to the ongoing success of magickal practices and, more importantly, to the evolution of human consciousness.

Yin and Yang: The Eternal Dance

According to general Taoist cosmology, before Creation there existed Nothing (Chin. *wu-wu*); not merely the absence of things, but a condition that cannot be defined by any known qualities including that of "emptiness"; it is, in effect, the Unnameable. This Absolute Void, symbolized by the unbroken circle or number zero, has neither beginning nor end (Chin. *wu ming*). It contains within Itself the vital potential for all types of manifestation; in Chinese lore, these are known as "the Ten Thousand Things," the figure being representative not of a precise number but simply another way of phrasing "infinite, endless." This Nothingness is merely an alternative way of describing the Tao, the eternal and abstract source from which all life ultimately springs and which continually permeates all of its many creations.

From the Wu-wu there came *Wu Chi*, "No Limit," and thence the heart of Nothingness known as *Hun-tun*, "Chaos."[2] From that central point of the Void there arose the first fixed and definable principle known as the *Tai-Chi* (see figure 3). This original One, or Unity, comprises the balanced and mutually dependent forces of Yang and Yin, the active and passive principles of the cosmos, which are eternally engaged in continuous

Figure 3. The Tai-Chi, representing the primal unity of Yin and Yang.

sexual congress with each other. For this reason, they remain undivided—that is, in the particular form of the Tai-Chi, Yang and Yin are not yet manifested as dualistic and limited polarities in the phenomenal universe.

From the intercourse of these two powers are born their reflexes of Heaven and Earth. These are the first phenomenal and divided representatives of the Tai-Chi. Heaven is thought of as an invisible and procreative force, while Earth is the visible matrix that receives the generative influxes from the Firmament. From Earth are subsequently born all the myriad varieties of dualistic life, both physical and spiritual. In planetary terms, these two polarities are then further subdivided to form the Sun and the Moon, which are respectively termed in Chinese as the *T'ai Yang* and the *T'ai Yin*, "the Great Light" and "the Great Darkness." These two cosmic powers are themselves reflected, still further, in bodily alchemy as the mature and sexually charged vital powers of men and women, and in the chakric centers of the psychophysical form wherein such alchemical energy is sublimated.

Phenomenal life is spawned from the conjunction of Yang and Yin through the motivation of its own spontaneity (Chin. *tsu-jan*); forms come into being because it is their Will to do so, in accordance with the movement of the Tao as it continues its ceaseless flow through Nature. In Shinto, a similar idea is acknowledged regarding the unstoppable urge for self-expression in the world of appearances; in Japanese, it is known as *musubi*. The bottom line of this idea is that all the diverse varieties of sentient beings and forms of life that exist in all the spheres of the cosmos, whether metaphysical or mundane, do so because they can, following out the requirements of their own Paths. It is not the right of human beings to make value judgments on the integral worth of other species with which they share a planet and a universe.

The act of creation does not mark an end to the interplay of Yang and Yin. Manifestation itself implies division and imperfection, for all the quantifiable aspects of existence can only be known by comparison to their diametric opposites. For example, the idea of heat is nonexistent unless there is also cold against which to contrast it, nothing can be considered to be big until there is also something that is small in relation, and so on. The term "imperfection" should not connote a view that life is just a sinful vale of woes, and therefore something to be looked upon with bitterness. Sadly, however, Buddhist influences on Taoism have seen this unnecessary idea take hold in the minds of a number of Taoist philosophers. In reality, Nature simply undergoes ceaseless transformations, as opposites of all types unite in order to transcend their sense of separation and limitation. In such conjunctions, they inevitably give birth to further manifestations that will themselves seek to become whole by union with their opposites, *ad infinitum*. In *The Book of the Law*, the core text of Thelema, the goddess Nuit expresses this same concept in the following words: "For I am divided for love's sake, for the chance of union."

Every event that we experience, irrespective of the plane of consciousness that provides the field for such a happening, comes about through the eternal and ecstatic dance of Yang and Yin. Every point of change in an object or set of circumstances is instigated by the action of its opposite; the transformations of the Yin require the energy of the Yang, and vice versa. This idea can be clearly seen in the symbol of the Tai-Chi, which shows the two universal polarities containing within themselves a dot, or portion, of their diametrical halves. To paraphrase the words of the artist-magician Austin Osman Spare, the entirety of Creation is engaged in a continuous procreative act![3]

Wu-Wei: The Art of Not Doing

"So then the Life of Non-action is not for thee; the Withdrawal from Activity is not the Way of the Tao; but rather the intensification and making universal of every Unit of thine Energy on every Plane."

Aleister Crowley, *Liber Aleph*.[4]

This essential Taoist concept has caused probably more confusion in the minds of Westerners than any other idea from the philosophy of the Way. It has also led some people to throw up their hands in horror at what they see as being a Taoist love of obscurity for its own sake. Much of the trouble has arisen from erroneous attempts to regard Taoism as just another face of Buddhist passiveness; a mistake derived from a too-literal understanding of the Chinese phrase wu-wei. Word for word, this translates as "not doing," or "no action." This, combined with the tendency of certain Taoists to reject mundane society, has led some commentators to declare that the goal of every true follower of the Way is, simply, to do nothing and remain in a quiet, nebulous, and physically inactive contemplation on life. By doing so, they may be attuned in some unknowable manner to the universal flow of the Tao. Nothing could be further from the truth; approaching Taoism from such a Western rational and reductionist viewpoint is a doomed enterprise. In order to appreciate the philosophy's real outlook, one has to be prepared to lose all these preconceptions and enter, instead, into the abstract and experiential mind-set of the initiate.

The concept of wu-wei underpins all Taoist activity, for it constitutes the essential formula by which magicians harmonize themselves with Nature. "Not doing" does not mean sitting back and simply watching the world go by, being inscrutably mystical to the eyes of the uninitiated. Rather, it defines the way in which all the earthly acts of the Taoist adept are one with the flow of the Tao, as it specifically manifests in his life.

The manner in which the Tao expresses itself through creatures is unique to each individual concerned. Through the regular use of meditative and magickal practices, this force can eventually be perceived. Such perception arises into the quietly receptive awareness of the magician when he is free of the conditioning and constraints imposed by his ears (the descriptions of his life's purpose as pronounced by others), and by his human mind (his own intellectual and rational view of his place in the universe). By subsequently understanding the direction that the Tao wishes to move—that is, the mode of existence that it desires to enact, through the human vehicle, in the phenomenal worlds—the magician is in a position to ensure that all his deeds are in harmony with that guiding power. He thereby fulfills his Destiny (Chin. *ming*), and is unconcerned with either the good or bad opinions of other people regarding such a road.

It may be that by following his own Way, he attracts the derision and mockery of those who are blind to their own selves and so cannot see anything worthwhile in the Taoist's attitudes. In the equivalent musha shugyo of the ninja, the Path sets the traveler against all his own preconceived notions of selfhood and role. This may cause friends to depart, the circumstances of his life may completely change, and new problems will inevitably arise to plague him. Yet the warrior moves without fear along the

Way, meeting every difficulty with a firm resolve, flowing like water along its natural course. Those who believe themselves to have superior intellectual prowess, or a "proper" idea of how life should be lived, may call the adept a "simpleton." However, the sage cares nothing for such insults; indeed, he may sometimes even appear to deliberately play out the persona of a fool. Yet at the same time he cherishes his views in his own breast because he knows that only in the light of the Tao may his deeds and opinions be truly judged, and not by the socially conditioned criteria of his detractors.[5] Does the bumblebee refuse to fly just because the orthodox "laws" of physics declare that it should not be able to? On the contrary, it simply, and successfully, goes about its own important business, mercifully oblivious to its supposedly anomalous state and the bewilderment of scientists.

The personal Fate signified by ming is not to be understood as "predestination" in the sense of an absolutely inescapable doom, but as the correct path in life that people should tread if they are to realize their true Inner Nature or Self. The Tao does not force people to move in a certain direction, and, in the main, they are theoretically free to carry out any action they desire. However, by living an existence that is out of step with their true Way, they merely create unnecessary problems for themselves, and others, too, for they tend to blunder into the Paths of other creatures in the course of deviating from their own.

Yet, what has all this to do with the idea of "not doing"? Surely the Taoists are specifically enjoined to act in the way that their Tao motivates them. The answer to this lies in the fact that those who have attained the knowledge of how the Tao specifically flows in their lives have also effectively found themselves. The road that adepts tread is one with their essential identities; the True Self, devoid of interference from the egocentric human consciousness, realizes its own potential by following its chosen Way, because the Self *is* the Way. The Path, and that which walks upon it, are ultimately the same thing. Hence, every truly harmonious act arises spontaneously, effortlessly, and naturally from a sense of unity with the Tao; each deed should be a genuine manifestation of the Inner Nature, rather than a forced and false action decided upon by the dictates of the human ego.

Therefore, all activity that conforms to wu-wei does so because it is free from the constraints of human calculation. The Taoist view of "doing," on the contrary, implies going out of one's way to achieve something, by mental, emotional, or physical effort, which is not in harmony with the real concerns of the practitioner's True Self.

For example, if the main thrust of one's Tao should be expressed through the medium of music, it would not be wu-wei to attempt to manifest it through sport.

Movement along the Path is not a question of getting from point A to point Z; it is not a frantic race to attempt to achieve a distant goal, viewing everything that comes in between as merely a variety of means to an end. Every act that arises from the Tao is equal in status; every step along the Way, be it creative or destructive, *is* the goal. This is not to say that Taoists may not have foreknowledge of future necessities, but simply that they do not see such distant occurrences as having greater or less relevance than the events that they may be currently experiencing. For this reason, Taoists should not yearn after those coming circumstances, but allow them to manifest in their own time and in the right place. Taoists should, at the same moment, be prepared if necessary to help their birth by any appropriate action, mundane or magickal, that may be required (such action being of itself a manifestation of Destiny, an integral and vital part of the act of Becoming).

Similarities to this view can be found in the Tantric philosophy of India, particularly in the sect known as Sahaja. This school encourages its adherents, known as Sahajiya, to operate from a position of true spontaneity and self-guidance, unencumbered by the trappings of social indoctrination that unnecessarily bind so many others. This includes the eschewing of class distinctions, such as those imposed by the traditional Indian caste system. The Sahajiya may happily engage in Tantric union with a member of the so-called Untouchable class (the poorest and "lowest" level in Indian society) without the sense of shame with which Indian social hierarchy would usually greet such fraternization.[6]

Of all the Western Hemisphere's own occult systems, one of the best comparisons to Taoism can be seen in the magickal philosophy of Thelema, as taught by Aleister Crowley. In this system of attainment, every man and woman is viewed as being a Star, a vehicle of Self-dependent Awareness, or God-consciousness, that seeks to experience Itself through the medium of the True Will. This latter represents the personal Path along which each person should travel in order to realize identity with that guiding force. Every act of the Will is a direct expression of the essential nature of the True Self. Path and Selfhood are one; by walking the former, the latter is achieved. Yet, as with the Way of the Tao, every stage of the Will is of equal importance, and all experiences that occur in conformity with that Path, whatever their outward form, should be enjoyed in the same measure.

The character of this sacred journey, as both Taoists and Thelemites understand it, is beautifully summed up in the following passage, which is taken from the second chapter of Crowley's *Book of the Heart Girt with a Serpent*:

17. Also the Holy One came upon me, and I beheld a white swan floating in the blue.

18. Between its wings I sate, and the aeons fled away.

19. Then the swan flew and dived and soared, yet no whither we went.

20. A little crazy boy that rode with me spake unto the swan, and said:

21. Who art thou that dost float and fly and soar in the inane? Behold, these many aeons have passed; whence camest thou? Whither wilt thou go?

22. And laughing I chid him, saying: No whence! No whither!

23. The swan being silent, he answered: Then, if with no goal, why this eternal journey?

24. And I laid my head against the Head of the Swan, and laughed, saying: Is there not joy ineffable in this aimless winging? Is there not weariness and impatience for who would attain to some goal?

25. And the swan was ever silent. Ah! But we floated in the infinite Abyss. Joy! Joy! White swan, bear thou ever me up between thy wings![7]

---

1. See James Legge, *The Texts of Taoism* (New York: Dover, 1962), 1:79, verse 37.

2. Compare this with the Qabalistic idea of the Negative Trinity: *Ain*, "Nothing"; *Ain Soph*, "No Limit"; and *Ain Soph Aur*, "Limitless Light." From these are manifested the Sephirothic structure of the Tree of Life.

3. See Kenneth Grant, *Images & Oracles of Austin Osman Spare* (London: Muller, 1975), 23.

4. See Aleister Crowley, "On the Mystical Marriage," in *Liber Aleph* (York Beach: Weiser, 1991), 23.

5. Compare this with the equivalent symbolism of the Fool of the Tarot.

6. In Tantric terminology, such a partner from the Untouchable caste is known as a *Shudra*.

7. See Aleister Crowley, "Liber LXV/Liber Cordis Cincti Serpente," in *The Holy Books of Thelema* (York Beach: Weiser, 1983), 60–61.

PART TWO

The Temple and the Magickal Tools

Introduction

In this section, the reader will find listed various implements and ritual weapons that are used in Chinese and Japanese magickal systems. These represent the magician's basic tools. However, there are many more that also have a place in traditional ceremonial operations, and some of these are listed in the Hexagram correspondences in part 4; they are all compatible instruments, though drawn from different schools of thought, including the shamanistic traditions, Taoism, Tibetan Lamaism and Bon, and so on.

In total, they represent a vast and somewhat daunting array of occult paraphernalia. However, it is not necessary for the aspiring magician to attempt to acquire every single one of these tools, for many are designed for use in very specialist situations that may never be encountered by many students. The basic tools described in the following sections will provide most of the tools required for general practice.

The important point to remember about any ritual object is that it is the focused concentration, and energized enthusiasm, of the magician who wields it that gives the instrument its power. The tool itself merely acts as a convenient vehicle for the magician's Will, and possesses no active virtues that the practitioner does not himself invest in it by his own force. This shows the need for regular training and development of essential personal faculties such as visualization and thought control. It also explains why those would-be occultists, who believe that the mere possession of magickal implements in a ritually theatrical setting is enough to ensure occult success, are forever doomed to failure!

The Temple

Whether magickal practices or meditations are carried out in an ornate and formal building, in front of a shrine by the roadside, in a forest clearing, or simply in a corner of an otherwise very mundane room, an essential factor remains common to all locations: that is, that the chosen area has been set aside and consecrated, either permanently or temporarily, as a sacred workspace—a Theatre of Magick—devoted entirely to esoteric acts. In practical terms, any such location can be defined as a temple; it need not be the venue for any specific acts of standard religious worship.

The Chinese term for a Taoist temple is *kuan*, which also means "to consider, to examine." Within the sacred space, the magician stimulates the subtle and penetrating action of his consciousness, so that it may apprehend the secrets of the metaphysical worlds and reveal the true nature of his Being. Yet, such inner knowledge also gives the ability to put the results of contemplation into action, to allow for the natural and spontaneous projection of energy into the outer world of forms; the continual process of balanced change ensures that after withdrawal there must come forward motion. Hence, *kuan* also means "to appear, to manifest; to experience." Therefore, it is within the sacred workspace that the magician, by his skills and expertise, orders the circumstances of his life according to awareness of the real needs of his True Self.

One of the main features of the temple is the ritual altar (Chin. *t'an*). This forms a consecrated table or "workbench" that may be used as a base on which to place candles, censers, ritual implements, and other paraphernalia, and also upon which talismans and other charms may be created. It is traditional in China for altars to be rectangular in shape. They are usually placed against the southern wall of the temple, so that when the magician stands before it, he faces the sacred direction of Heaven. The student may choose to follow this example, if desired, or else prefer the common

Western alternative of placing the altar at the center of the working area. Either way, the symbolism of the altar is, to all intents and purposes, the same in both oriental and occidental magickal philosophies. It signifies the embodiment of the Self in Nature; the manifestation or extension into matter of the magician's Will, as it flows in sincere and harmonious accordance with the Way of the Tao, and as it operates through the occult action of the elemental forces that he wields.

In etymological terms, *t'an* means "an area of raised earth given over to the offering of grain at the rising of the Sun." Hence, the altar is also an emblematic representation of K'un, the Earth, and indicates the fertile power of the Yin to reify magickal desires when offered the vitalizing and stimulating force of the Yang. For this reason, the Yin partner in the rites of sexual alchemy is often referred to as an "altar."

This essential temple accoutrement may be made of either wood or stone. If the altar has a hollow interior, this will be found useful to house the magickal tools when they are not in use. The surface can also be augmented by images or figurines of appropriate deities, according to individual taste and always bearing in mind the actual nature of any of your workings. It would, for instance, be self-defeating to place a consecrated figure of Kuan Ti on the altar if the object of your ritual were an invocation of healing energies!

If the practitioner lacks a decent amount of space in the temple area, making a full-size altar impractical—such as might be the case where only a small portion of an ordinary room could be given over to magickal work—an example of a useful alternative can be found in the traditional Japanese *kamidana*. This is an altar-shelf that forms the spiritual heart of Japanese homes. Affixed to the wall above head-height, the kamidana is used to house sacred emblems of the gods, and other items relating to ancestor spirits.

In Western countries, the magickal circle, marked out on the floor or carpet and in which the magician stands while practicing his ceremonial arts, is a well-known ritual device. Similar to the temple itself, the circle represents, in a concentrated form, the personal magickal universe in which the magician operates; that is, his particular cosmological view, and field of action, as seen from the position of his True Self. In the circle, which is also the emblem of infinite possibility and the continuity of existence, the magician must take the role of a sovereign. Taking his place at the heart of the symbol, the magician meditates on the qualities of Deity, and attempts to integrate his essential identity with them. It is this experiential understanding, and the consequent assimilation of a sense of divinity, that gives the ritual circle its power to act as a barrier against unwanted energies.

The use of such a device is also present in the East, though is not so immediately apparent as it is in the West. Limited uses can be seen in the novel *Monkey*, otherwise known as *The Journey to the West*. Tibetan Buddhism or Lamaism has its own traditional use of circular stone enclosures known as *Kyilkhors*. Of course, there are also the well-known pictorial mandalas in Tantric ritual that are commonly translated into English as "circles," though they usually consist of combinations of squares and circles. These constructions are used for meditative and magickal purposes, but are generally more complex and diverse in their symbolism and designs than the basic ritual circle under discussion here.

Another symbol that is generally held to have a protective power is the *fang-sheng*, or double rhombus. The single rhombus (Chin. *ling-hsing,* or diamond-like shape) is commonly looked upon as a symbol of victory over oppressors.[1] Hence, the subsequent duplication of the motif is considered to increase its natural strengths still further. The fang-sheng emblem is often seen on items of craftwork, such as pottery, and is inscribed on the walls of houses in order to ward off bad luck and hauntings by unquiet spirits. The two rhombus shapes are usually arranged linearly, but for practical magickal purposes, it is better if one is placed directly over the other, thus forming an octagram.

The illustration depicts an example of a fang-sheng design, for use in ritual work (see figure 4). The eight points of the octagram are complemented by their appropriate Trigrams (the topmost Trigram for Ch'ien should be aligned to the south), which represent the elemental and planetary powers that the magician evokes to achieve his goals. These figures also depict the extended and manifested cosmos in which the magician's Will is brought to pass. In the center of the design is the Tai-Chi symbol. This expresses the idea that the magician has harmonized the opposing polarities of positive and negative within himself, and that consequently there is no aspect of the universe with which he is not united in the all-pervasive current of the Tao.

The fang-sheng can be physically present in the temple as a floor embellishment, or else can be wholly visualized in an astral form. Indeed, the student will find it a very good practice to formulate an entire visualized temple in the imagination, either the same in appearance as its physical counterpart, or else according to imaginative desire. This provides helpful training for concentration, and improves the essential

Figure 4. The fang-sheng.

ability to mould plastic thought-forms. It also establishes a sacred workspace in the subtle planes of consciousness, which may then be used when the student is denied access to the usual physical temple environment, or during operations that are designed to take place wholly on astral level.

---

1. It is also emblematic of the Womb of Earth.

The Ritual Sword

The most important symbolic implement in Chinese magick is, without a doubt, the sword (Chin. *ta tao*, or *chien*). This influential weapon features heavily in many oriental tales, and it is the instrument of the warrior *par excellence*. Often, legendary swords are depicted as having inherent magickal properties; or else they acquire a semidivine nature by the fact that they are presented to heroes as gifts by grateful deities. Either way, this weapon is often used as a symbol that shows the warrior's connection to divine spiritual forces.

In Chinese magick, the sword represents the embodiment of the magician's Will, by virtue of which he controls the magickal forces that are useful to his work, or banishes those that are inimical to his own well-being or that of his friends. Exorcism of "demonic" powers has been, and remains, an important facet of both Taoist and Wuist rituals and legends. It is this process that has mostly gained for the sword its notoriety in the minds of Western commentators; the majority of these researchers, who do not appreciate the full implications of ritual sword symbolism, tend to concentrate too heavily on the tool's specific "demon-slaying" uses. However, certain Taoists do specialize in such rites of exorcism, and they are known as "Redheads."

To the Taoist magician, battle is often seen as being an essential part of life because it liberates the individual's True Self against egotistical forces that might otherwise attempt to subdue it. All things have their own place and function in the stream of time, and their individual Paths should not be interfered with. When such interference occurs, the natural harmony of Yin and Yang is disturbed and battle must commence in order to reassert balance. Disruption may come from mortal enemies, spirits, or, more usually, from one's own contentious personality. The type of battle waged, and the level of counterforce used, depends on the nature of the problem. For example, one would not use exactly the same methods both for dealing with a personality disorder and for defending oneself against a physical opponent. To fight a battle does not necessarily mean to resort to physical violence, but simply that one has recognized that a troublesome or dangerous state of disharmony has occurred, from whatever source, that must be rectified as soon as possible and by whatever means are appropriate. Fighting, to the Taoist, is not an opportunity for bullying or boasting over an opponent's defeat. Rather, it is an act that circumstances sometimes necessitate, and that should be indulged in for only so long as is necessary. In whatever manner such combat is to take place, and in whatever plane of consciousness, the ritual sword is the primary symbol of the need for the essential harmony of the universe, and is therefore always of paramount importance to magickal rites. The tip of the weapon is the symbolic axis upon which the Tai-Chi spins. However, because the tool is also the means by which the magician brings his Will into existence, its edge is also that which cleaves the Tai-Chi into the separate halves of Heaven and Earth, hence bringing about the conditions that are required for new birth.

Unlike the swords used in most Western magickal systems, which are typically made of steel, Chinese blades can be created from a number of different materials. In addition to steel, many are made wholly from wood; the types formed from peach or mulberry woods are considered to be the most potent, though willow is also sometimes used. Wood from a tree that has been struck by lightning is also eagerly sought after for the production of swords; in Chinese symbolism, swords and lightning bolts are compatible and interchangeable emblems.[1]

Threading old Chinese copper coins (commonly called cash) onto an iron rod creates another type of weapon. These are fixed in such a way as to form a short, cruciform sword. This might seem like a slightly odd way of making such a magickal tool, but symbolism and wordplay provide the reason. Cash coins are round with square holes in the center: the circle represents Heaven, while the square links to Earth; combined in one object, the coin represents the occult interaction of these two powers. The word *chien* is phonetically similar to *ch'ien*, "Heaven, male; that which is constant"—the name of the first Hexagram—and also to *ch'ien* (written with a different character), "copper coin, cash." Such homonyms are then brought together as a potent trio of ideas in one practical form: the ritual sword. If this type of weapon appeals to you, then you may have luck finding an original example in an antique shop; they do pop up occasionally. This is preferable to trying to make your own cash sword from scratch, which may be awkward to produce and rather expensive. In my own collection, I have a cash sword that dates from the time of the Manchu emperor

Ch'ien Lung (1736–1795 C.E.); it comprises approximately 140 coins that make up the blade, hilt, guard, and hanging ornamentation.

Antique swords are traditionally held in the greatest esteem by Chinese magicians, especially those weapons that have famous histories. However, such a choice is not practically available to most contemporary practitioners, and is ultimately not that important in terms of the success of one's work. A student's own committed efforts will make a new sword just as potent as any antique implement.

Whether your sword is of wood or metal, one of the most universally applicable designs to choose is a double-edged type, as shown in the illustration (see figure 5). Similar styles of weapon, particularly a type known as a Narrow Blade, can be found in the advanced stages of Tai-Chi Chuan practices. These can be obtained from martial arts suppliers. It is traditional to attach red tassels to the hilt of the ritual sword, in order to further emphasize and empower its active force. After consecration, it should also be wrapped in clean cloth, preferably of a red color again, when not in use. Remember to always treat your weapon with utmost respect, because it represents the extension of your essential spirit, and to abuse it is to insult your own self!

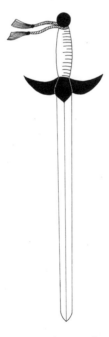

Figure 5. The ritual sword.

If possible, the sword's blade can also be embellished with dragon images, or other relevant designs; in both China and Japan, the sword is considered to be the special "god-body" (J. *shintai*) of the Dragon Spirit. It can also be inscribed with various traditional power-giving formulae, such as the following.

"Power over all spirits; power to make all things come to pass; the greatest power of all!"

The most important thing, though, is that the sword should feel right to you, however it looks and from whatever source it comes. You should sense that your own vital energy flows freely into it because you are fully at ease with it. Perhaps more importantly than for any other magickal tool, you must feel that you are truly one with the sword, knowing that you hold in your hand the very image of your soul.

In Chinese magick, the sword generally takes the place of the wand as it is used in our own Western traditions. It is often used to trace occult calligraphy directly in the air, or in the same media as for the Chinese spirit wand, to achieve "instant" talismanic magick.

In the magick of *mudra*—hand signs or gestures—"Sword" is represented by the first and second fingers tight together and pointing directly upwards, while the ring and little fingers curl into the palm with the thumb over them. This sign can often be seen being made by magicians and exorcists in Chinese illustrations. Often these figures are depicted in a one-legged "crane" posture, a ritual sword stretching out from one hand, while the other hand forms the essential mudra. This is a Tai-Chi Chuan posture, used by the magician who wishes to project his vital force through his body and into the blade, thus stabilizing it and making of it an extension of his power.[2]

"Sword" mudra may be used at any time when the power of the ritual weapon is required, but the physical tool is not available or felt to be suitable for the occasion (such as might be the case in a public area).

---

1. See Hexagram 30, Li, in part 4.
2. The Tai-Chi Narrow Blade is stiff at the hilt end and extremely flexible toward the point, making it a very difficult weapon to use properly. Only the most advanced practitioners of this martial art, skilled over many years in the projection of ch'i, can master it.

The Robe

As in many Western systems of magick, the use of robes is an important aspect of Taoist and Taoist-style occultism. The garment is a concrete emblem of the magician's aura. It also represents the personal magickal universe in which the magician operates, and consequently it embodies a function similar to the temple and the ritual circle. In addition, by wearing the robe, the magician declares both to himself and to any assistants that he has embarked upon the magickal Path. The act of putting on the item should be accompanied by meditation on the idea that one has departed temporarily from the world of mundane concerns and entered, instead, the Theatre of Magick. For the entire time that the robe is worn, petty thoughts concerning "everyday" life should be dismissed from the mind. Many non-initiates seem to think that the sole purpose of occult vestments is to make the wearer look impressive, thereby increasing that person's egotism. In reality, their primary function is to center one's attention on the new task at hand, to assist the mental and emotional leap from limited human expectations to an appreciation of the endless possibilities that the Theatre presents. Having adopted the regular routine of deliberately meditating on the robe's significance, the magician will eventually find that merely by placing it over his head he will experience an automatic shift of consciousness from human personality to magickal selfhood.

Wearing the robe helps to purify and attune the mind-body complex to the rite at hand. Due to its symbolic association with the auric shield, the robe also acts as a strong support for the magician's astral vehicle, so that it is better able to withstand any occult forces that may be ranged against it. Further, the costume is a certain physical reminder of the fact that the magician who wears it is an initiate, and should consequently behave like one. This is particularly useful when the human ego is acting petulantly and is tempted to attempt to gain the upper hand, to the ruin of all of the magician's otherwise well-intentioned efforts. Those readers who have experienced the personality clashes that are common within many occult groups will understand this situation only too well.

To the Taoist or Wu, the ritual robe is aptly known as the "Gown of the Universe," and is usually colored red or yellow. The red type (Chin. *kang I*, "red garment") is generally sleeveless, and like all oriental ritual robes, it lacks a hood. Blue silk is often used to embroider the hem, with further blue ribbons hung down the front from the neckline. The yellow version tends to have wide-flaring sleeves. Both types open at the front and are often decorated with various power symbols, such as dragons, spirals representing the vibrant energy of thunder, the Tai-Chi emblem, the figures of the Pa Kua, and so on.

If the student is unable to procure or make such a vestment, but is already in possession of some other kind of garment that is used in occult practices, such as a simple black robe, this may be used instead. In this case, concentration upon the idea that the color of the garment represents the primal Void of the Tao may assist your ritual efforts. Wearing it, you are, like the unity of Yin and Yang, encompassed by the blackness of the Cosmic Egg from which all life and all abilities are born, and to which all things will eventually return.

If you can make the robe yourself, then this can help you attune to the garment on a very personal level, which is always good. However if your skills do not run to such dressmaking, then you may employ someone else to make it for you. The important thing is that you approach the finished article with the correct attitude; the robe is a sacred costume and should be worn with great respect. As with all other magickal tools, it must never be used for mundane activities, but kept wholly apart for magickal work. Nor should it ever be donned merely to impress others, or treated as if it were almost an item of fancy dress. If someone asks to see you togged out in your regalia, simply to satisfy his or her curiosity—and it does often happen—then it is best to refuse politely. There are many depressing sights in the world, and one of them is the spectacle of pagans and other occultists parading around on television chat shows dressed in their ritual garments.

Equipment for Making Talismans

In Taoist magick and related Chinese practices, the use of talismans (Chin. *hufu*) has always held a position of great importance. Over the centuries, such charms have been made from a number of different materials. For the most part, paper has been used as the base for the majority of talismans, and this remains the case today. However, some spells have also been written onto peachwood, or even on tablets made from gold or precious stone, such as the symbolically and ritually important jade.

In Japanese Shinto, an interesting variant of the magickal talisman comes in the form of the *taima,* an amulet that uses part of a dismantled Shinto wooden shrine as the body on which the charm is drawn. Such shrines, particularly those at Ise, are demolished every twenty years and then rebuilt in order that the structures designed to accommodate the kami may themselves be part of the natural fluctuation of creation and destruction. Naturally, this wood is considered to be highly potent.

If paper is the medium that the magician chooses, its color, and that of the ink used for the calligraphy, depend on the nature of the desired result. In other words, if a variety of colors are employed in this magick, they should always correspond symbolically to the types of force that the charms are intended to set into motion. However, as a general rule, the contemporary student may follow certain basic rules for talisman creation, though of course you should always feel free to experiment with new ideas. In order to make the most common styles of talismans, you will need a brush or pen, red coloring material to use as ink, and yellow paper.

Traditionally, the stem of the brush had to be made from peachwood, due to the special and sacred nature of that tree. The instrument also had to be virgin—that is, previously unused. Given the fact that it is somewhat difficult to obtain peachwood brushes (unless you could make some for yourself!), it suffices that the brush should at least be new. Size and type are up to your own convenience; you may wish to use traditional Chinese calligraphy brushes, or else prefer an ordinary paintbrush.[1] In order to achieve the correct look for proper Chinese calligraphy, it is difficult to avoid using a traditional Chinese brush; the specific shape of the brush-head allows the user to form the strokes in an authentic manner that is difficult to replicate exactly with an ordinary paint brush. However, for those people who do not wish to practice calligraphy as an art form, but only desire to make effective Chinese talismans, a normal brush is an adequate instrument.[2]

For red ink, the ancient magicians used cinnabar as a pigment, mixed with gum that acted as a binder. Cinnabar, otherwise known as sulphuret of mercury, has symbolic connections to longevity, blood, and so on. The ancient pictogram for the mineral shows it being transformed in the crucible of the alchemist, which, in Taoist sexual terms, refers to the bodily alchemy of the female genitalia and menstruation; "Cinnabar Cave" and "Cinnabar Crevice" are Taoist phrases used for the inner vagina and vulva of female partners in the sexual mysteries. In the practices of chi-kung, the same pictogram also represents the universal ch'i energy that is refined in the body's own "Cinnabar Field," situated at the navel.

However, it would be very unwise for the modern student to attempt to replicate such an ink recipe, as cinnabar is dangerously toxic. Choose a safer alternative instead. For most talismans, I use either Chinese calligraphy ink that must be ground from a stick and mixed with water, ordinary artist's ink, or natural food colorings that I can blend together to make a blood-red hue. My reason for using the latter is that I can safely use it for talismans that are destined for consumption. The drawbacks with food colorings are that they tend to fade on paper more quickly than ordinary ink, and the vibrancy of their hues is not so rich as that for calligraphy ink, which can result in talismanic characters that look rather listless and dull.

Yellow paper can generally be used as the body upon which all characters and signs are painted. Sometimes red paper may be substituted, with white paint for the characters, but in order to avoid confusion I will discuss only the former arrangement which is the most usual in practical Chinese magick.

Yellow is the color of Earth, the womb of Nature, which receives the creative and impelling energy of Heaven (represented by the red ink), and which in turn gives birth to form and substance. The use of red and yellow in combination draws upon the essential partnership of these two polarities in order to create the change that the charm seeks to achieve. The magickal result of the rite is the child, or product, of the union of Heaven and Earth.

The ritual writing brush (Chin. *pi*) is symbolic of the phallus in Chinese art. Hence, in the creation of talismans it also signifies the sexual power and energized Will of the magician, by virtue of which the generative and active Yang power of the cosmos is projected into its receptive Yin matrix.

If you desire to use talismans in a "eucharistic" manner, for such purposes as internal alchemy (Chin. *neidan*), the development of personal faculties, and so on, rice paper may be used as the body for the charm. However, as stated before, natural food colorings should be used as ink so that the finished talisman is safe to consume.

In circumstances that require a talisman to be kept for a period of time, especially one that is designed to be carried around on one's person, an appropriate container is essential for its safekeeping. This could be a pouch or a wallet. Alternatively, I often keep such talismans rolled-up inside small wooden tubes; these were originally meant to hold embroidery needles, but they are perfect as attractive and secure homes for fragile paper charms.

As with all consecrated tools, these items must never be used for any other purpose once they have been dedicated to the magickal Path.

An interesting alternative to traditional practice is to use your own body in the place of paper; the magickal characters are drawn directly onto the skin, using a thick henna-based mixture such as Indian mehndi paste, which gives an orange-red color. The henna permanently stains the top layer of skin, but the body sheds this naturally over a period of one to four weeks. The design is eventually lost, so you need not fear ending up with a permanent tattoo that could never be removed. The virtues of this particular method are that you are continually carrying the talisman around, it cannot be misplaced accidentally, and its action upon the physical body is that much more direct and dynamic. Those working with a particular deity in a series of regular devotional invocations might find this technique especially useful; they can draw the signs or characters of their patron onto themselves, in order to have a literal bodily link to that god or goddess for the duration of their work.

---

1. On a personal note, I would encourage students to avoid the use of Chinese calligraphy brushes that have heads made from soft, dark brown bristles. These are usually wolf hairs. I think that wolves, globally, have a hard enough time as it is without the additional burden of being turned into brushes!

2. Those who are interested in studying the techniques of Chinese writing would benefit from reading *Chinese Calligraphy*, by Chang Yee (London: Methuen & Co. Ltd., 1938).

The Bell

The ringing of ritual bells (Chin. *chung*) is an exceedingly important aspect of ceremonial worship in the temples of China and Japan. Folklore and mystery surround these sacred objects, which hold an equal measure of importance for both Taoist and Buddhist sects.

The primary function of the bell is to summon the gods and spirits to be present in the temple precinct; its resonant sound draws the attention of the magickal worlds to the priests/magicians, notifying their preternatural inhabitants that divine assistance or blessings are required. The same idea lies behind the acts of Shinto devotees who clap twice before the Jinja, and pull on ropes that cause wooden clappers to bang together, prior to offering prayers to the resident kami.

In magickal work, knocking upon the bell at the beginning of any rite also has a potent psychological effect. It signifies the magician's intention to focus concentration upon esoteric matters. As such, the act marks a distinct point of departure from the mundane world of human, everyday matters. Once the bell has been rung, no prosaic thoughts regarding "trivial" matters should be entertained by the magician, who must not be distracted from directing all his personal power to the work at hand. The sudden ringing sound, or the sharp clap of the hands, acts as a slap to the mind, driving away all rambling and undisciplined mental activity, leaving an alert awareness in its place. For this reason, it carries out a similar role to the donning of the occult robe.

Such important magickal significance was attributed to this tool by the ancients that many legends arose concerning the incredible supernatural abilities of certain bells, such as the power of flight, the dispensation of great good fortune to worshippers, a capacity to sound themselves, and so on. In some Japanese stories, the integral spiritual essences of some bells have even been visibly manifested in the human world. For instance, in a tale from Kamakura, the spirit of one such bell is said to have taken on the form of a gigantic priest who wandered about the locality.

Oriental, ceremonial bells are cast from bronze and are often highly ornamented. Some can be huge, weighing five tons or more, and they are rung by means of a large beam of wood that is suspended from the roof that covers the bell; the beam is swung against the side of the instrument by one or more people. It is said that in ancient times some folk believed that the tone of a bell would sound sweeter if a young girl was pushed into the molten metal during the casting process. This horrific idea is pure symbolism and the result of linguistic wordplay, and is certainly not to be taken literally. It probably derives, at least in part, from the fact that the Chinese word for "bell," *chung,* comes from the same phonetic series as *t'ung,* meaning "a virgin." This emphasizes a link between the instrument's function and the magician/priest's emotional and mental purity, unsullied, as it were, by influences from the outside world.

Eastern bells are different from their Western counterparts in that they are more akin to open-ended cylinders, being virtually the same diameter, top and bottom. However, Taoist and Buddhist practitioners often replace this standard instrument with large bronze bowls, which are rung by means of hand-held hammers.

In the case of the contemporary student, there is no set type of bell that must be used. Individual pitch and tone are more important than design, size, or the metal from which it is formed. Take your time and try out a number of different examples before you settle on one in particular. Choose that which has a sound most pleasing to your hearing, or whose tone best conjures up a sense of magickal atmosphere. The sound of the bell should not disturb your ears, which would otherwise only disrupt your essential equipoise during rituals. In my own case, I have a relatively small silver bowl that is handy enough to be transported easily from place to place, and yet which gives forth an evocative and sustained resonance (lasting more than fifteen seconds) when hit with a padded striking-rod.

In the pictorial language of Chinese art symbolism, the bell generally represents respect, obedience, and the bringing to pass of one's wishes.

The Magick Mirror

In Chinese and Japanese magick, mirrors (Chin. *ching*) are held in great esteem and are prized and indispensable possessions for anyone traversing the magickal path. Many Shinto shrines in Japan contain these objects. They are regarded as the special instruments of the sun goddess Amaterasu, and one in particular, at the Great Shrine in Ise, is said to be the original mirror into which the shining deity gazed at the very beginning of the world. It is for this reason that the Japanese view bronze mirrors as general solar symbols. The Ise icon acts as the *shintai*, the "god-body," of Amaterasu; it is the sacred housing for her divine essence upon Earth. A ceremonial mirror also constitutes one of the Three Imperial Regalia of the Japanese Mikado (emperor), the other two being the *Mi-Tama* (sacred jewels) and the Divine Sword.

The role of the oriental magick mirror is essentially the same as for its Western equivalent. In its depths, the adept gazes in order to perceive clairvoyant images of the deities, spirits, and demons, and also to have knowledge of events happening, or events that have yet to happen, in both the physical and spiritual worlds. The mirror also has the power to show the true forms of magickal beings, if they should be otherwise wearing false guises in an attempt to deceive the magician. Similarly, it is used to show the true inner emotions of the viewer. It is said that if the person is calm and spiritually at ease, then the mirror will show a clear and unsullied image; otherwise, the surface of the metal may be dim and the viewer's reflection distorted or in some other way lacking in clarity. As a Japanese proverb has it: "When the mirror is dim, the soul is unclean." If looked at from a rationalistic perspective that only takes physical matters into account, it would be easy to sneer at such an idea. However, to the initiate, it is not really the bodily reflection that is being referred to. In terms of an exercise in occult skrying, the Japanese idea has great validity; any emotional turbulence that might plague the magician at the time of the operation will inevitably affect the clarity of the astral imagery that he sees in the mirror; and if he happens to have personal or emotional problems, and he sees a clairvoyant personification of his own troubled self, then it's likely that such an image may indeed appear in a highly distorted manner to his inner vision.

Magick mirrors can also be used as "lenses" to actively project occult energy into the ritual workspace. Students who wish to learn more concerning the utilization of these objects as active working tools, rather than as simple passive aids to skrying, would do well to study *Initiation into Hermetics*, by the late Austrian occultist Franz Bardon, where the subject is discussed at some length.

The mirrors of ancient China were usually made from bronze and were of a convex shape. One side (the convex face) was smooth and highly polished to produce the reflecting surface, while the concave side was decorated with various symbolic animals and other figures in relief (such as dragons, horses, squid, signs of the Chinese Zodiac, etc.) and had a central boss. Tradition declared that the most effective and potent mirrors that the magician could get his hands on were made at Yang-Zhou, in central China.

In addition to the classical bronze examples, another type of mirror that is often used in magick is the Pa Kua ("Eight Diagrams") Mirror, otherwise called the Feng Shui Mirror. This is generally octagonal in shape, and consists of ordinary mirrored glass that is set in a black or green-painted wooden frame. Around the glass, the I Ching Trigrams are depicted in red. Such objects are used as part of the ancient art of feng shui in order to deflect destructive earth energies away from houses, office buildings, and so on. In this regard, however, they seem to have been rather overused in recent years. The tendency has been for people to place them in various arbitrary locations as a general precaution, with little understanding of the actual feng shui arrangements and necessities of the sites concerned. This is a situation that could harm far more than it helps, as it is possible that the sort of fortunate energies that are desired to be brought into the buildings could actually be repelled by careless placement of the mirrors.

Taking their use in feng shui as an example, it is obvious that the magician can also use Pa Kua Mirrors, or any other type, in a defensive role against the offensive magickal acts of his rivals. In such cases, the mirror's purpose is to deflect the energy of a psychic attack away from the intended target, and return it to its sender. When used in this way, the mirrors are called *Hu Hsin Ching*, "Mirrors that Protect the Mind." Four such ritual instruments can also be placed at the Quarters of the temple, to help keep the practitioner's concentration free from disturbance by outside influences. As well-known tools of defensive magick, they figure widely in the stories of Chinese thunder deities who use them to "flash lightning" at their enemies.

If neither of these suggested mirrors appeals to you, then an effective multipurpose alternative can be made. Take a piece of round, clear convex glass, such as you might find covering some types of clock-faces, and degrease it by washing it with mild detergent. When dry, paint the back of the glass (concave side) with black paint until you have completely covered it; this will take several coats to achieve. As you are waiting for the paint to dry, make up a strong infusion of mugwort, and use this to soak a circular piece of blotting paper that has the same circumference as the glass. Allow this to dry completely and then glue it to the back of the mirror, over the top of the black paint. One more coat of paint and the mirror will be ready for consecration. If the student thinks it desirable, an appropriate consecrated talisman may also be burnt and its ashes placed in the mugwort infusion, prior to wetting the paper.

The ancient Japanese conception of magick mirrors was that they had the power to draw in and hold the soul or life-force of those who owned them and gazed at their reflections over long periods of time; it was believed that there was a vital kinship between a person's reflection and his or her spirit. This gave rise to many legendary tales, wherein the spirits of the dead suffer at the hands of new possessors of mirrors that had once belonged to the deceased. In a similar way, some elemental beings are said to use mirrors as physical bases, in order to anchor themselves to the material world. This latter idea embodies a very functional and effective magickal formula, whereby the magician may use a mirror as a talismanic body for a particular occult force that he has evoked, instead of relying on paper charms for the task. This usage is reminiscent of widespread and frequently recounted tales of great Taoist magicians who, not unlike the legendary Arabic adepts, were able to capture spirits in bottles made from gourds. When the bottles were opened, strange clouds would emanate from them and trap the hapless beings before returning to the containers, their prizes being quite unable to escape.

In the state rituals of ancient China, a bronze basin called a *chien* sometimes took the role of the mirror. Both these objects represent the same symbolic values in ritual and art—e.g., conjugal contentment—but the chien was also used to hold sacred water for ceremonial ablutions and anointing. It seems credible that this water would also have then been available to the presiding Wu as a suitably reflective surface for any skrying practices.

The Drum

At the start of battles in ancient China, drums would be played to arouse the fervor and bravery of the troops, to instill within them the force and fire of Nature's storms. The reverberation of the drum-roll was likened to the cry of thunder as it crashed in the heavens, spitting out fury at the enemies of the gods. Consequently, the instrument was a primary emblem of martial defiance.

Yet, the thunderstorms that the drum seeks to imitate are not only destructive, but hold within themselves the potent power of generation and movement away from stagnation. Spring tempests release the fructifying rain so that it may fall upon ground previously parched by drought (in China, winter is a dry season), allowing new life to grow. For this reason, to the magician the ritual drum (Chin. *ku*) presents an effective means to excite great personal and creative power in both himself and any other participants of his rite. Its use also accompanies shamanistic practices such as wild trance-dance. Flowing with the beats, the dancer flings off any shackles of reticence, allowing the rhythm of the dance and the hypnotically repetitive sound of the drum to alter the state of his consciousness and project it beyond the human world and into the realm of the spirits.

Drums are also emblematic of the primal force of Creation, of the Chaos that exists at the very heart of the Void. It represents the hub of the Universe Wheel, from which all manifestation has emerged. The beats of the drum, therefore, are like the rhythm of the root-sound of Creation, symbolized by such mantric seed-syllables as AUM, AUMGN, and OM.

The Chinese word-character for *ku* can also mean "bulging," and "to stir up." Consequently, it refers to any state wherein energy is pent-up prior to explosive release as the drum cries out. Therefore, the ritual employment of this instrument may accompany any act whose essential formula is one of power-arousal and its subsequent projection outward to create change in the manifested universe.

Traditionally, Chinese drums are made with earthenware resonators and animal-hide tops. Sometimes, however, they were also formed entirely from bronze, and were decorated with ornate embellishments such as frogs on their outer rims, incised fish around the circumference of the bowls, and elephant-head handles. These instruments are treasured family heirlooms, and other collectors, such as diplomats, also eagerly seek for the bronze varieties. In the latter case, however, these sacred instruments have often been reduced to a sadly degraded and banal end by being used as ornamental coffee tables!

These types of drums have existed in Sino-Japanese cultures for more than two thousand years, during which time there has been little or no change in their essential designs and characteristics. Contemporary students, however, are not obliged to slavishly follow tradition, but may choose any sort of instrument that fits their purpose. Choice of pitch is also up to individual preference, though the deeper the sound the more reminiscent the beats become to peals of thunder.

If you are a vegetarian/vegan, you may wish to seek out a craftsperson who can make drums that use canvas skins in place of animal hides, or perhaps the skins of creatures who have been allowed to die from old age rather than slaughter. Yet, whichever type you employ, the occult effects of all of them can be enhanced with painted sigils or ideographs, appropriate to the instrument's magickal purpose. For instance, you could decorate the skin and resonator with the I Ching signs and word-characters for the fifty-first Hexagram, Chen, "Thunder." As in the practices of Haitian Voodoo, the student should treat the drum with great reverence, for it embodies a powerful spirit. It may also be found helpful to rub a small amount of mild ritual anointing oil into the skin on an occasional basis—though not so much that it becomes drenched!—in order to nourish the tool's occult energy.

The Spirit Wand

In the section on the ritual sword, I stated that in Chinese magickal practices, that particular weapon generally takes on the role of the wand as it is used in Western occult systems. However, Chinese magicians do utilize a type of wand in acts of spiritism—that is, communication with various spiritual or magickal beings.

The art of mediumistic contact via this spirit wand (Chin. *chi*), which is sometimes also referred to as "the magickal pencil," has an ancient history in Chinese culture dating back several thousand years. In Western countries, automatic writing and drawing, whether transmitted through a simple pen or pencil, or by a device such as a planchette, has been generally associated with Christian spiritualists and partygoers out for a spooky thrill. This has led to the technique being viewed with some ridicule by many non-Christian initiates, who might benefit from its use but too often reject it because of its unfortunate popular image.[1] However, such a negative view does not prevail in the East; here, the chi is seen as being a most potent device by which the magician can access the deepest levels of knowledge that are usually the guarded secrets of the ancestors, spirits, and gods.

The act of *pu-chi,* the reception of oracles obtained through preternatural manipulation of the wand, goes hand in hand with the very beginnings of the Taoist magickal system. Having entered into states of profound trance, the ancient magician-priests, or Wu, would allow their bodies to act as the conduits for the beings they had invoked. These spirits would then transmit messages and spells through the wand to the outer world. Many of the drawings and characters that resulted from this were deemed to have such a powerful effect that they were copied onto paper and were eventually incorporated into the collection of "official" Taoist talismans in later years. Hence, it is to this spiritistic source that we should turn when considering the development of the wholly esoteric symbols that are sometimes used by Chinese magicians in their spell casting, which are varyingly called Celestial Calligraphy, Ghost Writing, Thunder Script, and so on.[2]

The spirit wand is usually carved from the wood of the ubiquitous power-tree—peach. However, as with the sword, willow can also be used, as it has many ancient associations with traditional shamanistic and divinatory practices. The conventional lore regarding the creation of such an implement is very specific, though in your own case you may wish to alter the ritual to suit your particular circumstances. The chosen branch should be roughly one-and-a-half feet in length; this is approximately the distance of an adult arm, from the fingertips to the elbow.[3] Its direction of growth on the tree should be toward the Sun in the east. The tree as a whole, however, represents the lunar West and is the sacred emblem of the goddess Hsi-wang-mu. The choice of the branch, therefore, is not arbitrary, but signifies the necessary union of these two vital spiritual polarities. Prior to the branch being lopped off, the Chinese word-characters for "Spirit of the Clouds" must be carved onto the trunk of the tree, on the opposite side from which the branch has been taken. Below these words, the characters for "Wondrous Revelation of the Celestial Secrets" should also be cut. This is followed by a specific incantation that the magician should chant with vigor:

"Magickal pencil, potent tool that harbors secret force every day; I have cut you so that you may reveal all mysteries to me!"

Sometimes, one end of the wand is carved into a hook and is fitted into another piece of wood that acts as a handle. Otherwise, a branch is chosen that is naturally forked, rather like the hazel twig that a water diviner might use. Either way, the purpose of the wand is to provide a flexible implement for the transmission of talismans or other messages from preternatural beings. Such oracles are drawn into a thin layer of sand, rice, bran, or incense-ash, which is spread upon a shallow tray or board. The stylus-end of the wand rests upon the tray, while the handle or fork lies lightly in the medium's upturned palms, in such a way as to make physical manipulation near impossible. The possessing spirit then communicates by causing the wand to move upon the surface of the sand, etc., making pictorial images, word-characters, and other significant designs that are then interpreted by the diviner.

When not in use, the chi should be kept wrapped in red silk or similar material, and housed with all the other magickal implements.

The talented trance-medium can also use the *pi*, the ritual brush or pen used to write charms, instead of a specific spirit wand. Ultimately, the important point is the magician's own ability to enter into altered states of consciousness, and his capacity to act as a controlled and disciplined conduit for the preternatural forces with which he seeks contact. There is no genuine reason why there has to be a single instrument that must be used in all circumstances.

---

1. The powerful and intriguing pictures of artist-magicians such as Austin Osman Spare, and of a small number of the surrealist school who also used this technique, show the fascinating results that can be obtained by those who can transcend the common notions.

2. See the section *The Magick of Talismans,* in part 3.

3. In some of the traditional, Qabalistically influenced books of European ritual magick, such as the *Grand Grimoire*, the practitioner is counseled to make a "Blasting Rod" from a branch of similar length, with which to command evoked spirits. See Idries Shah, *The Secret Lore of Magic* (London: Abacus, 1972).

The Fan

A quintessential symbol of the Eastern spirit and identity, appearing in numerous forms in the visual arts and in past times having a complex place in social structure, the fan (Chin. *shan*) is also an important magickal weapon in Taoist occult practices.

The esoteric secrets of this implement owe much to Taoist cosmology, and ideas regarding the psychophysical make-up of the human body. According to the sages, all living things are invested from the time of their birth with a limited amount of ch'i, the vital and subtle energy that sustains physical being. This power, symbolized by Air or the spiritual Ether, is apportioned from the universal source of existence, the Tao, which in its function of life-giving is known as *Ch'i Mu*, "the Breath of the Mother."[1]

Death comes to animal life when a creature's store of ch'i is exhausted. So great is the fear of this loss of vital breath that belching and flatulence are frowned upon by some Taoists, who perhaps take the idea rather too literally; it is thought by them that quantities of precious ch'i are irretrievably lost through such bodily acts!

The fan, especially when wielded by an adept such as the immortal Chung-li Ch'uan, is considered to have the power to give new life to the dead, and so has an important function in necromantic experiments.[2] This regenerative capacity is due to the fan's magickal ability to "waft" currents of additional ch'i into the dead matter, thereby vitalizing it with new life energy. This idea is borne out further by the fact that the Chinese word for "fan" is phonetically identical to *shan* (written with a different character), which means "to give; to supply, etc." It is also similar to another word, pronounced shan, meaning "to excite; to inflame." A more important application for the average occult student lies in the fan's potency in operations of banishment or exorcism. Together with the sword, this tool is the major offensive device against harmful or disruptive ghosts or other errant spirits. By natural extension, it is also of use in any general state of psychical unrest where the cause lies in the disturbed emotions of human beings. The reason behind this function also has connection to Taoist cosmology, on the basis that what has the power to restore life also has the ability to drive it away. For example, Chinese lore is replete with tales of the possessed bodies of the human deceased, which then become *chiang-shih*, "vampires," otherwise called *hsi-hsueh kuei*, "ghosts that suck blood." In these cases, the fan is used to drive out the intrusive and "false" ch'i energy that has temporarily reanimated the corpses. In Chinese folklore, this type of horrific possession may occur for several reasons. For example, if a cat—a Yin animal of sorcery and the Moon—jumps over a corpse that is awaiting a burial, the body may then be prone to becoming one of the Undead. Another possible cause may be that funeral arrangements have been sloppily or disrespectfully carried out, thereby denying the dead a protection from destructive feng shui energies or attacks by malicious entities. In all these cases, the invading force takes command of the *p'o*, the lower "animal soul," that remains for a brief time with the body after physical death.[3]

To the magician or clairvoyant, kuei can often appear in the form of smoky, or indistinct and vaporous, figures. The fan is capable of dispersing such apparitions by its ability to manipulate currents of spiritual Air, thereby blowing apart the wraiths' coherency. All these various acts, plus those pertaining to necromancy, should be viewed in a symbolic, magico-spiritual manner. It should be understood that ch'i never refers to ordinary air, set into motion by the physical movement of the fan, but to a subtle, nonphysical, and universal energy that penetrates and connects all manifested things. The magician may utilize this vital power by virtue of his initiated knowledge of symbolism, and his own training and self-development.

In terms of its appearance, a ritual fan may be of the universally recognizable folding type, or of the static "sail" design that is attached to a central rod (see figure 6). Of the two types, the latter is the older, and figures most prominently in Chinese art. The Japanese favor folding fans, which are, in their country, aptly enough, symbols of life. They are of importance in the festivals of the sun goddess Amaterasu.[4] This style did not enter China, however, until the tenth century C.E. Whichever you choose, ensure that your fan is durable and can sustain handling; some modern fans, ostensibly made just for house decoration, can be pitifully flimsy and would probably fall apart within a short space of time if you tried to actively use them in ritual.

In Chinese art symbolism, fans signify "goodness," not only because of their exorcistic use in magick, but also because *shan* has vocal identity with *shan*, "that which is good or virtuous."

Figure 6. Two types of ritual fans.

1. This concept is echoed in other cultures, such as in the Hebrew Qabalistic notion of the animating energy of the *Ruach*, the spirit or soul of life that can also be translated as "air, breath." This is derived from ancient Sumerian views. The same idea is also emphasized in the ancient Egyptian civilization, as evidenced by certain chapters of the *Pert M Hru*, usually called *The Egyptian Book of the Dead*, particularly chapters 54 to 59. See either R. O. Faulkner, *The Ancient Egyptian Book of the Dead* (London: British Museum Publications, 1989), or E. A. Wallis Budge, *The Egyptian Book of the Dead* (New York: Dover, 1967).

2. See appendix A, *The Eight Taoist Immortals*.

3. *Chiang-shih* literally means "a cataleptic body." This accounts for the modern representation of vampires in Chinese films, where they are depicted as hopping along stiffly after their victims, their arms straight down at their sides. In the Chinese terminology, there is also a hidden suggestion that the vampire might also be a living person whose body has become rigid as a result of trance-induction, but whose spirit roams freely abroad, invisibly drawing out the life force from others. Such astral seeking is a function of the Yin polarity, as indicated by the traditional Chinese idea that vampires can fly with great speed through the night sky, being empowered by moonlight. There is a very great similarity in this practice to the sending of the fetch in northern European magick. Underneath all the respective layers of folklore, the two cases are probably identical.

4. At one time, they were also used as unorthodox weapons for self-defense, and they still play a minor role in some martial arts traditions.

The Ritual Light

The profuse and colorful adornments of paper lanterns (Chin. *teng*) are a common sight in Chinese and Japanese festivals. They are also important implements in the magician's collection of occult paraphernalia. Unless otherwise specified, however, all the following symbolic and ritual attributions also apply to naked candles (Chin. *chu*). Practically speaking, it will matter little if you choose one over the other in your own work.

Specific festivals within the Chinese calendar serve to illustrate the cultural importance of lanterns. At the end of the New Year celebrations, the Festival of Lanterns is held on the fifteenth day of the first month.[1] This is a time given over to the honoring of ancestor spirits, who return to the physical world to take their own part in the festivities of the changing year. In order that the way back to the Otherworld may be clearly visible to their sight at the end of the celebrations, the invisible spirit paths are lit up by a great profusion of lanterns that are hung all around on houses and along streets.

These lights are also used later in the year during the infamous Festival of the Hungry Ghosts. This is held over a whole lunar month, but the main rites are usually carried out on the fifteenth day of the seventh month.[2] This notorious time of the year is concerned with minimizing the harm caused in the world by the so-called hungry ghosts. These are the spirits of those killed by violence, the drowned whose bodies were never recovered—thereby denying them proper burial in accordance with the laws of feng shui—and all the ancestors who have been denied or ignored by their descendants. For all these types of enraged kuei, the journey back to the Land of the Dead is near to impossible. They are hungry because they yearn for the attention of the living. Stuck in a state of limbo, they cannot pass on to the next world, and their aching desire becomes aggressive. They roam the world in a condition of utter torment, a mass of unquiet and vengeful ghosts whose presence creates potential dangers for humankind. Accordingly, lanterns are hung for their comfort, and to guide them, hopefully, to the gates of the Otherworld. Communal efforts are also made to provide the souls of those dispossessed by their families with votive sacrifices of food, drink, "spirit money," and so on, so that they will not prey on the peace of the living or molest the shrines erected to other ancestral beings.

Japan also has a nationwide Festival of the Dead, called *Bommatsuri*, or *O-Bon*. This is held over four days in July, and like its Chinese equivalent it also utilizes lamps to conduct the discarnate ones back to their own realm. In addition to being hung in the usual fashion, these lights are also placed in the prows of small model boats that are then floated down rivers. Riding in these diminutive vessels, the spirits can return from wherever they have come.

Such is the public use of ritual lanterns. For the magician, these basic attributions are extended still further; in the temple, the magickal light takes on a multi-layered character. The flame of the light, whether from lanterns or bare candles, represents the Sun as it rises at dawn in the eastern sky. It is an exterior depiction of the creative forces of the Yang which are also present in the body of the magician, giving him the power to actively project the shining rays of his own Will into the world. As the light from the Sun illuminates all the dark corners of the world, so too is the spiritually powerful flame of the lantern or candle a very special and hallowing sign. It represents the light of the magician's magico-spiritual awareness, by which he seeks to clarify and direct his lesser human thoughts. Attempting to elevate his consciousness to a oneness with the flow of Tao, all his subsequent occult actions are truly wu-wei.

To illuminate the temple with such sacred incandescence is tantamount to calling upon the gods to be present and to assist the magician's endeavors. This is particularly true of the magician's own inner self, and of the essential call to that deity within to flood his ego-consciousness with the wisdom to act in true alignment with the Way, instead of being at odds with it, as is too often the case. As with the ringing of the bell, the act of lighting the lanterns or candles is a beacon to the magickal universe, an indicator of the magician's intentions to embark upon some kind of magickal activity.

Ritual lights, placed upon the altar, have been traditionally used by Chinese magicians to draw in powerful spirits to the temple, like moths to a flame. Attracted by the magickal authority that the glow conveys, such intelligences are drawn into the sacred area, and may then be put to the service of the practitioner's wider aims. Yet, paradoxically, the Chinese word for a candle, *chu*, is phonetically similar to another word pronounced *chu*, which means "to drive out; to exorcise." In other words, the flame of occult command and spiritual wisdom that summons, is also a lashing fiery whip of punishment, repelling unwanted presences from the temple and keeping the magician free of psychical interference.

Chinese lanterns come in a variety of shapes and sizes and are readily available (see figure 7). Most are generally made from strong paper or silk. Find examples that are visually pleasing to you and that can be easily suspended in your working area. Some styles can be supported upon poles, while others work better if hung from the ceiling. Those that have a rectangular shape can also be placed directly onto the altar. Choose the type most convenient to your own circumstances.

Figure 7. Examples of Chinese lanterns.

If you don't wish to purchase a lantern and are happiest with bare candles, that's fine for most operations. For rites designed to promote fertility, however, you may find it expedient to utilize a lantern; in Chinese symbolism it is an emblem of great fruitfulness. Those who are already experienced in the use of candles in magick will know that it is also helpful to choose the color of the wax to fit the nature or goal of the ritual. In the case of active exploration of the influences of the various I Ching Trigrams and Hexagrams, appropriate colors can be found in the lists in part 4 of this book.

---

1. Roughly corresponding to the end of February in the Western calendar.
2. Corresponding to our August.

71

Incense

Fragrances (Chin. *hsiang*) have been used in oriental religious and magickal practices for thousands of years. Initially, such perfumes were smoldered in specially constructed thuribles, an essential part of temple furniture. Nowadays, however, it is a more common practice for incense sticks (joss sticks) to be used. Although this has also become a regular custom in the West, it does have to be said that the quality of scent derived from a stick, though adequate in most cases, can rarely match that of loose-grain incense smoldered on charcoal.

The word *joss* properly means "an item of Chinese spiritual devotion," such as a statuette of a deity.[1] Hence, the fragrance from a joss stick is sacred to the divine powers of the cosmos. A *joss house* is another name for a Chinese temple, whether Taoist, Buddhist, or otherwise. The word is possibly a corruption of Portuguese *deos*, which comes from Latin *deus*, "a god." One thing that the devotee must never do is to blow out the stick once it is lit; it should always be allowed to reduce to a smolder by itself, or else the initial flame may be fanned out with a wave of the hand.

The burning of perfumes plays an important role in different types of Chinese magickal work. Incense can be offered to deities, both at public temples and at domestic shrines, during acts of invocation. It may be used as a fumigant to help banish "demonic" forces and to purify the magician and his temple prior to further work. Burning particular scents helps the magician to create the correct atmosphere for the particular energy that he wishes to summon.[2] The people who practice external alchemy (Chin. *waidan*) may also need to burn specially created incense mixtures in their laboratories as an essential part of the process of transformation. In the latter example, such recipes can be very complex; a Chinese alchemical text, written in 116 B.C.E., recommended that the alchemist smolder a scent that had been carefully and harmoniously formed from one hundred ingredients!

Shamanistic practices by the Wu also include the presence of incense. Indeed, in China, the term "incense-head" specifically refers to anyone of a shamanic persuasion.

In the most common types of ritual or meditative acts, sandalwood acts as a basic fragrance that is generally appropriate for most needs. However, other plant substances are also popular as incense material. Aloeswood, for instance, is appropriate for all types of sex magick or Tantric meditation; it was a custom at one time in China for bedsheets to be perfumed with the burning wood prior to lovemaking. Mugwort, one of the most sacred of plants to the Chinese magician and considered to be highly potent, is burned to assist in the summoning of magickal beings to the temple. Other favored scents include lotus, ylang-ylang, patchouli, jasmine, cinnamon, orchid, henna, and many more. The exact ingredient chosen depends on the nature of the rite. If the student requires assistance in choosing an appropriate incense, then the examples given in part 4 may help.

In the Chinese cosmological system known as The Ten Celestial Stems, the smoldering of incense is associated with the cosmic element of Fire. Naturally, this is due to the application of heat being needed to release the scent. However, the specific magickal action of fumigation itself is, in practice, rather more akin to the element of Wind/Wood. Like air, incense smoke has the qualities of freedom of movement and the ability to penetrate into the tiniest cracks. For this reason, incense is the symbol of spiritual liberation, of the consciousness of people who may enjoy the revelation of great mysteries by meditation into the hidden areas of their own being. The smoke is also symbolic of the ch'i, or Vital Breath, infuses all of Nature with life, and which is of such importance in Taoist breathing exercises; the Chinese word *hsiang* literally means "that which breathes forth a sweet odor." It is probably for this reason that joss sticks are not blown out when lit; to do otherwise would symbolically pit the ch'i of one's own breath against that of the incense.

Ancient censers or thuribles were generally made from bronze and came in myriad designs, some plain and simple, others very highly ornamented. One example, made during the Sung era, depicts the Old Master, Lao-tzu, riding on the water buffalo that took him into the unknown West.[3] Certain censers were also formed into the shape of the Cosmic Mountain, which is a Taoist symbol of the very heart of Creation; these implements were called *po-shan-lu*, "mountain-shaped censers."

For your own practices, basic modern and inexpensive thuribles, many in a vaguely Eastern style, are readily obtainable from all occult shops. They are, of course, made from brass rather than the more pricey bronze. It is not necessary to go out on a limb and purchase an antique Chinese censer for the purposes of ritual fumigation, nor is that recommended on the grounds of conservation; a regular modern one will do just as well. This may seem like a self-evident and unnecessary warning, but having come across a few people in the past who refused to do any magickal work until they could acquire "the real thing," I feel obliged to make the statement nevertheless.

For those who wish to make use of a compound incense recipe, in loose-grain form, I have devised the following simple and easy-to-make formula that can be utilized as a general scent appropriate for many different rituals:

1 part sandalwood

1 part gum benzoin

½ part myrrh gum

  A few drops of jasmine essential oil

1 drop ylang-ylang essential oil

Grind all dry ingredients down to a powder, and then mix them together thoroughly. Allow this mixture to sit for a while. In the meantime, blend the two essential oils; always swirl them gently, never shake them. Then add this to the dry powder, and stir it in well. Again, leave the finished incense to sit for a time, overnight at the very least, then use when desired by placing small quantities onto hot charcoal disks. For extra safety, line your censer with fine sand first.

---

1. In Hong Kong, it also has the simplified connotation of "luck."
2. This is known as the Doctrine of Correspondences, or Similars. Individual plants and perfumes are linked to particular types of occult practice or category of spiritual being, so that by the employment of the one, the other may be sympathetically contacted or called forth. For example, the burning of willow during an invocation of the Chinese gods of thunder, and so on.
3. See Buffie Johnson, *The Lady of the Beasts* (Vermont: Inner Traditions International, 1994), 286, plate 284.

Mudra

Oriental magick and meditation are often accompanied by the employment of occult hand gestures. These are most commonly known by the Sanskrit word *mudra*, but to the Chinese they are also called *chuang-tai*. A Japanese term for the ritual use of several mudras in a sequence is *kettsuin*. The various finger combinations of the different gestures, which can sometimes be quite complex, can be used in association with other ritual tools, or else on occasion they may replace such paraphernalia altogether.

The connection of mudra to the Buddhist religion is well-known to many people, being noticeably depicted in the icons of its various sects. However, to the Taoist magicians and priests, mudras also provide an important method for directing energized will power. Both these religions owe their knowledge in this field, and a great deal more besides, to influence from the Tantric and yogic schools of India where gestures are used extensively with the practice of *asana*, for the purposes of *Chakra Puja* ("circle worship"), and during such rites as *Nyasa*. The latter is concerned with the occult empowerment of the psychophysical form by the visualization of deities in one's bodily parts, while mudras are simultaneously formed and placed over the areas to be energized.

When the magician employs appropriate gestures, he is following essentially the same line of reasoning as for the process of ritual as a whole. By the adoption of specific finger combinations, certain thoughts or potent emotions are actively engendered in the practitioner's mind, or else are given added strength of purpose if he is already concentrating upon them. The psychic energies resulting from such internal pressure are then released and directed by the mudras toward the goal of the rite. In this way, the magician's own body becomes a primary occult tool, energized with force and assimilated into the flow of the Tao. Magickal gestures constitute a form of silent language that can synthesize a series of complicated mental ideas into concise, powerful, and direct modes of expression, thereby transcending the limitations imposed by words.

Chinese medicine teaches that vital energy courses through the physical body by means of meridian channels; acupuncture, for instance, seeks to bring about healing by the redirection or activation of this energy, through the careful placement of needles in specific bodily locations. In a similar way, a properly constructed mudra also has the effect of activating this same internal power, focusing it through the magician's hands to wherever it is needed. By this method, he harnesses the active and the passive forces in his own body; he becomes a unity of Yin and Yang. He is a passive vessel that contains and nourishes the essential power of his magick, and simultaneously the active and literal means by which the energy of change is propelled into the outer world.

Each of the five fingers has an association with a particular element of the Wu Hsing: little finger = Earth; ring finger = Water; middle finger = Fire; index finger = Wind/Wood; thumb = Metal, though it is also sometimes listed as Void.[1] Some or all of these cosmic elements are then brought into play by mudras according to the specific combination of fingers. So, for example, in the "Sword" gesture, the fingers that take on the prominent and directing roles are the index and middle fingers. This causes a combination of the forces of Wind and Fire. It is not hard to see that this partnership is violently active, explosive even, the Wind feeding the Fire so that the magician's Will bursts forth in a blast of pure power; it is a gesture that is concerned with energy in motion. In the case of exorcism, where "Sword" plays a principal part, it is obvious that spirits cannot long stand in the way of such force if the exorcist knows how to correctly wield it. Yet, "Sword" is not a blind activation of energy that unthinkingly crushes all obstacles before it; Wind is the magician's intelligence or wisdom, which focuses the actuating power of Fire toward a justified and necessary end. It also signifies his refusal to be bound by those things that are not true aspects of his Tao, but to move continuously forward, instead, as an independent and self-motivated being. Many other gestures can also be profitably analyzed in this same manner.

In the practices of hatha and laya yogas, *mudra* can also refer to deliberate muscular contractions in other areas of the body, such as the stomach and sphincter.[2] These are employed in order to facilitate the free flow of prana through the yogi's subtle chakric centers, and hence to assist him to reach a state of transcendence from the worlds of causality. A mudra may also be one's earthly sexual partner in the rites of Tantric alchemy, through whom union with an object of meditation, such as a deity who is temporarily embodied in the partner, may be achieved. This practice is known as *kama mudra*.

As with any other occult implement, the effectiveness of mudra is increased if the practitioner has understanding of the deeper mysteries that lie behind the outward physical action. The gestures should also become familiar to the magician through repeated practice. Ultimately, their repetition over a period of time will create psychological signposts, so that the correct reservoirs of energy within the magician's own being will then be tapped automatically each time the mudras are formed. Power accrues with use!

It should never be forgotten, however, that simply forming the required hand shapes will not achieve your magickal aims; there must be real concentrated will power behind each and every act. In any genuine system of occult attainment, this is the most important factor that leads to success. Without it, the student will achieve nothing and will merely play at being a magician. The need for the serious practitioner to embark on a committed series of exercises designed to strengthen visualization and mental concentration cannot be stressed too often. If such exercises are considered to be too much hard work, then the student should wave goodbye to any further attempts at magick!

---

1. These are the standard Chinese and Japanese attributions. The Austrian occultist Franz Bardon gives the following alternative Western list in *Initiation into Hermetics* (Wuppertal, Germany: Dieter Ruggeberg, 1981): little = Air; ring = Earth; middle = Akasha; index = Fire; thumb = Water. The Hermetic Order of the Golden Dawn presented yet another version: little = Air; ring = Fire; middle = Earth; index = Water; thumb = Spirit/Akasha.

2. These yogas are, respectively, that of physical postures, and exercises designed to awaken the Kundalini by the use of pranayama, muscular contractions, and energized visualization. The Kundalini, or Fire Snake, is the magickal energy or vital spiritual power within each person, and ordinarily it sleeps at the basal chakra known as the Muladhara, until it is deliberately aroused or released in an act of spontaneous psychic catharsis.

Practical Magickal Work

Introduction

And how then (sayst thou?) shall I reconcile this Art Magick with that Way of the Tao which achieveth all Things by doing Nothing? But this have I already declared to thee in Part, shewing that thou canst do no magick save it be thy Nature to do Magick, and so the true Nothing for thee. For to do Nothing signifieth to interfere with Nothing, so that for a magician to do no Magick is to commit Violence on himself.

Aleister Crowley, Liber Aleph.[1]

The following sections give examples of various types of magickal operation. They are not intended to represent the entirety of either traditional or experimental work, but merely to introduce the reader to the potentials in certain Sino-Japanese occult philosophies and related systems, particularly in their links to the I Ching. The chosen techniques represent various levels of difficulty ranging from relatively simple exercises for beginners, to more advanced ones for those with more experience. As soon as the basic principles have been mastered, the student should not feel obliged to stick slavishly to the given frameworks, but is always encouraged to personalize or expand them whenever the Tao motivates.

At this point, a few words on verbal invocations are necessary. Those that are provided in this book are only intended to be examples of their type; they are not mandatory. Use them, or fire up your own imagination to create something better. I find that it is excellent practice for students to construct their own orisons or chants or, sometimes better still, to allow them to arise spontaneously during ritual sessions. In this way, the student is encouraged to enter into a very personal relationship with the forces that he or she seeks to invoke. This consequently raises the degree of emotional input given to rites, thereby increasing chances of ultimate success.

It often seems to me that lengthy verbatim invocations can be used to mask the absence of other techniques that are vital to magickal success. Certain specific chants, such as the Enochian Calls of Dr. John Dee and Sir Edward Kelly, can doubtless have very definite magickal effects by virtue of their own mysterious and inherent force, even if such happenings are not always exactly what the magician expects. However, for the rest of the time, the main value of spoken words in rituals is that they serve to inflame the emotions and provide the magician's mind with a sense of direction and purpose. If they are used as a substitute for other methods, rather than as an important addition to them, then they tend to fall flat and merely pander to a shallow feeling that the practitioner is somehow "doing something magickal." Too many people who desire to involve themselves in magickal practices seem to be of the opinion that basic techniques, such as visualization, focused concentration, and so on, involve too much hard work. They believe that all that is required is to read aloud invocations, written by themselves or other people, in a ritual environment. Yet it is the mastery of the basic "drill" practices that they ignore that provides the framework for genuine success. For further advice on this theme, read the books of Aleister Crowley, Israel Regardie, Franz Bardon, or any good book on Raja Yoga.

Nothing succeeds like persistence. As with physical exercises, magick and meditation are best done regularly and in graded levels of difficulty. If you're new to such things, don't expect to be able to play the role of the adept successfully from the very start. Real progress takes time and enthusiastic effort. Such enthusiasm has to be assiduously maintained, even during those times when nothing seems to go right; all practitioners experience such periods, no matter how advanced they may be. Try to derive something positive from these periods rather than simply becoming depressed. They are there to teach us needed wisdom, not to make us feel sad or guilty.

If possible, try to carry out some kind of esoteric exercise every day. This can be a period of quiet meditation and reflection, an active ritual, divination, or anything else that is required. If you pick a very specific time of the day at which to do it, make the effort to stick to that, and only deviate from it if an unforeseen and unavoidable obstacle arises. It may be that you are away from your temple when the time comes around, in a place normally considered to be anything but spiritual. Even so, you should still find a way, if possible, to surreptitiously honor the letter of your oath, perhaps by carrying out your rite on a wholly astral or mental level. For instance, I once set myself the daily task of carrying out a series of invocations at particular times of the day and night over a period of months. Modern life being as it is, it often happened that at those moments I could not avoid involving myself in mundane activities such as traveling on Britain's often crowded and uncomfortable public transport. So, if I was with a friend, I would ask that person to keep an eye out for troublemakers, shut my eyes, and settle down to my rituals on an inner level, outwardly showing no sign of doing anything more exciting than sleeping. If I was alone, I trusted to the gods to look after me. I was never mugged. If one is honest, such efforts don't always appear on the surface to be very productive; sometimes they seem totally mechanical and you may feel that you are just "going through the motions." Yet they do have a long-term effect by increasing the vital sense of determination to succeed in spite of difficulties, and this can only be beneficial. A certain Taoist sage once declared that the true followers of the Way should be able to enact their life's purpose next to a busy highway, if necessary; they should not always expect to be able to escape to a sacred mountain refuge!

An indispensable aid to the aspiring magician is the magickal record. This is a log-book in which the results of any work attempted are recorded, whether negative or positive, as well as additional and relevant incidents such as dreams, spontaneous phenomena, and so on. This might seem like old news to some people, but in my own experience I have found that too many students still neglect this vital tool and see it as irrelevant. The main benefits of keeping a truthful record are numerous:

1. The sheer act of keeping a diary helps to train the mind to concentrate in a disciplined and focused fashion.

2. It promotes a necessary scientific balance to the emotional forces used in magick.

3. It is a vital account of the magician's spiritual progress and helps to give lasting evidence of personal development, improvement in skills, changes in attitude, and so on.

4. Students may learn important lessons from examples of practices carried out by others, as documented in their records.[2]

5. Sometimes, when in the midst of a period of magickal stagnation and mystical drought, it is easy to become despondent and forget that we ever had successful results prior to such a bleak time. Looking back over previous entries helps to dispel such notions and boosts self-confidence.

6. An unforeseen event occasionally happens, the significance of which is not always immediately apparent. Sometimes, understanding is only granted after long periods of time have elapsed. The diary entry helps to avoid the adverse consequences of a foggy memory, so that the revelation, when it finally occurs, can be fully appreciated.

Like me, you may choose to be a traditionalist and write all your records by hand; it lends an attractive personal touch. The downside of this is that you can begin to run out of storage space if your accounts stretch for many volumes over a number of years. You may choose, instead, to place everything onto a computer disk, or even record it on an audiocassette. The method doesn't really matter; what is important is that the entries should be as honest as possible, otherwise there's little point to them.

Finally, it is worth remembering a few key concepts that are true for any kind of occult system. Firstly, magick is a subversive practice, in the sense that it runs counter to the dominant rationalist view of the universe. However, this still does not absolve the practitioner from common sense. For instance, the magician must always ensure that the intended results of his rites have a natural course along which they may travel. In other words, there must exist exterior conditions that link the magician to his aims, thereby helping his desires manifest. For example, it's no good calling upon the gods to help increase your knowledge and wisdom if you're not actually prepared to put in the long-term commitment and study at ground level through which such understanding would be gained. And if you cast a spell to attract friends or lovers, you must still get out to those places where you're likely to meet them; if you stay at home, no amount of magick is likely to help you!

Secondly, there is a longstanding debate over whether magick is a science or an art. In truth, it is both. It is a science because it possesses intrinsic formulae and laws, albeit very peculiar to itself, and because its postulates require the magician to rigorously test them for himself rather than accepting them as articles of faith. Yet, it is an art, too, because its success or failure also depends on the emotional force, personal temperament, and latent skill of the practitioner. Anyone can learn the theory and practice of basic occult techniques, and gain some proficiency in them, but real, energized enthusiasm must be present if such actions are to be successful in the long-term. Also, the best magicians are born, not made. For this reason, one person may be very skilled in a certain type of practice, such as divination, but only be able to achieve average competency in other areas. It is therefore up to each student to discover his or her particular talents, through a wide-reaching and systematic training, and then develop these for the overall good of themselves and their fellow human beings.

Whatever the practical usefulness of magickal rites, the ultimate aim should not be the attainment of mere short-term gains or quick fixes. Magick, properly understood, is about a greater understanding and integration of Selfhood, with all the changes that such assimilation brings. If magick fails to permanently alter the magician's whole approach to life, in all its forms, then it is at risk of becoming a vacuous and egotistical exercise leading to a spiritual dead end.

---

1. See Aleister Crowley, "On the Necessity of the Will," in *Liber Aleph* (York Beach: Weiser, 1991), 57.

2. For intriguing examples of such records, see the published diaries and extrapolations of such notables as Aleister Crowley, Leah Hirsig, Frater Achad (Charles Stansfeld Jones), etc.

Banishing and Purification

Assuming the Form of Fudo

Prior to any ritual or meditation, the temple must always be cleansed of intrusive forces that might seek to disrupt the magician's work. The area must be fortified as a sacred zone that will be receptive to, and supportive of, all magickal efforts. Such a cleansing, or banishing, also acts as a purification for the magician's body-mind complex, thereby assisting the essential psychological transition from the mundane world to the mind-set required in the Theatre of Magick.

A certain method employed to this end by Japanese Buddhist priests involves the use of specific mudra combinations that call forth the power of a god known as Fudo. This deity, originally of pre-Buddhist origin, is a god of wisdom and fire. Artistic illustrations usually depict him in either a red or blue form; he has a deliberately intimidating face, and his body is enclosed by an aura of divine flame which is known in Japanese as *funagoko*. In his right hand, he holds a sword that represents his wisdom and authority. From the left hand there hangs a coil of weighted rope, which is used to bind discordant supernatural beings and other chaotic forces that are antagonistic to the process of enlightenment. Some authorities have identified him with the supreme Japanese Buddha, Dainichi Nyorai, whose name Joseph Campbell has translated as "Great Sun Buddha." Therefore, Fudo is also a solar deity whose shining, invincible fire illuminates the darkness of ignorance and controls those entities who seek to interfere in the initiate's Path, either through deliberate malice or just simple lack of awareness. In practice, such problems do not generally arise from the machinations of spirits or "demons," but more often from the trouble-making capacity within the initiate's own human personality, which needs to be subdued before any further progress along the Way can be attained.

The following procedure is adapted from the traditional Fudo invocation, and is eminently suitable as a preparatory rite. It may also be found to be useful in situations where rampaging psychic energies are bringing about a situation of poltergeist activity, or some other kind of unwanted haunting. It is not necessary to be an actual Buddhist in order to carry out the rite successfully; the mudras are just as effective and meaningful to the Taoist or Tao-jen, provided that person can understand and assimilate the various gestures and their attendant processes of thought and emotion. Remember that simply mimicking the signs will not do the job for you; every part of the procedure is essential, as is a proper respect for the deity and his sacred gestures.

Figure 8. Fudo, god of wisdom and fire.

Before attempting the rite for the first time, ensure that you have a good idea of Fudo's image and can visualize him comfortably. The accompanying illustration can be used as a basis for concentration (see figure 8), or else a more traditional form can be found in *Buddhist Art and Architecture*, by Robert E. Fisher.[1] Although the technique may seem a little complicated at first, with practice you should find it to be relatively simple, yet very potent.

PROCEDURE

1. A battery of eleven strikes upon the ritual bell should open the temple.[2]

2. Visualize the image of Fudo in front of you. Take special care to include his sacred symbols and weapons, held in the correct hands. Invest this image with life; see the flames flickering around his form, feel that his body is swelling with power. When the image is sufficiently real to your imagination, invoke the god formally by word.

3. You should then endeavor to merge the image of Fudo with yourself, identifying your being with his; become the god in your thoughts! Then make the mudra known as "The Fists of Anger" (mudra 1): crook the little fingers and place them together, do the same for the forefingers, and curve the thumbs under the second and ring fingers. This is your affirmation that you are one with the deity; concentrate on this idea as forcefully as possible as you make the gesture.

Mudra 1. The Fists of Anger.

4. Extend the forefingers until they touch each other, forming a triangle; the other fingers stay in the same position as before (mudra 2). This is "The Triangle of Fire." Accompany this with concentration on the flames around you (as Fudo); see them grow in strength and visualize fire flickering around the fingers that form the gesture.

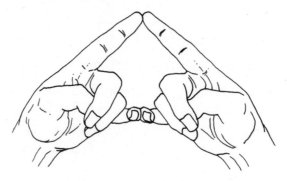

Mudra 2. The Triangle of Fire.

5. Now, form "Sword in its Scabbard" (mudra 3). With the left hand, put the fore and second fingers together and stretch them out, then curl the ring and little fingers into the palm and fold the thumb over the top. This mudra points vertically upward and represents the Scabbard. Then make the gesture for Sword with the right hand; this is basically the same as Scabbard.

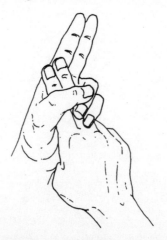

Mudra 3. Sword in the Scabbard.

Slide the fingers of Sword under the thumb and ring fingers of Scabbard and make the fit nice and tight. In your mind's eye, see yourself holding the actual sheathed weapon of the god, with which you will bring order to the temple.

6. The Sword is then to be drawn from its Scabbard, and the latter placed on your head (mudra 4). This signifies that you have recognized that there are potentially disruptive energies in the temple, and that you are preparing yourself to deal with them.

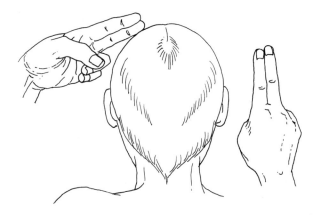

Mudra 4. Sword drawn from Scabbard; Scabbard placed on head.

7. Place Sword back into the Scabbard (mudra 5). Concentrate on gathering your strength for the "fight."

8. When you feel that you are mentally and emotionally fortified for battle, draw the Sword once more (mudra 6). Brandishing the weapon, know that you have total control of your environment. See light bursting out from your body into all corners of the temple, purifying it, and driving out unwanted forces. You must have confidence in your ability to bring order; quash your fears!

9. As soon as you are satisfied that the temple has been successfully prepared, replace the Sword in its Scabbard (mudra 7). Allow feelings of calm to infuse your mind; know that all energies are in balance.

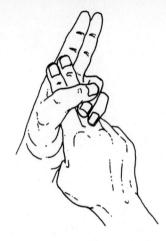

Mudra 5. Sword in the Scabbard.

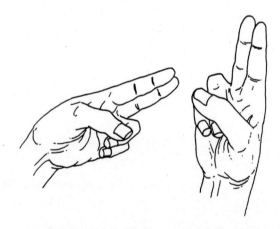

Mudra 6. Sword drawn from Scabbard, ready for use.

Mudra 7. Sword in the Scabbard.

10. Separate the image and identity of Fudo from yourself. Thank him for his assistance.

---

1. See Robert E. Fisher, *Buddhist Art and Architecture* (London: Thames & Hudson, 1993), 152, plate 136.
2. This is an extremely important number. In the I Ching, and also the system of Thelema, it represents the harmonious union of the male and female principles, the end of old situations, and the consequent birth of new circumstances. See Hexagram 11, T'ai.

Stone Warriors

The following ritual is based on a traditional feng shui technique, designed to dissuade "bad" earth energies from traveling down roads and over bridges. This was customarily used to keep the settlements to which such routes led free from misfortune. To achieve this, rocks painted with the characters for *shih kan t'ang*, "the stone dares to resist," were placed as obstacles to stand in the way of the unwanted energy and deflect it elsewhere.

It's possible that one reason for this practice might lie in the high regard with which Tai Shan Mountain is held. This is one of the holiest sites in China, and the god who personifies it has the special power to ward off malicious spirits and other destructive energies. Hence, he is represented in miniature in the feng shui technique. Rocks are also strong and sturdy, and are therefore pertinent magickal symbols to use when a blocking force is required, their inherent powers of defense being enhanced by the addition of the painted charm. This method is obviously linked to the fifty-second Hexagram, Ken, which is associated with the cosmic element of Earth, and its manifestation in the forms of stones, mountains, and so on; aptly, its name means "resistance, defiance."

With a little imagination, it is possible to expand the technique for general use in the temple, so that it may act as an additional guard against disruptive psychic forces, either as a precautionary device or because the magician may be feeling particularly hard-pressed. In this particular case, four stones would be used, one placed at each cardinal compass point. These then take on the traditional role of the Fang-hsiang; these are Chinese tutelary deities, often represented in the form of pottery figures, whose task is to magickally defend temples and tombs. Such "stone warriors" do not have to be restricted to one location, but can be transported from place to place. By placing them at the Quarters, the magician effectively marks out the area wherein any occult work is to take place; this is particularly useful if the fang-sheng itself is to be wholly visualized.

PROCEDURE

1. If you can get to an area of countryside or beach, take a little walk around and look for suitable stones on which the characters can be painted. You will need to find four that are similar in size and shape. Flat granite pebbles from the beach are particularly good for this purpose. Whatever their origin, the stones should be large enough to accommodate the painted charm and be psychologically effective in a visual sense, yet not so large that they cannot be transported easily. Let your intuition guide you to the right stones; choose those that "call" to you. Always treat them with respect, and don't take them with a grabbing attitude.

2. Back in the temple, carry out a banishing by Assuming the Form of Fudo.

3. Using your talisman brush, paint the characters for shih kan t'ang on each stone, in consecrated black ink or paint (see figure 9); these symbols should be written vertically. On the reverse side, paint the character and Hexagram for Ken.

Figure 9. Chinese characters for shih kan t'ang.

4. With the forefinger, or the hand in the mudra for "Sword," retrace all these characters once they are dry. Imagine that each one shines with power as you do so.

5. Meditate on the spirits of the stones; strive to awaken them to your Will. Concentrate on the desire that these elementals will act as firm defenders for your temple, and that they will successfully repel all forces that might seek to cause harm. Have the strong conviction that they will form an impenetrable wall around you.

6. If you intend to go on to further work from here, place one stone at each quarterly point of the fang-sheng. Because they are identical, you do not have to allot each one permanently to a particular point; they may be interchanged quite happily. Then form visualized telesmatic images of the stone warriors, standing over their host stones; they look like massive gray golems, armed with shields, facing outward towards any potential threats. Reinforce these images with further concentration on their strength and power to defend; know that they will only allow those energies that you seek to contact in your rituals to pass through their barrier. Here, once more, "Sword" mudras may be used to give added impetus to your efforts.

7. When all work is finished, imagine that the warriors are disappearing into their stone bases. Then wrap these in clean cloth and put them away somewhere safe.

8. Finish with a final banishing by Assuming the Form of Fudo.

If you have an area of land that you use regularly for magickal work or worship, and you wish to keep it permanently protected, you can carry out the alternative practice of burying the stone warriors in the earth at step 6 of the rite. In that case, you would have to concentrate on the desire that they will continually defend the sacred space from intruders. This won't necessarily keep out other people, but it might make them feel decidedly uncomfortable if they do stray in, so that they probably won't wish to hang around for very long.

As alternative imagery for the visualized warriors, the practitioner could choose to follow the Chinese example completely and see the spirits as tigers instead. The power of the shih kan t'ang charm has been thought to manifest spiritually in that creature's form.

Consecration of the Ritual Tools

Before the first attempt is made to use the ritual implements for practical magickal purposes, they must be purified and consecrated to the Path. This is essential in order to rid them of any previous influences, and to "program" them to your aims.

The following simple rite is concerned with consecration of the ritual sword. However, the framework can also be used to consecrate all of the basic tools if a few simple changes are made. Simply select the implement required, alter the ritual's compass orientation and mental focus according to the nature of the chosen tool, and pick a deity or immortal that is most appropriate to the task at hand.

Prior to beginning the rite, you will need to make an infusion of mugwort, and then allow it to cool. If this herb is not available, saltwater can be used as an alternative.

PROCEDURE

1. Set up the stone warriors, and banish by Assuming the Form of Fudo.

2. With a clean cloth, lightly wash the sword with the mugwort infusion. As you do so, concentrate on the idea that you are cleansing the weapon of any influences from previous use, and that henceforth it will be a sacred tool for yourself alone, wholly devoted to the purposes of your Tao.

3. Dry the sword, pass it through your incense smoke, and then lay it on top of the altar.

4. Facing south, make the mudra of "Sword," and focus your concentration upon the weapon on the altar. In your mind's eye, see it begin to blaze with a bright red fire all the way along its length. Accompany this with concentration on the idea that the sword represents the embodiment of your Will in matter, that it is an extension of your essential Self. Focus on the desire that through

101

its use you will have command of your own vital power to cause change in the universe, and an ability to call upon the assistance of any spirits or other beings or forces necessary for your work. Have unshakable confidence in the weapon's authority.

5. Hold the sword aloft and focus your mind upon an appropriate deity or immortal, such as Chang Tao-ling, P'an Kuan, or Lu T'ung-pin. Invoke formally as in the following example, and have the firm conviction that the deity is bringing about a successful consecration; know that he or she has heard your call and is manifesting your desire:

> I invoke you, Chang Tao-ling,
> Heavenly Master, lord of the Five Elements,
> At whose command the Two Powers move.
> The sword reaches forth into light and darkness,
> Calling to the ten thousand things;
> Lightning-bolt of my Will,
> Voice of my Self in all the worlds.
> The divine blade is the symbol of godhead,
> Bringer of harmony, creator of change,
> Essence of battle and avatar of truth.
> God of magick, master of exorcism,
> Empower the blade so that my Tao may manifest.
> In the name of the Will, let this be done!

6. Unless you intend to go on to other rites straight away, wrap the sword in a clean red cloth and put it away.

7. Finish by giving thanks to the deity, and purify the area with a final banishing by Assuming the Form of Fudo.

Investigating the Hexagrams

An interesting way to begin your magickal practices with the I Ching is by intuitive investigation, or skrying, of the Hexagrams. With this exercise, the goal is to allow the figures to speak spontaneously and directly to you, to allow them to relate their own individual stories without initial recourse to the actual I Ching commentaries.

The procedure utilizes the force of "random selection" to choose the character that is to be investigated. Don't try to influence the choice by concentrating on a question or thought, as you would if a divination were being carried out. Act neutrally toward it, accepting whatever symbol is chosen without complaint.

Although the Three Coins Method of casting the Hexagram is specifically used here, being the most common technique, you may also employ the traditional yarrow sticks if you prefer. For the former method, you will need three coins of the same denomination; if they have been previously used for I Ching divination (Chin. *chan-kua*), so much the better. Any country's coinage will do, though symbolically and psychologically the employment of Chinese cash coins would be an advantage. Heads are always counted as Yang, and have a value of three; tails are Yin, and are valued at two. For I Ching divination, by throwing down the three coins, six times consecutively, the "random" Hexagram is constructed according to the following values:

Total for One Throw		Result
6	___ ___	moving Yin line
7	_____	Yang line
8	___ ___	Yin line
9	_____	moving Yang line

If a moving line has been selected, it is always read, in the final analysis of the divination, as its opposite. Hence, for a total throw value of six, ＿＿＿ ＿＿＿ becomes ＿＿＿＿; and for a throw value of nine, ＿＿＿＿＿ becomes ＿＿＿ ＿＿＿. For each time that the three coins are cast down, one line of the Hexagram is constructed. This continues until all six lines have been formed. The resulting character is then found in the Hexagram table (given on page 171), and the appropriate oracle read as an answer to the seeker's question. In the case of the operation that we are concerned with here, however, the oracular commentary should only be studied after intuitive investigation has taken place.

PROCEDURE

1. Set up the stone warriors and banish by Assuming the Form of Fudo.

2. Place your I Ching coins in the center of the fang-sheng space, on a clean cloth that you should henceforth retain for divination purposes.

3. Take some time to relax and quiet your mind of all thoughts. Then take up the coins, shake them in your hands for a few moments, and then cast them onto the cloth.

4. Draw the first line of the Hexagram, which is always constructed from the bottom upward. Continue the process until all six lines are formed. If the final figure includes any moving lines, you may choose to investigate either the Hexagram in its initial form, or the new Hexagram that will be formed after the moving lines have gone through their transformations.

5. Concentrate on the figure that you have drawn, and try to memorize its composition. Avoid the temptation, at this stage, to analyze it.

6. Close your eyes and bring up a visualized replica of the Hexagram before your inner vision. See this with as much clarity as you can, and hold on to the image as steadily as possible for at least a couple of minutes. Allow no other thought to enter your mind; absorb yourself thoroughly in the shape, making sure that all the lines are in accordance with your casting.

7. Relax and enter a state of mental reverie. Observe dispassionately any thoughts, images, or feelings that may arise, but don't attempt to alter them or to hang on to any one in particular. The aim is to be a detached observer

of events, rather than an active participator. Allow the mental ideas or forms to arise spontaneously, but attach no particular validity to them at this stage.

8. When you are ready to finish, and have gained all that you wish, or can, from the investigation, put your coins away and banish by Assuming the Form of Fudo.

9. By referring to the chart, find out which Hexagram had been selected. Compare the traditional nature of that figure to the results of your own skrying; see if any points of your experience concur with any of the qualities, symbols, or circumstances that the I Ching associates with that particular Hexagram.

Don't be disappointed if at first you receive little more than mental rambling that seems to have little or nothing to do with the figure. The process of stimulating genuine intuition by assimilation of the Hexagrams into your consciousness is, for most people, a gradual affair. It will, however, bear great fruit if sustained; this is true both for the people who wish to expand their magickal practices with the I Ching, and for those whose main desire is to work with its standard divinatory function.

Pathworkings

The ritual use of guided visualizations, otherwise called pathworkings, can provide an interesting way to explore the worlds of the Hexagrams and their symbolic inhabitants. The exercise can be done as a valuable operation in its own right, thereby helping to give greater insights into the natures of the sixty-four signs. Otherwise, it can also act as an additional aid to the magician's concentration, prior to more complex rites, so that his mind is wholly in tune with the specific energy that he desires to invoke.

It is best if the magician constructs such mental scenarios for himself, using the appropriate emblems, creatures, plants, and so on, some of which may be found in part 4 of this book. However, as an example, let us say that I wish to investigate the nature of the fifty-first Hexagram, Chen. I might start by visualizing myself in warrior's garb, walking in the midst of a troop of fighters along a wide road. This crosses a boggy plain upon which grow willow trees and water-loving sedges. On either side of the road flit the capricious dead-lights of the will-o'-the-wisp, which Chinese folklore declares to be the souls of those killed in battle. The livery of each warrior is colored azure blue and flaming red. Each one also holds an appropriate weapon, such as a trident or mace, apart from a group at the front who beat marching time on drums. Above our heads, lowering storm clouds disgorge the sound of thunder, and rain beats down upon the world in a seemingly never-ending downpour. A furious gale blows, and dragons can be seen sporting and fighting in the tempest. Although the scene appears to be all violent energy, paddy-fields that can be seen in the distance, which require great quantities of rain, confirm that life often needs the active and extreme stimulation embodied by Chen if it is to continue and prosper.

These images and ideas can be extended as far as you like. Using the same method, it is a simple process to construct an appropriate guided journey for any of the Hexagrams. Of course, the more that you discover about the signs and their areas of influence, the deeper will be the content and satisfaction of such journeys.

Chi-Kung and the Cosmic Winds

Chinese magickal philosophy, being very much interested in the different occult influences that emanate from and are associated with the various compass directions, ascribes eight types of so-called Winds to the "gateways" of the cardinal and intercardinal points. These, in turn, can also then be linked to the Eight Trigrams of the I Ching. Such Winds are further connected with eight mythical giant pillars that, according to legend, are said to separate the vault of Heaven from Earth.

In practical magickal work and meditation, as opposed to purely geographical considerations, these Winds are not to be understood as common air, but as different types of prana or ch'i energy. They may be inducted into the body by appropriate breathing and meditative exercises, such as those used in the ancient Chinese practice of chi-kung. These techniques are carried out in order to achieve *yang-sheng*, nourishment of the vital life-energy in the human body. The ancient magicians considered this process to be of such importance that it was even symbolically depicted on certain magickal talismans. One such charm, known as "the Left and Right Hands of an Immortal," seems to show, in an abstract manner, a Taoist magician making a chi-kung posture that is known as "the Monk's Form."[1] This gesture is also used in Iron Palm meditations for kung fu, and involves a specific breathing sequence while the hands are simultaneously raised to the level of the chin and positioned as if holding an invisible ball.

The individual natures of the different Winds, and their possible effects upon the psychophysical body, can be intuited by contemplation on the epithets that the Chinese ascribed to each one, and to the characteristics of their associated Trigrams:

Compass Direction	Trigram	Wind[2]
South	Ch'ien	The Great Storm
North	K'un	The Cold Wind
East	Li	The Roaring Wind
West	K'an	The Wind that Lasts
Southeast	Tui	The Cheerful Wind
Southwest	Hsuan	The Cool Wind
Northeast	Chen	The Burning Wind
Northwest	Ken	The Sharp Wind

Novices in breathing exercises should not be tempted to jump in at the deep end and experiment with complicated and sustained chi-kung or pranayama techniques without supervision; there is always the risk of hyperventilation if you don't have someone on hand who can guide you safely. Always seek the advice of an experienced practitioner before you set out to try such methods.

However, the simple operation that is outlined in this section can help to introduce students to the basic process of chi-kung in a relatively safe manner. It will also help to increase experiential understanding of the different types of personalities that the Trigrams exhibit.

The exercise is best done in the morning, and preferably after only a light breakfast. It may also be found useful to drink an infusion of ginseng root before starting. Another traditional herbal practice is to inhale the steam from dried ephedra that has been placed in a bowl of hot water.[3] In this case, the aim is not only to help clear the chest and nasal passages of inflammation and mucus blockage, but also to assist the awakening of the chakric centers so that they will become receptive to an influx of additional ch'i. Recently discovered archaeological remains in China also suggest that it was an ancient practice among the Wu to use ephedra as part of shamanistic trance ceremonies and invocations of the gods. The plant is a very primitive gymnosperm, and has been profitably used in oriental medicine and ritual for thousands of years.

However, all such additional supports are quite optional. Indeed, a certain degree of caution should be adopted when using ephedra, especially if the infusion is also drunk as a tea; it has a potent chemical action. I make mention of it here only for educational value. Those who are determined to try out the plant for themselves, however, should only do so occasionally (not more than once a week). Also, those who suffer from ailments such as hypertension, diabetes, thyrotoxicosis, coronary thrombosis, and other heart diseases must never use ephedra. If in doubt, consult a qualified medical practitioner first, or else avoid the plant altogether. In any case, ephedra is now a restricted plant in some countries, so you may find yourself legally prohibited from its use. Any experimenter would also do well to read *The Magical and Ritual Use of Herbs and Aphrodisiacs*, by Allan Miller, before embarking on the enterprise.[4] Ginseng, however, is a freely available and very popular root, and is generally considered to be nontoxic. Yet, even so, it may be wise to consider that some experts have counseled against its use by those suffering from severe pulmonary diseases, as there are indications that it may push those illnesses deeper into the body and thereby increase their severity.

Do not try to experiment with all the Winds at one setting. Take the time to work with each one singly and in a regular fashion. Ensure that each is given the same degree of attention; never allow any of the powers to dominate the others. In this way you will obtain the maximum benefit from them and will not suffer the sort of problems that can be caused by an excess of one type of energy in your body.[5]

PROCEDURE

1. Banish by Assuming the Form of Fudo.

2. Using the sword, or better still the fan if you have one, trace the relevant Trigram in the air at its appropriate compass point. See it glowing before you, vividly, in a pertinent color (see the Hexagram lists for suggestions).

3. Remain facing the Trigram and imagine that a wind is beginning to blow upon you from the compass zone. Feel it playing against your skin and affecting your thoughts and senses as it does so. The nature of the wind should be fitting to the Trigram. For example, for K'un you would imagine that it is an icy blast, reaching out to touch you from the dark realm of winter, chilling you to the bone; for Chen it would be an electrifying experience, filling you with an exhilarating feeling of energy; the breeze from Tui would be light and perhaps perfumed with the scent of flowers that instill in you a sense of happiness, and so on. Concentrate, as well, upon the idea that this is not mundane air, but dynamic ch'i, the energy of life itself.

4. Without strain, deeply inhale the ch'i through your nostrils to a slow count of four seconds, imagining that it is moving down your body until it reaches the area of the solar plexus.

5. Hold your breath for eight seconds, and allow the ch'i to energize the chakric center at the solar plexus. Visualize this area aglow with an intense light.[6]

6. Exhale through your mouth to a count of four, and then hold your breath for another eight seconds.

7. Immediately begin the whole cycle from step 4 again.

8. Continue this for as long as you wish, though it is best to keep the sessions short at first until you have greater experience with them. However, you should always stop the practice if at any time you begin to feel light-headed. You might find it useful to keep note of the number of breathing cycles that you complete by using a set of "telling beads" (a string of japa or mantra beads, like a rosary, that is also known as a *mala* in yoga), or a piece of simple knotted string; every time you finish one circuit of breath, move your fingers along the beads or knots by one place. This is preferable to trying to keep a mental note, which could be distracting to the exercise. Try to gradually increase the number of cycles at each session.

9. When ready to finish the cycles of breath, sit in a comfortable asana and empty your mind. Allow the force of the inhaled ch'i to "speak to your senses." As in the section on investigation of the Hexagrams, pay attention to any spontaneous thoughts that may then arise, though don't dwell on them to the exclusion of all else. Also take note of any unusual phenomena, such as an increase in internal heat in any part of your body or the activation of profuse sweating.

10. Finish the session with a final banishing by Assuming the Form of Fudo.

Adepts in Chinese magick are famed for their ability to use internal heat actively, which has been generated by chi-kung practices, for the healing of people's ailments. A few are even said to be so advanced that they can stoke up their inner magickal fire to such an extent that they can actually boil water by placing pans of liquid on their abdomens or thighs! Similar well-known tales are told of Tibetan lamas who have used this heat, called *g-Tum-mo* or *Tumo* in their language, to rapidly dry wet sheets that have been wrapped around their bodies, even while sitting in the midst of snowy terrain.

Although it is obviously not a requirement for most people to aspire to such levels of proficiency, these anecdotal stories do serve to illustrate the famed potency of ch'i power. In the case of healing, it also shows a potential outlet for your practice that can be of possible use to others as well as to yourself. With diligence, a reasonably intense degree of inner heat, and thereby a strong personal level of ch'i, can be achieved by any serious practitioner.

After any chi-kung exercises, it is wise to disperse surplus energy from the body. A simple cleansing cycle can do this. Take the deepest breath possible, and draw in your lips as if you are about to whistle. Expel the air in short, strong blasts, pausing for a few seconds occasionally, until the lungs are completely deflated. Repeat this a few more times, but once again beware of lightheadedness.

---

1. See Lazlo Legeza, *Tao Magic: The Secret Language of Diagrams and Calligraphy* (London: Thames & Hudson, 1987), 89, plate 63.

2. Richard Wilhelm's translations, from the Li Chi, "The Book of Rites." See Wolfram Eberhard, *A Dictionary of Chinese Symbols* (London: Routledge, 1986).

3. *Ephedra nevadensis*, commonly called Mormon tea. The Chinese form of the plant, *Ephedra vulgaris*, goes under the name of *ma-huang* and is said to be more potent in its effects than the Western variety.

4. Sadly, this medicinally and spiritually important plant has received bad press in recent times. This has been due to abuse by several commercial manufacturers. The potent alkaloid in ephedra, known as ephedrine, has been included in some stimulant drinks and confectionery, often with little caution and few warnings to customers about the possible side effects to those people whose illnesses should preclude the plant's use.

5. The effects resulting from energy imbalance are many. Mostly, they tend to pose only minor problems. However, on rare occasions the result can be a little more serious. As an example, I can state from my own past experience that the overaccumulation of Yang energy, for instance, can cause some decidedly irritating symptoms such as the protracted disturbance of vision. This can last for some time until the energy naturally dissipates or is balanced by the deliberate counteraccumulation of Yin power. Provided the student always strives to harmonize the polarities, gradual experimentation with ch'i can be done safely and is an important aspect of Chinese magick.

6. This center is called "the Cinnabar Field" (Chin. *tan tien*) by Taoists who think of it as being the body's own subtle crucible in which the ch'i is transformed into a vital alchemical "elixir." In acupuncture, this same region is known as "the Ocean of Ch'i."

The Magick of Talismans

The briefest glance at Chinese magick, both ancient and modern, is enough to show that there are few methods in the magician's armory that rank as highly as the creation and use of talismans (Chin. *hufu*). For the Taoist specialist, such potent charms are indispensable, yet they also play an important role in virtually all Chinese occult practices. Even very specialist contemporary practitioners such as mediums, whose field of expertise usually lies in a different direction, are able to create simple talismans for the benefit of their clients; these are usually concerned with healing, the acquisition of good fortune, and the removal of curses.

The official Taoist collection of talismans, the *Tao-tsang*, contains more than three thousand designs. The origins for some of these have already been discussed in the first section of part 1, *Chinese Magick and Taoism*, and in the section dealing with the spirit wand. The genius and wisdom of individual fang-shih have also created many more over the centuries.

One of the most famous of all Chinese magickal charms is a composite collection of four archaic, graphic word-characters, commonly called the Seal of Lao-tzu (see figure 10). This is said to have been created by Chang Tao-ling, the deified magician and founder of the Taoist religious system. As such, the design is nearly two thousand years old. Its purpose is open-ended, in that the result obtained from its use depends on the particular desire of the magician who wields it. The idea behind the talisman is that the magician employs it in order to tap into a spiritual source of power discovered and established by Chang, the "Heavenly Master," all those centuries ago; it is the authority of this magickal force that brings the required wish into being.

This concept is similar to that of talismans that operate by association with various spirits and deities, whether such designs are revealed through mediumistic activities or by the imaginative use of characters already associated with those beings. In either case, the charms themselves act as the essential link between the magician and the

Figure 10. The Seal of Lao-tzu.

spirits, providing an ongoing point of ingress into the pretermundane realms and enabling the magician to call upon those magickal beings in order to achieve his goals.[1]

This process has its equivalent in the West, where the sigils or seals of elemental and planetary intelligences, which may be commonly found in various textbooks of ceremonial magick, are viewed as being the "signatures" of those particular beings. The sigils represent abstract expressions of the spirits' essential qualities, and provide a means whereby they may be embodied and controlled in the physical world. Through the process of ritual evocation, such sigils can be utilized as talismans, in order to bring about results that are consistent with the areas of influence that those spirits traditionally govern.

There are several other methods for spell-casting using charms. For instance, the magician may also create potent talismans using the Chinese writing system; the precise characters that are used depend on the specific desire to be achieved. So, for example, if you wished to create a talisman to help ensure general success in life through the productive use of personal abilities, you could write the characters for *ch'eng*, "to succeed," and *kung*, "personal merit" on yellow paper with red ink.[2]

The theory behind this particular style of talisman is that the Chinese word-characters are not looked upon as being mere exoteric shapes, designed only for the convenience of expressing human thought in writing. They are actual sacred designs. As well as describing circumstances, ideas, objects, and so on, in the mundane world of everyday communication, they also share essential magickal sympathy with the subjects they represent. Hence, in the worlds of magico-spiritual perception, symbols become living forms; in these realms, Chinese characters are, effectively, that which they describe. Subject and object blend, so that the use of the one can cause changes in the other. Writing the appropriate word, or phrase, coupled with the correct ritual or magickal technique enables the magician to form the conditions or outcomes that he desires, using his Will to mould the plastic and protean spiritual dimensions.

This is essentially the same idea that motivated the occult utilization of hieroglyphs by the ancient Egyptians. By painting the symbols for objects such as food, beer, and so on, onto the walls of tombs, plus descriptions of other circumstances that were required for a safe and successful afterlife, the priests ensured that those very same things were given an astral existence. Consequently, they became available, in a visible and tangible form, to the *ka* or spirit-double of the deceased. This same concept was also a fundamental principle in the day-to-day and nonfunereal ritual activities of living Egyptian magicians.

If the Chinese writing characters are considered to be so inherently potent, some people may wonder why they are not used in a talismanic manner by everyone, irrespective of whether or not they have had any formal magickal training. As a matter of fact, they are used in this way, to a degree. The characters very often appear as amulets in Chinese art; for example, various versions (and there are many) of *shou*, "longevity," are a popular choice in the hope that they will sympathetically promote a long life for their possessors. Yet, the real art of charm creation remains the province of the initiated magicians, the potency of their spells being increased by the fact that they are occult specialists, whose contact with the secret forces of Nature is far superior to that of the lay person. It is the magician's training, personal power, knowledge of the inner meanings of symbols, and his overall understanding of the flow of Tao that lie at the heart of a successful talisman.

As with many other systems, Taoists also use mysterious, occult writing in their spells, as well as the usual word glyphs. These signs, variously called Ghost Writing, Celestial Calligraphy, Thunder Script, and so on, are true magickal symbols that can only be fully understood and used by initiates. In 317 C.E., a magician-priest by the name of Ko Hung, the grandson of the notorious Ko Hsuan, wrote a famous but now rarely seen treatise called the *Pao-P'o-Tzu*. This was concerned with the art of talismans, alchemical philosophy, and other similar Taoist ideas. It also described the various signs of the Ghost Writing, and their associated occult meanings.

Some of these characters share certain visual characteristics with the ancient forms of the usual Chinese script. However, it is possible that for the many more that seem to have no philological origin, their sources may be discerned in traditional mediumistic practices using the spirit wand. As far as the Taoist magicians are concerned, this esoteric form of writing represents the special "language" of spiritual beings, the correct use of which subsequently allows the human to gain direct access to the divine powers.[3] Each sign signifies a command, a magico-religious idea, or the object of supernatural force that the user seeks to control. They are considered to be extremely effective when used on talismans, or when merely traced in the air with the ritual sword or an appropriate hand mudra.

It is a common occurrence for talismans to be burned as soon as they have been created and empowered. The ashes are then placed in liquid and drunk, thrown into rivers, or disposed of in other ways that are appropriate to the final outcome sought from their use. The reason behind this is that by setting light to a charm, the desire that it represents is liberated from thraldom to the physical world. The energy, which has been loaded into it during the process of ritual, is released and can concentrate itself wholly on the spiritual doubles of the painted symbols. These then present their case to relevant deities, as it were, or give appropriate instructions to the spirits that come under their control. It is through the intervention of such beings that the desire is brought into being. By destroying the physical talisman, the whole charm—characters, color symbolism, ritual force, and all—is transmuted into a wholly spirit-based state.[4] It should not be thought, however, that all Chinese talismans are burned in this way; many are retained intact. The exact process depends on the goal of the rite.

Whichever technique you may wish to use in your own magickal operations is very much up to the results of personal experimentation. However, as a general rule, you may find that charms that require a very specific result work better if they are burned after consecration. Those that are intended for a more protracted effect, on the other hand, such as a daily ward against ill fortune, might do better if kept in their finished form and placed somewhere safe. If you wish to burn your talismans and consume the ashes in a drink, which is a common practice in the East to assist the healing of illnesses, please make sure that the ink and paper used for the charm are nontoxic.[5] To be on the safe side, avoid this method in favor of the harmless "rice-paper technique."

The following steps outline a basic way to charge and consecrate simple magickal charms.

PROCEDURE

1. Banish by Assuming the Form of Fudo.

2. Burn incense appropriate to the nature of your rite, and purify blank talismanic paper by moving it several times through the smoke that rises from your censer. This should be accompanied by the thought that you are thoroughly cleansing it of all spiritual impurities.

3. With the ink and brush, paint your chosen talisman design onto the paper, all the while concentrating on the desire that you wish to accomplish with it.

4. With your ritual sword, or "Sword" mudra, retrace the lines of the characters, while imagining that each line is glowing like fire, infused with the concentrated power of your Will. Again, accompany this with thoughts of your intent, and a firm conviction that the talisman will bring it to pass.

5. Invoke an appropriate deity, i.e., one whose area of influence is in accordance with your goal. Call upon that god or goddess to assist your efforts and help empower your rite. Let this invocation be as simple or as complex as needed.

6. Pass the talisman through the incense smoke once more, and then, if appropriate, offer it to the flame of your candle or lantern. Allow it to burn safely in a dish or the like. As the fire consumes your charm, know with full confidence that your desire is in the process of becoming; see it being enacted in your mind's eye.

7. The ashes should then be disposed of in a suitable way. For example, in workings connected to the element of Earth, they should be buried in the ground; for Wind/Wood, they should be cast to the vagaries of the moving air; and so on.

8. Thank the deity whose help you have called upon, and finish with a final banishing by Assuming the Form of Fudo.

It is not generally a good idea to dwell on the desired outcome of any operation. Worrying about when it will manifest is a sure way to keep it in limbo. Carry out the rite, record it accurately in your record, and then try to forget about it. Lust of result merely acts as a barrier to successful magickal work.

The exact timing of any operation lies in the hands of the magician, and is up to the requirements of his own Tao. However, traditional Taoist wisdom also states that the cycle of the Chinese Zodiac (Chin. *huang-tao*, "the imperial way") can be profitably employed in the calculation of auspicious times for rituals. In other words, the chance of a successful outcome is enhanced if the nature of the rite coincides with that of the zodiacal sign that rules at the time.

Finally, when considering which talisman is most appropriate for your needs, it may help to consider the traditional Chinese view of "assisting and opposing elements." Basically, this idea states that the five elemental forces of Nature—Water, Fire, Metal, Wind/Wood, and Earth—are naturally helpful or antagonistic to each other, depending on where they fall in the overall cosmic cycle, and by the interaction of the physical elements that reflect their natures in the material world. These relationships are listed below:

	ASSISTS	OPPOSES
Water	Wind/Wood	Fire
Fire	Earth	Metal
Metal	Water	Wind/Wood
Wind/Wood	Fire	Earth
Earth	Metal	Water

Hence, Water assists Wind/Wood because its life-giving fluid allows trees to grow, yet has an obvious quenching action on flames. Heat from Fire/Sun warms Earth and allows seeds to germinate, but flames also melt the metal ores that can be found in the ground. The rest of the cycle continues in the same manner.

This way of looking at the elements will be familiar to those people who are already conversant with Golden Dawn philosophy, and also with the Tarot where the suits of the minor arcana are paired in a similar way. In practical terms, if the magician has recognized that a certain problem or weakness in his life can be linked to a particular elemental quality, then he may combat it by actively using a rite that evokes the force of that element's diametric opposite; or, looked at from another angle, he can enhance particular strengths by calling forth the element that helps the one that is associated with his talent.

As in Western systems of occult attainment, Taoist magick sees great importance in the control and use of these five interacting powers, which together form a subtle framework for manifested life. In the text known as *Yin Fu Ching,* "The Classical Book of the Harmony of the Seen and Unseen," their value is greatly praised (albeit using the strange term "foes," which is probably a reference to the sort of dynamic tension between opposite forces that so often leads to needed change):

"To Heaven there belong the five mutual foes, and he who sees them and understands their operation apprehends how they produce prosperity. The same five foes are in the mind of man, and when he can set them in action after the manner of Heaven, all space and time are at his disposal, and all things receive their transformations from his person."[6]

Here, clearly stated, is an equivalent theory to that held by Hermetic philosophy: "As above, so below." By learning how to control the essential magickal forces within the microcosm of his own person, together with an accompanying understanding of the Path along which he should travel, the magician may then act with potent effect in the wider macrocosm.

---

1. In one translation, the Chinese word *hufu* literally means "an agreement (with the spirits) for protection."

2. Idries Shah depicts this charm (listed as D) on page 215 of *Oriental Magic* (St. Albans: Paladin, 1973).

3. Compare this with the well-known Enochian language and alphabet revealed by Dr. John Dee and Sir Edward Kelly in the sixteenth century C.E.

4. For more information on this theme, read the chapter for the Anglo-Saxon rune Cen in my book *The Whispering Signs*.

5. Not wishing to alarm anybody unduly, I feel beholden to relate a personal experience. I once created just such a talisman to help cure a cold that I was suffering from. Without checking the toxicity of my implements, I painted the talisman, empowered it, burned it on the altar, and then drank a small glass of water in which I had placed the ashes. Within a relatively short space of time, I experienced a violent and frightening bodily reaction, presumably from a residue of the chemical dye used on the talismanic paper. Needless to say, this was not the effect I was after!

6. See James Legge, *The Texts of Taoism* (New York: Dover, 1962), 2: 258, verse 2.

Mu-Jen

There is a long tradition in the West of magick that utilizes puppets or dolls. The East also has a similar long-standing custom. In China, these diminutive figures are known as *mu-jen*, "wooden people." As the words declare, they are generally carved from wood, usually from that obtained from peach trees or paulownia, though other types of symbolically important trees can also be used. Sometimes, the root of mandrake forms the image, the legendary occult potency of this plant being esteemed in China in exactly the same way as in the traditional magickal lore of Europe. If mandrake is not available, then ginseng (Chin. *jen-shen*, "man-plant," or "like a man," so called because of its crude resemblance to a human figure) may be used instead; it has the same symbolic value as the former root. In Chinese folklore, ginseng is also considered to be especially powerful because it is supposedly formed from the elemental union of lightning and water. This is nothing more than a secret reference to the marriage of the solar male and lunar female essences in sexual alchemical symbolism, which results in the birth of a magickal child that is represented by the ginseng root.

Mu-jen have often been used to bring harm to enemies, and to this end they are sometimes provided with miniature weapons to symbolize the desired aim. Such use makes them practically identical to the Siberian shaman's *tupilak*, which is an anthropomorphic effigy through which the shaman projects destructive force at his opponents. In a legend concerned with the carpenter's god Lu-pan, the same magick is used when the deity carves a magickal figurine to bring drought to a town whose residents had previously attacked him. Sometimes, mu-jen may also be made of paper, and are then thrown in the general direction of the intended target. The underlying reason is the same as for other traditional occult weapons such as the Australian Aborigine's pointing bone. The object is considered to have a potent spirit double, and this is sent to invisibly attack the victim, embedding itself in him after having been propelled from the physical tool by the act of throwing or pointing.

Effigies are also used in the form of crude simulacra that are intended to represent the unfortunate recipient of such magick. In an identical manner to equivalent types of Western image magick, the doll is subjected to attack from sharp objects such as nails, which are hammered into its body at various "sensitive" locations after the victim's date of birth has first been painted upon it.[1]

An ancient legend concerning a Chinese god of wealth, Ts'ai Shen, illustrates the long history of this destructive art. At one time, the deity was a mortal magician who went by the name of Chao Kung-ming. He fought on the side of the Shang dynasty against the armies of the rival Chou, and his magickal skills were famed throughout the country. For a time, he was able to cause havoc in the ranks of his enemies; none could stop him. However, one Chou commander, Chiang Tzu-ya, conspired to destroy the Shang adept by means of the mu-jen. First, he made a simulacrum of Chao Kung-ming and painted his name on it. For twenty days thereafter, he fumigated the image with incense smoke, and called forth the demons of destruction. Then, on the twenty-first day, he impaled it with ritual peach-wood arrows fired from his bow. As a result, Chao Kung-ming died, creating a bitter blow for the Shang cause. However, after the war, his spirit was raised from the Land of the Dead by the gods, and he was deified and renamed as Ts'ai Shen, "the Spirit of Riches."

In spite of the above passages, it would be wrong to assume that such militant and sometimes downright antisocial purposes constitute the entirety of the wooden people's capacities. Among other things, they can also provide an important mediumistic link to the spirit world. *Tao-nu,* "Tao women," carry the figures around with them and use them as temporary bodies for the spirits and gods with whom they are in psychic contact. Seekers put questions to the Tao-nu, who then deliver the answers as they receive them from the effigies. To the Mongolian shaman, this type of magickal doll is called an *ongon,* and is often used to house the discarnate soul of a deceased and honored predecessor who will then be responsible for assisting a new shaman in his or her work. In Japan, the oracular person, nearly always female, is called *miko,* or *itoko.* Often she is blind, and is considered to be under the special care of the gods. These women also carry dolls for spiritistic purposes, but in their case the wood used is normally from the mulberry tree. These days, such itoko are less numerous than in past times, but may still be found in certain remote areas of Japan, such as Tohoku in the north of Honshu Island.

Apart from such examples, the imaginative magician can find many more useful applications for the mu-jen, and will understand that they provide an important and versatile extension of the talismanic process. However, the important point to remember is that merely to form the image is obviously not enough. It must also be properly consecrated to the magician's desire and given a form of life, as it were. In order to achieve this, the mu-jen must be charged with *ling*, "spirit-essence" or "supernatural power." The magician must also have a clear idea of what he wishes the doll to accomplish; in effect, it must be programmed to carry out a certain role. In most cases, it is better if the figure is limited to one specific task.

As an alternative to wood, clay may be used. If the intention is to create a magickal result for the doll's creator, rather than a client, a spirit-link should be formed between the two. This is achieved by mixing in a small amount of saliva, blood, or hair into the clay while it is being shaped. Obviously, given that the doll will then effectively be an extension of the creator's body, it should never be allowed to come into another person's hands.

The following rite follows a form of magickal practice that is known in the West as "the creation of elementaries/elementals." This also has marked similarities to the magickal use of shabti figures in ancient Egypt.[2] Prior to beginning, you should create and empower two talismans; one should be a charm representing your desire, and the other should depict the Chinese characters for *sheng*, "life," and *ch'i*, "vital breath" (see figure 11).

Figure 11. Chinese characters for *sheng* and *ch'i*.

Procedure

1. First, the body of the mu-jen must be created. It can either be very basic and unadorned, or else may show a depiction of the role that it is to carry out; for example, if the end result is to strengthen your ability to study and assimilate knowledge, then the figure could be shown holding a book. If clay is used, don't forget to blend in body substance, if appropriate. During the shaping process, the talismans should be burned and their ashes mixed in with the clay, or placed inside a hollow in the wood which can then be sealed. Always make sure that you give the figure a rudimentary navel.[3] It should also have a mouth and nostrils, which at this stage should be open.

2. Prior to beginning the ritual proper, banish in the temple by Assuming the Form of Fudo.

3. Take the mu-jen in your hand. Draw in a deep breath and then expel your air in a controlled manner into the image's nostrils or mouth. Repeat this several times. As you do so, imagine that this vital force is filling the body like smoke or mist, giving life where before there was none. Give a brief affirmation of that which you have done:

> The Primal Void was still;
> Chaos slept alone in the embracing silence.
> No forms, no movement.
> Then the Mother's breath streamed forth;
> The Way stirred up matter and motion,
> Imparting destiny to all things.
> Creature of my own hands,
> Living spirit,
> Take breath from my breath;
> Life from my life,
> Destiny from my destiny.
> Arise! Awake! Move to my Will!

4. Seal up the nostrils and mouth (this is easier if you have used clay), symbolizing the desire that no ch'i should escape from the image.

5. Concentrate on the goal that you wish the figure to achieve; in your mind's eye, see your new creation bringing your desire to pass. Say:

   "Magickal child, instrument of my Will,
   Walk the Road with me."

6. Conceal the mu-jen somewhere safe, away from prying hands and eyes, and in a location most appropriate to its task (for example, if assistance in studying is your aim, then this could be a locked drawer of a desk at which you regularly sit to work).

7. Banish by Assuming the Form of Fudo.

A final cautionary note: Some Western magicians often deem it unwise to keep the same elementaries/elementals for long periods of time, preferring to make new ones relatively frequently. In such cases, the old figures should always be destroyed and their life-energy reabsorbed by the magician who made them.

---

1. In certain areas of China, some people still consider it dangerous to give away information concerning their dates of birth, and as a result have been known to be deliberately vague with regard to their ages. Their fear is that if such personal information were to be revealed, making it potentially available to all, it could be used by particular types of sorcerers known as *da siu yan*, "little people hitters."

2. For more information on these themes, see Franz Bardon, *Initiation into Hermetics* (Wuppertal, Germany: Dieter Ruggeberg, 1981), 152–171. See also chapter 6 of either R. O. Faulkner, *The Ancient Egyptian Book of the Dead* (London: British Museum Publications, 1989), or E. A. Wallis Budge, *The Egyptian Book of the Dead* (New York: Dover, 1967).

3. In the human body, this area is the seat of the animating ch'i power that gives life to dead matter.

The Gate of Dreams

In common with many ancient cultures, Chinese tradition looks upon the adventures experienced in dreams (Chin. *meng*) as being of equal importance to the events that happen during waking lives. Once asleep, a person's consciousness is thought to depart from the physical body and the everyday world and enter, instead, the mysterious worlds of the spirits and the gods. As many Chinese tales indicate, in these dream-realms, events are often deemed to be as causative, in a variety of ways, for an individual's future fortunes as any act that takes place in the corporeal domain. Instruction and advice regarding all aspects of life, esoteric and mundane, may also be given to the sleeper. Such information may be direct and to the point, or given in oracular or coded form. In the latter case, a type of divination (Chin. *chan meng*) is then used to interpret important symbols. Ancient Chinese ritual law declared that all such inquiries had to be carried out during the daylight hours immediately following the night of the dream; as soon as another sunset had occurred, the act of divination was taboo.

Initially, this task was the job of a professional, but over time ordinary people were also given a means to decode their own dreams for themselves, to a certain extent, through the use of books that gave explanations for particular symbols and actions. One such book, the *Chou-kung Chieh Meng*, is traditionally ascribed to the Duke of Chou, a figure so influential in the development of the I Ching.

Akin to traveling in the spiritual realms during sleep is the shamanistic magician's deliberate soul flight into other planes of being during trance states. This consciousness projection may be achieved by a number of methods, but one particular way that we will discuss here calls upon the assistance of a "spirit horse." This supernatural creature acts as the magician's vehicle, by which he is enabled to travel into the astral realms and explore their topography. "Getting off the horse" is a phrase that is used in China to refer to a shaman or Wu who has entered into communion with the gods.

In such a guise, the horse is considered to be a force of feminine energy, and its magico-religious potency is widely acknowledged. In the system of the I Ching, for instance, horses, especially mares, are particular totemic emblems for the second Hexagram, K'un, which relates to the polarity of Earth and the Yin current as a whole. Also, when a girl first begins to menstruate, it is said that her Yin path is opening, that is, that she is becoming personally attuned to that cosmic force within her own being; the menses itself is often referred to by the euphemism "riding the horse."

This concept of the horse as Otherworld guide is not confined to Chinese culture, but may also be seen in many other parts of the globe. To the pagan Celts, a supernatural white horse was often responsible for carrying the spirit of a dead person to the Isle of the Blest; this creature seems to be an avatar of the goddess Epona/Rhiannon, though it may also sometimes signify the waves of the western sea. In Norse lore, the All-Father, Odin, is able to traverse all the different worlds of Yggdrasil, the Cosmic Ash, thanks to his magickal eight-legged steed, Sleipnir. The later European "witch cult" also adopted the general idea into its notions of astral flying, and it remains an important element in Anglo-Saxon runic magick.[1] In Islamic tradition, a white, human-faced mare called Al Borak ("the lightning") carried Mohammed into Heaven.

At Japanese Shinto shrines (J. *jinja*, "kami place"), this shamanistic practice is also the origin for a horse charm, by the use of which worshippers' prayers are sent to the gods for their consideration. The plaintiff approaches the shrine, bows, claps twice, and pulls upon a rope that is attached to wooden clappers. He then throws some money into a collection tray, or makes an offering of incense or *nusa*, before making his prayer.[2] The procedure finishes with a final bow to the kami, and the devotee's desire is then written on a prayer tablet that is called an *ema*, "horse picture." As explained in the section on talismanic magick, the fundamental reason for the magickal use of symbols in the physical world is that they are considered to have living reflexes in the spirit realms that help to bring about the magician's aims. So, the astral counterpart of the ema is charged with the task of carrying the wish to an appropriate kami, just as if the plaintiff himself were a powerful shaman with the capacity to ride the spirit horse into the divine realms and address the gods directly. The tablet is then hung upon the walls of the jinja, together with many others previously placed there by other seekers.

For similar reasons to this Shinto practice, it has also been a tradition in certain Buddhist schools to burn white paper horses during funeral ceremonies. By doing so, it is hoped that magickal doubles of these models will then take on life and act as faithful steeds for the deceased in their journeys into the afterlife. However, in more ancient times, it was a custom in Indo-Iranian societies for actual white horses to be sacrificed as part of burial rites. In our modern age, these symbolic horses have often been replaced by paper cars; this imparts a somewhat materialistic and prosaic edge, but the background reasoning remains the same nevertheless. The general idea is also to be found in the use of special flags that have fluttered from the hills and mountains of Tibet for centuries. Called "wind-horses," they depict a running horse surrounded by Tibetan prayers and with sacred fire in the place of a rider. Their purpose is to elicit good fortune from the gods. There is probably another link, as well, to the legendary fly-whisk of the Taoist Immortal Lu Tung-pin. Made from a horse's tail, it gives him the power of flight, and for similar reasons actual ritual fly-whisks are instruments used by Taoist magicians to assist their own spirit-projection.

One way by which the contemporary magician can use the spirit horse involves the deliberate creation of trance. Here, the aim is to summon the steed by the employment of active physical techniques that cause ecstasy, such as wild dance accompanied by hypnotic rhythms beaten out on the ritual drum. In shamanistic settings, this instrument is often regarded as a physical representation of the summoned spirit and is symbolically ridden. Concentration focused on calling forth the horse, and the exhaustion brought about by protracted dancing, cause the human earth-bound awareness to be overwhelmed by an upsurge of the spiritual Self and a consequent opening up of vision to a worldview denied to mundane sight. In this state, the magician then employs the spirit horse as a vehicle with which to explore the other realms of existence that have suddenly become accessible to him.[3] This is an advanced practice, however, and should not be attempted until a fairly advanced degree of occult proficiency, in general, has been attained. It should also be carried out, initially, under the supervision of an adept who is expert in it.

An easier way to begin to experience the nature of the horse is by the production of lucid dreams. This is an exceedingly important exercise in its own right, and all students would do well to practice with it as regularly as they can in order to gain its fullest effects.

PROCEDURE

1. Begin by choosing a comfortable place where sleep can be indulged without interference or distraction from other people. If this can be carried out in the

temple space, then so much the better. You may find it useful to sleep in the midst of the protective fang-sheng. The consecrated ritual drum should also be at hand.

2. Banish by Assuming the Form of Fudo.

3. A comfortable asana position should be adopted. You should be capable of maintaining this posture without physical strain, though it should not be so relaxing that you fall asleep at this stage.

4. You should then imagine that you are walking down an inclined and rough path in the wilderness. The sun is setting in the west; darkness is swiftly descending upon the land. All around you are rocky outcrops that make strange silhouettes in the half-light, and before you the path leads to a mysterious cave set into a cliff face. You are aware that this is your Gate of Dreams. Concentrate on the symbolism of the place as being a crossing-point where the preternatural worlds connect with the human realm.

5. When you arrive at the cave, sit down just within its entrance. In front, you can see that a tunnel stretches back into the rock and down into the bowels of Earth.

6. With an imaginary finger, trace the character for K'un and its Trigram or Hexagram into the earth before you.[4]

7. Being careful to avoid losing your awareness of the visualized scene, take your drum in your hands and begin to beat a regular rhythm; if you don't have a drum, you can visualize one instead and imagine the sound that it would make. As you do so, focus attention on the traced signs, and mentally call upon the spirit horse to come from the Underworld, to ride up the tunnel toward you. Imagine that the drumbeats are also calling the creature, its beats resonating throughout the hidden places of the Dark Land, irresistibly enticing the guide to come to you.

8. Continue with this until the horse appears before you in the cave. When it manifests, accept the image as it is presented to you; don't try to alter it to fit your own ideas. It is better if you can allow it to come in its own time, but if there seems to be no response to your call, it is acceptable to visualize the creature proceeding up the tunnel to the cave entrance. In such a

case, it should be seen in an earthy yellow color, like ochre, or in white if you prefer, in order to emphasize its occult nature.

9. Go to the horse and ask it to carry you into the lands of the spirits during sleep. Tell it that you wish to be guided through all events that may happen, and then be brought back safely to the physical world when you wake. Then climb onto the horse's back, and allow it to take you down the tunnel into the Underworld.

10. At this point compose yourself to sleep as normal on the physical plane, remaining in the place that you have chosen for the exercise. Continue to concentrate on the inner journey at the same time; relax into it, dreamily imagine the roughly hewn walls that surround you as you ride deep into the realm of K'un. The sound of the horse's hooves on the rocky floor makes a regular and hypnotic beat. Allow sleep to take your consciousness as you travel; don't try to stay awake in order to concentrate on the descent.

11. When you wake, make an instant and careful record of all that has been experienced during the dream-state, no matter how trivial any individual events might seem. In particular, take note of any companions that may have been present in the dream scenarios; you will probably find that the horse accompanies you for the duration of your sleep, provided there is no disturbance that wakes you and hence disrupts the efficacy of the exercise. However, the spirit creature will not always remain in a horse shape; it is not bound to that form, and its exact image will very much depend on the nature of the dream being experienced. Pay attention to anything that your companions may say or show to you, for they may contain useful information.

12. Finish by Assuming the Form of Fudo.

The association of dreams with the cosmic polarity of Yin is further shown in the following alternative rite, which is also designed to achieve lucidity in sleep. It is based on a traditional Chinese method that aims to induce temporary projection of consciousness into the Otherworld of the ancestors. The procedure involves the use of mu-jen, and invokes the presence and assistance of the goddess Tsi-ku, who also goes by the names San-ku and Tsi-ku Niang. This deity, whose name means "the Purple

Lady," is an enigmatic and abstruse character whose areas of influence are all concerned with psychical activities such as clairvoyance, spiritism, divination, and so on. In the past, those who wished to have contact with the spirits of their forebears routinely called upon her power.

In the following technique, Tsi-ku is called upon to temporarily take up her abode in the mu-jen figure, which you will have to specifically make for this purpose. The image then becomes a charm, by the use of which your dreams may be influenced and made more satisfying. Once chosen for this particular exercise, the mu-jen should not be used for any other kind of magickal rite, but kept wholly as a sacred habitation for the goddess. When not in use, keep it wrapped and concealed in the altar (if that is hollow).

Figure 12. Chinese characters for Tsi-ku and *chao*.

PROCEDURE

1. Make your mu-jen image. This does not have to be a work of art, though the female gender should be made clear. On the back of the figure, paint the Chinese characters for *chao*, "to call; to summon," and those for Lady Tsi-ku herself (see figure 12). Traditionally, the doll is given a set of clothes to wear, but you may omit this if you wish.

134

2. Place the figure upon the altar, and banish by Assuming the Form of Fudo.

3. Smolder appropriate incense and visualize the goddess in the air above the altar and the mu-jen. From the waist up she is the image of oriental beauty, her luxuriant black hair rolling in waves down her back. However, the lower half of her body is composed only of a fine smoke that seems to mingle with that of the incense. Concentrate on this image for as long as possible.

4. Formally invoke Tsi-ku. The following incantation is based upon a Chinese original:

> Hear me, Lady Tsi-ku, Mistress of Divination; San-Ku, goddess of the secret ways of the spirits, to whom no door is shut and no path blocked. May your being enter this image and invest it with life, so that it may empower my Hun body to tread the roads of the Realm of Night. What do I wish to accomplish in the lands of the Yin? I wish to search there for the knowledge of my ancestors and converse with Keepers of Power. Guide me back safely to the living world as I wake from sleep, to the kingdom of the Yang. Help me to remember that which I will have learned.

5. See the visualized form of the goddess descending and entering the mu-jen. Then, take the figure in your hands and concentrate strongly on the desire that the talisman will act as your guide in the dream worlds, and will enrich your night-time adventures.

6. When you are ready to sleep, place the image in a safe place near your head, and relax.

7. As before, make a careful record of your dreams as soon as you wake.

8. Wrap the mu-jen, pack it away, and banish by Assuming the Form of Fudo.

According to the Chinese occultists who called upon the goddess, the mu-jen becomes physically heavier after Tsi-ku takes up residence. You may find that this is so, or you may not; it doesn't matter. The ultimate proof of a successful invocation is to be found in the increased lucidity of your dreams, and the subsequent wisdom that you will gain from them.

1. For more information, see the chapter for the nineteenth rune, Eh, in my book *The Whispering Signs*.

2. Nusa are pieces of white paper, bought at the shrines from the attendant priests, that represent the purity and honesty of the devotees' intentions.

3. This process should not be mistakenly compared to the acts of possession that take place in Voodoo, where it is the worshipper who takes on the role of a *chual*, "a horse," upon which the divine loa ride. Such communion is a reversal of the shamanistic technique given in this section.

4. See Hexagram 2, in part 4.

In O Musubi

In both China and Japan, the number nine has always been considered to be extremely powerful in magickal terms. It is generally associated with the Yang current of energy, and consequently it embodies the power of creativity and projection of the Will.[1] Much of its potency is derived from the fact that it is the last single digit number, and that if it is multiplied by any number from one to nine, the resulting total will always reduce to nine once more (e.g., 9 x 6 = 54; 5 + 4 = 9). Nine is also the final repository of all the magico-spiritual qualities of the previous numbers, prior to the movement into double digits and the subsequent manifestation/sub-division of those forces.

Basic grid patterns are also held to be potent containers of magickal energy. They appear in many guises in various Taoist talisman designs, especially in those that are used to procure good fortune. One reason for such use can be found in the Chinese word *ko*, which means "a check pattern formed from crossed lines." This is phonetically identical to another character that means "to change, to transform," and hence it is one with the process of magick. Perhaps there is also a symbolic link to a Chou dynasty agricultural practice, wherein farmland was divided into nine equal and adjoining lots; eight being for private use, while the ninth, in the center, was a communal plot the produce of which was the portion of the rulers. For many generations in China, this was considered to be the fairest and hence most productive method of farming. Its grid pattern would therefore have the extended symbolic meaning of abundance. It may also be relevant to note that with those people who have attained "hallucinogenic" or visionary states of mind, grids are some of the most common images seen. These may just be purely chemical products of brain activity, or they may not, but either way they still signify a shift from the ordinary mindset into an alternative, and hence magickal, state of consciousness.

It is clear that a combination of the power number nine and the talismanic grid pattern would be deemed by magicians to be a particularly potent occult device. In

Japan, the practitioners of Ninjutsu have been famed for their proficiency in a technique known as *In O Musubi*, "Making the Signs." This obliged the ninja to make slashing motions with one hand, while imagining that he was forming a grid made of five horizontal and four vertical lines before his eyes. The resulting design was called a *kujikiri*, and was intended, among other things, to protect the ninja from harm as he went about his secret business.

Each line of the grid has a particular esoteric meaning, and the entire message or spell of the pattern is determined by reading the lines in the following arrangement, from top to bottom: first vertical line, first horizontal line, second vertical line, second horizontal line, and so on. This produces a final statement that can be roughly translated as "Succor to the warrior who must fight all men, before he is torn asunder in battle." The whole construction, therefore, was used by the fighter to calm his fears and give him additional strength while on perilous missions that would often put him in danger of losing his life.

By the addition of another visualized character on top of the kujikiri, the technique of In O Musubi is capable of being expanded into a focus for deeper meditation and spiritual catharsis. In a practical magickal sense, it also becomes a matrix for the magician's extended desires. This additional symbol is known as the *juji*. It is the tenth power to the grid's nine, and therefore signifies the concrete phenomenal expression, or child, of the kujikiri's creative potential. The precise form of the juji depends on the goal of the rite; for instance, a pentagram is sometimes used as the focus for meditation, or, if a more particular result were required, then an appropriate word-character would be placed on the grid instead. The following rite is based on this traditional technique, and can provide an interesting alternative to the usual form of talismanic magick.[2] One of its advantages is that it may be carried out in any location, without the specific need for any of the ritual implements.

PROCEDURE

1. Banish by Assuming the Form of Fudo.

2. Quiet your thoughts and endeavor to focus concentration on your navel. Form the mudra of "Sword in its Scabbard," and visualize the ch'i energy as if it were a ball of bright light like the Sun at the solar plexus.

3. A line of this light is then to be imagined as traveling up the body and down the right arm until it reaches and energizes the Sword hand. Imagine that

your fingers are alive with this vital power; at this point, you may feel a manifestation of the energy in the form of a tingling sensation.

4. "Sword" is then to be drawn from the "Scabbard," and should be used to construct the grid before you, following the order previously given. After each line is formed, you should vocalize the Japanese mantric word with which it is associated. These are (1) Rin; (2) Hei; (3) Toh; (4) Sha; (5) Kai; (6) Jin; (7) Retsu; (8) Zai; and (9) Zen. Each line should be strongly visualized as it is traced, and seen to be glowing with the same intensity as the ch'i that empowers it. Care should be taken to ensure that the kujikiri is complete before passing on to the next step.

5. Using the same mudra, an appropriate juji is then to be traced on top of the grid, making sure that it does not spill over the edges.[3] This can be accompanied by a vibrational vocalization of the name of the word-character, if appropriate. Concentration should also be focused strongly on the outcome desired from the rite. If you find it helpful, this stage can also include any other invocations to specific deities whose areas of influence are in accord with your aim. It is important that the kujikiri should be seen as glowing with ever-increasing intensity as you focus your concentration; the energy in the matrix must be built up as far as one is able, so that in your mind's eye it is almost too bright to look at. Any verbalization carried out thus far can also be done mentally, if you happen to be in a public place at the time and do not wish to attract undue attention from others.

6. Using "Sword," you must now liberate the charm and allow it to become. This is achieved by forcibly stabbing the juji with the mudra, while visualizing the whole image—both kujikiri and character—as exploding outward in a sudden burst of energy, leaving no trace of itself behind. As you do this, concentrate on the knowledge that your spell has been "sent" to the spirits, and that the desired result is already in the process of coming about. Those people with a background in the martial arts might find it helpful to enhance the act of liberation with a pronounced *kiai*, in order to emphasize further the active energy projection.[4]

7. Banish by Assuming the Form of Fudo.

1. To the Chinese, all odd numbers are Yang, while even numbers are Yin.

2. The traditional Japanese technique also often employs nine additional kettsuin that relate to the nine lines and words of the grid. As these take the exercise into areas not covered by the current section, they have been omitted here.

3. See the Hexagram lists in part 4 for information on the association of particular magickal operations with the relevant I Ching Hexagrams and their word-characters.

4. *Kiai* is a Japanese term, derived from Chinese *ch'i ai*, which means "spirit shout." It signifies a loud cry that is an essential aspect of karate punches, and is indispensable for point scoring in the sword-fighting discipline of kendo. Apart from its obvious application of focusing the mind upon the "target" and causing him or her disconcertion, the deeper mysteries of its use are concerned with the forceful projection of ch'i, known as *ki* in Japan. The intention is to inflict more damage than could be achieved by mere physical strength; this is sometimes known by the sarcastic euphemism "black medicine." The greatest experts of the technique do not have to even touch the other person physically in order to create the desired effect; it is their projected ch'i alone that does the job. The ancient origins for all of this are probably to be found in the global use of "shouts of power" by shamanistic magicians, uttered or chanted in the ecstatic trance as a projection of spirit-force and magickal authority.

Invoking the Dragon Force

In the West, Christian animosity and ridicule have attacked the essentially pagan symbol of the dragon so thoroughly and for so many years that now, for many nonpagan people, the image has been made to look ridiculous. It tends to figure merely as an emasculated character in children's stories. Otherwise, academics rationalize the legendary creature as a simplistic folk interpretation of dinosaur bones. However, in the East, the symbol is treated with greater respect and has played a continuously important role in social custom, art, and magico-religious thought for several thousand years. One of the earliest artistic representations of the creature, showing a snake-like form with feet, can be seen on a Chinese red pottery amphora/wine jar that dates to the late third millennium B.C.E.[1]

The dragon (Chin. *lung*) is considered by the Chinese to be the most sacred creature of the Yang principle. It signifies imperial power, the authority of Heaven and its generative force in Nature, the projecting energy of male sexuality, and so on. This important connection to the Yang polarity is also doubly emphasized in the traditional Chinese idea that dragons have eighty-one scales on their bodies. Nine is a very powerful Yang number, and when its force is doubly strengthened by multiplying it by itself, a total of eighty-one is created. This final number can be read as the extension, or phenomenal action, of the essential power of nine in matter. It is known as a "perfect number" by the Chinese philosophers, and it is no coincidence that the seminal tome of Taoism, the *Tao-teh Ching*, also has eighty-one verses.[2]

The dragon's magickal body, capable of shape-shifting into myriad different forms, and being equally at home in both the celestial abodes of the gods and in the depths of the sea, is also the very archetype of change. It is a pure symbol of Taoist magick. Moving invisibly beneath the vast expanse of Heaven, it stimulates the clouds to release their bounty of rain. By extension, it also signifies the Tao that moves through all manifested life and urges beings to seek Self-expression by the bringing forth of their essential Wills. The pantheistic and pagan idea that this actuating power is present in all Nature has been aptly illustrated by the Japanese writer and influential artist Okakura Kakuzo, who declared that the essence of the dragon is embodied in the very features of the world and in the elemental forces that sweep across it. The wet bark of trees are the dragon's scales, the cry of its mighty voice is heard in the roaring wind, and forked lightning darts across the sky like the dragon's suddenly outstretched claws.[3]

Legendary sightings of the creature are notoriously momentary; the witness sees an unexpected vision of the dragon, which captures his attention before disappearing from view as quickly as it had come. In the deepest esoteric sense, this is an allegory of the swift eruption into human consciousness of awareness of the Tao. Like the *Mezla* of the Qabalah—the lightning flash of influence that streaks down the Tree of Life from Kether to Malkuth—it is the burst of magico-spiritual immanence and inspiration that illuminates the adept's mind, thereby uniting it with divine presence and stimulating fresh activity.

Within dragon mythology are also enshrined many secrets of sexual alchemy, the coded references to which were initially intended only for the understanding of initiates. An example of such an occult double-entendre can be found in the legendary idea that dragons eagerly seek after a strange and mystical gem, known as "the Stone of Darkness." This supernatural jewel is said to be hollow and to hold within its center "the vital essence of copper." If you understand that the dragon is here intended to mean the phallus of the initiate, and that copper (Chin. *t'ung*) is synonymous with the color red and has important associations with the darkness of the feminine Yin, then the sexual implications of the story become obvious.

The symbol of the winged or flying dragon also signifies the magickal power of the Kundalini, or Fire Snake, as it rises in the body of the yogi or Tantric practitioner.

In the following invocation, the practitioner's aim is to call upon the combined forces of the so-called Four Dragon Kings of the World.[4] These spirits are said to exercise influence over the cardinal points of the compass and to rule over their respective oceans. I have termed the operation "The Fountain Breath" for reasons that will become clear, and it may be used to stimulate the magician's own winged-serpent power by increasing essential *ling* within the psychophysical body. Before commencing, you will need a ritual sword, bell, a consecrated talisman for the dragon force (see figure 13), and a shallow bowl or shell filled with seawater. If you do not have easy access to the sea, you can create an acceptable alternative by making up a strong saline solution with spring water and sea salt. A good picture of a Chinese dragon should also be used

Figure 13. An example design for a Dragon Talisman.

Figure 14. The dragon, symbol of the continuous creative movement of the Tao.

as a device for mental concentration (see figure 14). You will find it helpful, as well, to employ the ritual drum, but don't worry if you do not have one.

PROCEDURE

1. Banish by Assuming the Form of Fudo.

2. Facing the south, ring the bell an additional nine times and take up a comfortable asana in front of the altar. For obvious reasons, a good posture to

use is "the Dragon"; here, the practitioner should kneel on the floor with the heels tight up against the buttocks, ensuring that the spine and head are straight. If you are using the device of a dragon picture, this should be in front of you at eye level so that you are not obliged to bend your neck to see it.

3. Take up the Dragon Talisman, and form your hands into the mudra known as "the Diamond Thunderbolt" (see mudra 8). Hold the charm between your outstretched forefingers and focus attention upon the dragon picture in front of you (or close your eyes and concentrate on an appropriate mental image, if you prefer). Mentally summon the dragon force, using those attributes that you know to be connected to this symbol as "signposts" to direct your mind. Avoid carrying out the process in a mechanical or intellectual manner; allow strong emotions to build in you—need the power to come to you! The dragon is the moving and mysterious power of creation, not a cold and rational concept.

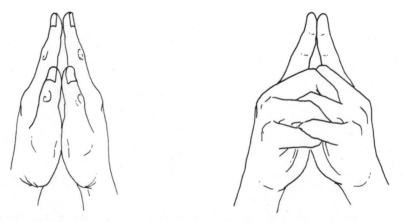

Mudra 8. The Diamond Thunderbolt. Front view and back view.

4. When you feel that a sufficient level of emotional power has been raised, burn the talisman in the flame of your candle or lantern, with care, and then place the ashes in the seawater. Concentrate on the idea that by doing this you are forging a spirit-link between yourself and the forces that you

are evoking. At this point you should also anoint the base of your spine and the top of your head with the charged fluid.

5. Stand up, point the ritual sword toward the south, and visualize the Dragon King of the Southern Ocean. His color is red, and he moves in a serpentine fashion in the air before you. His name is Ao Ch'in. Invoke him with your own appropriate words, preferably spontaneous as the spirit moves you in keeping with the dragon's nature.

6. Go to the north, point the sword to that Quarter, and visualize the Dragon King of the Northern Ocean. He is called Ao Shun and his color is black. Invoke him.

7. Go to the east, point the sword to that Quarter, and visualize the Dragon King of the Eastern Ocean. He is called Ao Kuang and his color is azure blue or blue-green. Invoke him.

8. Go to the west, point the sword to that Quarter, and visualize the Dragon King of the Western Ocean. He is called Ao Jun and his color is white. Invoke him.

9. Take up your asana once more, facing east so that the red and black Dragon Kings are to your right and left hands respectively. At this point, you may begin a steady but forcible rhythm upon the drum, if you have one.

10. Imagine that these two Kings descend, shrinking to an appropriate size, and then enter your body at the base of the spine.

11. Inhale slowly and deeply, and concentrate on the two Kings rising parallel to each other up the spinal column, until they reach the cranial cavity. Try to time it so that they reach the top at just the point when your inhalation is at maximum.

12. Exhale slowly, and visualize the Kings descending through your body, this time with one on either side of the spine (the red King to the right, black to the left), until they return to the base of the spine.

13. Repeat this process for as long as you feel is necessary or desirable, before allowing the Kings to return to their respective Quarters.

14. Face the south, so that the blue and white Kings are to your left and right hands respectively.

15. Repeat steps 10 to 13 for these two Dragons.

16. When you are ready to finish the rite, thank the Kings for their assistance and bid them leave to return to their own abodes.

17. Banish by Assuming the Form of Fudo.

18. Dispose of the seawater in a suitable and respectful manner, such as returning it to the sea, or perhaps bottling it for future use. It is not a courteous act to simply pour it down the sink.

If you wish to carry out this rite again, you will not have to make another Dragon Talisman if you use the seawater that has already been consecrated at your first attempt. If the fluid is new, however, you will obviously have to follow the entire procedure again. As an alternative to either seawater or a saline solution, you could also try water that has been collected from a lake or river, which traditional folklore connects to the presence of dragons or dragon-like spirits. This adds to the fluid another helpful symbolic importance, and thereby enhances its psychological impact. In my own case, for instance, I often use water that I took from Loch Ness, Scotland, several years ago; its Fortean link to the legendary "monster" is well-known, but I also have deep emotional and spiritual ties to this area of the world. Any such additional and personal elements that you can bring to your work can only help you succeed in your efforts all the more swiftly.

---

1. See William Watson, *The Genius of China* (London: Times Newspapers Ltd., 1973), 53, plate 37.

2. There is some evidence to suggest that the *Tao-teh Ching* was not initially intended to have eighty-one verses, and that this number only came about due to later deliberate alteration with the structure in order to make it fit the magick "perfect number." This may have occurred around the year 50 B.C.E.. For more information on this idea, see Robert Henricks, *Te-Tao Ching* (London: Bodley Head, 1990), xv–xviii.

3. In John Boorman's yet-to-be-rivaled cinematic evocation of the Arthurian legend *Excalibur*, Merlin uses Kakuzo's metaphorical description almost word for word when trying to explain the nature of the dragon-power to a young Arthur.

4. Chinese lore states that there are traditionally five Dragon Kings. In this case, the role of the fifth, whose place is at the center of the other four, is taken by the practitioner himself.

Working with the Astral Body

Numerous occult and magico-religious systems hold ideas, sometimes quite complex, regarding the multiple nature of the human spiritual being. In contradistinction to orthodox Judeo-Christian teachings, where the soul is seen as a single entity, but with a somewhat uncertain role, the magickal schools of thought acknowledge the existence of several specific and subtle, nonphysical bodies that form integral parts of a person's overall psychophysical make-up. Such bodies act as a necessary framework upon which physical organic life is based, and without which such life could not manifest.

Chinese esoteric lore states that human beings possess essentially two spirit-bodies, or, looked at from another point of view, one soul with two component sections.[1] The first is known as the *P'o*, literally meaning "the white spirit," which possibly refers to a traditional ghostly appearance that it presents to those with the eyes to see. This is the denser of the two, and the one that is particularly attached to the basic actions and needs of physical existence (hence, it is sometimes called the "lower soul"). Of the two spirit-bodies, this is the first to become linked to its physical host, it being thought that the P'o manifests at the exact point of a human baby's conception. However, at this stage it is little more than a vehicle without awareness. It has nine vital sections, which correspond to the nine apertures of the physical body. These are the eyes, ears, nostrils, mouth, phallus or vagina, and anus. Taoist sexual lore also states that the vital sections are linked to various conditions of female arousal during sex, which are collectively known as "the Nine Spirits of Woman." These, in turn, are connected to nine specific sexual positions, as described in an ancient Taoist text known as *The Sex Handbook of the Dark Maid,* which dates from the time of the Sui dynasty.[2] The nature of the P'o partakes of the cosmic polarity of Earth, and as such within the physical body it acts as an agent for the Yin force.

The second spirit-body is called *Hun*, literally meaning "the spirit that speaks." Its subtlety is greater than that of the P'o, and it acts as the vehicle for a person's transcendent and guiding consciousness (hence, it is commonly called "the higher soul"). Traditionally, this becomes associated with the human host after the P'o, not attaching itself until the baby takes its first breath. It is linked to the cosmic polarity of Heaven, and is therefore associated with the power of the Yang.

When the two souls are held in perfect balance within the human body, thus corresponding to the overall and universal harmony of Yin and Yang, good health and general physical well-being are maintained with a corresponding opportunity for long life. This balance can be brought about by various techniques, such as chi-kung, sexual practices, and so on, which produce an inner alchemy that is known as *neidan*. As the word implies, this particular process of transformation takes place mainly within the spiritual being of the practitioner. In contrast, exterior alchemy (Chin. *waidan*) uses various elixirs and other substances, prepared in an alchemical "laboratory," to secure the harmony of Yin and Yang from the outside.

The concept of two highly interactive souls is also present within the Japanese culture. Here, the natives traditionally believe that both of them should be deliberately nourished during a person's life, in accordance with each soul's individual nature. Hence, sexual fulfillment and pleasure making are very important because they refresh and strengthen the "lower soul," while spiritual contemplation and other similar acts are vital to the well being of the "higher soul." Such an attitude, when properly approached, makes for a balanced and sane personality, and a tolerant outlook on life.

At the point of physical death, the Hun is said to leave the corpse first, whereupon it becomes known as a *shen*, "a divine spirit." This ascends to the celestial abodes of the gods, or, in the case of Taoist adepts, may take up its abode in the western paradise of Hsi-wang-mu. The P'o, on the other hand, remains for a time with the interred body, before it, too, passes into its own Underworld realm, and then, according to some authorities, eventually disintegrates. If the P'o remains earthbound, such as in the cases of those who have died violently or have not been granted a respectful funeral, then it becomes known as a feared *kuei*.

Such is the general Sino-Japanese view of spiritual anatomy. In practical magickal work, the magician is in a position to use this dual soul actively during life, by using it as a vehicle to project his consciousness into other realms of being. The section *The Gate of Dreams* gave information on such astral traveling during sleep. However, the following four exercises allow, progressively, for investigation of the astral realms during the waking state, in a manner akin to Western methods for projection of the so-called Body of Light.

In these techniques, it is the Hun aspect that is the specific vehicle used by the magician, while the P'o remains within the vacated physical form, nourishing it and providing an earthly link to the magician's roaming consciousness.

PROCEDURE 1

1. Sit in a comfortable asana and relax thoroughly. Breathe slowly and deeply, and imagine that all tension is disappearing from your muscles.

2. As soon as full relaxation is achieved, close your eyes and imagine that a hole is opening in the top of your skull.

3. The sense of personal awareness, or consciousness, should then be imagined as rising out of your physical body through that cranial opening, until it hovers in the air above the physical body.[3] For this exercise, no visualized astral body is yet required.

4. Your point of consciousness should then be allowed to scan the room you are in, taking in as many details as it can with regard to the layout of furniture, decorations, and so on.

5. Allow the consciousness to return to the physical body through the cranial "hole." Finish by comparing your astral vision of the room to its actual physical form, to see which points of detail, if any, concur. At this stage, the two will probably be drastically different, but you shouldn't allow this to deter you from further efforts.

PROCEDURE 2

1. You should try to procure a large household mirror, preferably one in which the entire body can be reflected or that at least allows for the torso and head to be seen. This mirror does not have to be specifically consecrated to magickal work.

2. Sit in a comfortable asana, or on a straight-backed chair, in front of the mirror. Take time to relax the body and mind and gaze calmly at the reflection before you. In particular, pay attention to the image's chest as it rises and falls in time with your breathing. Imagine that real air is being sucked into the reflected body and then expelled in the same manner as for your physical body.

3. You should then endeavor to transfer your point of awareness from the physical body to the reflected image. Begin by focusing your concentration on the brow of your reflection, at a point roughly equivalent to the position given to the Third Eye or Ajna Chakra in Tantra and Yoga. Imagine that a strong pulling sensation is emanating from that point, dragging at your own forehead and drawing your consciousness out of your physical body and toward the reflection. Shut your eyes, go with this sensation, and imaginatively transplant your awareness into the reflection. Look upon your mirror-body as being your real form, feel its solidity and its potential for mobility, and use its eyes to look around at the objects that surround you in the mirror-world (remember that these will be in opposite positions to their physical doubles).

4. When you are comfortable with your new body, look straight in front of you through its eyes and visualize your vacated physical body. See it, and the room it is in, as if *they* are now the reflections; feel that the vacated body is wholly dependent on the actions that you carry out in the mirror-body in order to give it life and motion. Imagine that the mirror-body is breathing normally, and that the physical action is but a mere copy (this is a reversal of stage 2).

5. Try other imagined actions, such as raising and lowering your arms or turning your head. These should also be mimicked simultaneously by the physical form.

6. Finish the exercise by withdrawing your consciousness from the mirror-world and returning it to the physical body. Open your eyes and look at the reflection in the glass before you; see it as once more being but an ordinary copy of the mundane world.

PROCEDURE 3

1. Sit in your chosen asana and relax.

2. Visualize your Hun spirit leaving your physical body through the hole in your crown, in the form of a cloud of smoke.

3. Shape this "smoke" with your mind, until it resembles a rough copy of your physical body. Ensure that you can visualize this image accurately, and with no breaks in your concentration, before you proceed further.

4. Transfer your point of consciousness to the Hun; feel it to be the new vehicle of your awareness. Identify yourself with it; become it!

5. Using this new vehicle, make an exploration of the room that you are in. Concentrate, initially, on the way that it looks as in procedure 1. In later sessions, you can use the Hun to explore other senses by touching objects, smelling incense smoke, and so on, enhancing all such feelings with your imagination.

6. When you are ready to finish, withdraw your awareness from the Hun and return to your physical form.

7. See the vacated Hun becoming a shapeless cloud of smoke once more. Draw it back into the physical base via the fontanelle area. Care should be taken to ensure that every particle of the visualized image is reclaimed; it is not a good idea to allow any part of yourself, as this truly is, to waft around independently outside of your body and beyond your control.

As soon as the magician has become thoroughly familiar with the foregoing exercises through repeated practice, he will be ready to move onto the next operation. This is designed to allow the magician to explore actively the astral planes associated with individual sacred characters or emblems, such as those pertaining to the Trigrams or Hexagrams. For this it will be necessary to have a properly consecrated magick mirror; for reasons that will become obvious, a round, black mirror is most suitable for this particular exercise. The entire process should be treated as a proper rite and be carried out in the temple area.

PROCEDURE 4

1. Banish by Assuming the Form of Fudo.

2. Clear the mirror of the influences of any previous work by visualizing a cleansing burst of light within it; know that this is purifying your mirror for the rite at hand.

3. Sit in a comfortable asana in front of the altar, and meditate on the dual spirit-bodies of the Hun and P'o. Contemplate the fact that it is the Hun that you will use as your vehicle within the inner planes, allowing the P'o to remain in your physical body so that it will be safe during your excursion into the beyond.

4. Place the mirror upon the altar and gaze into its depths. Imagine that you are looking into a long, dark tunnel that stretches into the distance beyond your sight.

5. Project the Hun and identify yourself with it, in the manner that you have learned.

6. In your new vehicle, stand before the mirror and see it expanding in size before your eyes until it takes on the form of a large tunnel in front of you.

7. Walk down the tunnel for some distance, and then see a closed door in front of you. On this portal, visualize the symbol that you wish to investigate in a color appropriate to its nature. It is probably best to begin with the Trigrams, as they are the easiest to visualize.

8. When this symbol is firmly before your eyes, use your Hun body to open the door, and then pass into that which awaits you beyond the threshold. At initial attempts, don't be surprised if you can see nothing but blackness beyond the door; persistence is the key to opening the astral sight.

9. When you have experienced all that you wish, or all that you are able to, leave the astral world and walk back up the tunnel until you stand once more in the temple.

10. Withdraw consciousness from the Hun and return it to your physical form. See the spirit-body losing its structure and becoming smoke once more. This is then to be drawn back via the fontanelle "hole."

11. Banish by Assuming the Form of Fudo.

When skrying any aspect of the worlds of the spirits, care should be taken to retain control of the emotions. No encounter should result in the magician losing the power to discriminate between true and false imagery. Never unquestioningly believe anything that you may be shown; this is a common pitfall for many people in the occult world. Treat all your encounters and visions fairly and with an open mind, but don't accept their validity until you have checked the results against the known attributes and natures of the symbols that you have investigated.

1. Compare this with the Voodoo tradition that states that each person houses two souls, known respectively in the Creole tongue as *gros-bon-ange* and *ti-bon-ange*. Of the two, the former spirit is the one most associated with the material world.

2. For a description of these positions, see Nik Douglas and Penny Slinger, *Sexual Secrets* (Rochester: Destiny Books, 1979), 256–260.

3. In Taoist magickal lore, it is mostly through the area of the one-time fontanelle, associated with the Head Chakra the Taoists call "The Flowery Lake," that the magician is exhorted to project his astral consciousness. Regular training in certain esoteric practices, such as chi-kung and the sublimation of sexual energies that are then directed up the spinal column to the head, are thought to effect a gradual loosening of the cranial sutures. This allows for the easy departure and return of the traveling spirit. Some Buddhist practitioners in Tibet are known to carry out a similar practice called *powa*, which also seeks to open the skull, but which is primarily concerned with directing the reincarnation of a person's consciousness after physical death.

The Mountain Invocation

The following ritual serves to illustrate just how readily the I Ching can be turned to a practical and therapeutic use in order to help overcome the sort of deep-set problems that beset people all too frequently. In this particular rite, the invocation/meditation is concerned with the alleviation of a perennial troublemaker: lack of confidence and determination to follow through one's own destiny, when faced with outside pressures to conform to an orthodox view of one's role in life.

Prior to beginning, you will need to make a talisman that depicts the word-character for Ken (archaic, classic, or both) and its Trigram or Hexagram.[1]

PROCEDURE

1. Banish by Assuming the Form of Fudo.

2. Form the mudra known as "Outer Bond" (see mudra 9). Accompany this with reflection on the society that you live in, how it derives its strength from social interaction and cohesion, but which becomes a hollow sham if

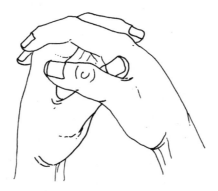

Mudra 9. Outer Bond.

individual Wills are squashed in an attempt to create a state of controlled homogeneity and orthodoxy. This is like a mountain that has weak foundations; it looks impressively strong from the outside, but must inevitably collapse.

3. Now make the mudra known as "Inner Bond" (see mudra 10). Understand that the strength of a mountain relies on a strong core and a firm base. So, too, does the evolution of your life rely on the voice of the god within you, the spiritual Will that is there to guide you to Self-realization. Be prepared to heed its advice in spite of opposition from others who are divorced from their own destinies; take the time to listen to its lessons and don't be dissuaded by the cries of those who would have you follow a different path. Take care, however, to differentiate between the true voice of the god, and the mutterings of the ego. Confusing the two would lead to megalomania.

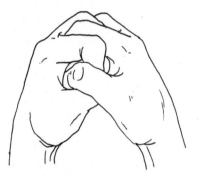

Mudra 10. Inner Bond.

4. The word-character for Ken, or its Trigram or Hexagram, should then be visualized at your feet.

5. The symbol should then be brought up the body, along the spinal column, until it reaches your head. Hold it there for a few moments and then allow it to descend to the solar plexus.

6. Contemplate that you are as strong and defiant as a mountain. Weak traits, such as the tendency to show only token dissent to the arguments of other people, are being expunged. Convince yourself that you have strengthened your power to be more assertive and determined, and that you possess the self-assurance and courage to follow your own Way.

7. Take up your prepared talisman for Ken, and load it with this new sense of confidence. Feel and see the power flowing from you into the charm, and know that from that moment om it will work continually to bolster this new sense of purpose.

8. Put the talisman somewhere safe, preferably on your own person. Then banish by Assuming the Form of Fudo.

---

1. See Hexagram 52, in part 4.

K'un Meditation

The ancient Taoist sages are considered by some people to have been the first environmental scientists. Such an assertion comes from the fact that it was common for such people to withdraw into the wilderness, away from other human habitations, in order to study the natural world firsthand. From their observations arose much knowledge concerning the medicinal value of herbs, and their studies also developed and encouraged the proliferation of landscape themes in Chinese artwork. In their solitude, the Taoist hermits also acquired a particular love for dwarf trees, which were found growing naturally in mountainous areas. These were later used as ritual ornamentation for temples and monasteries. The Chinese magician-priests were the first people to attempt the deliberate cultivation of such trees. However, the flowering of the art of bonsai really occurred in later times when it was taken up by Shinto practitioners in Japan.

Taoist contemplation on the environment was not carried out merely as an academic exercise. It was a sincere attempt to discover the manner in which the Tao effortlessly flowed through and motivated the entirety of Nature when freed from the restrictive and artificial desires of human beings. As a consequence, it could also guide people to a more fulfilling existence, if only they'd let it; opposition to the Way, on the other hand, merely resulted in self-impoverishment and abuse of the natural world. Aleister Crowley expressed this same concern when he declared: "'Do what thou Wilt' is to bid Stars to shine, Vines to bear grapes, Water to seek its own level; man is the only being in Nature that has striven to set himself at odds with himself."

By their meditations, the sages were able to discover how to integrate themselves into the balanced and spontaneous flow of life. Taoist observations on the natural behavior of other creatures under different circumstances were probably also responsible, in part, for the later development of animal styles of kung fu by the Shaolin Buddhist priests. Through attempts to achieve a unity with Nature, the Taoists also

159

formed magickal and mystical contacts with the various divine powers existing behind its outward appearance; some of these later figured as deities of the Taoist religious pantheon, and were to greatly influence the practices of feng shui.

The following meditation is also designed to assist the human consciousness to harmonize itself more successfully with the natural world, to feel itself to be a part of Nature rather than an aspect set apart from other living beings. It allows for a better appreciation of the ever-moving cycles of creation and destruction that are so necessary to the continuation of life.

PROCEDURE

1. Banish by Assuming the Form of Fudo.

2. Contemplate that the planet Earth is a vast, living being, and that the objects and creatures that dwell upon and within it are component parts of the overall planetary form.

3. Earth should then be thought of as breathing, taking in great quantities of air and ch'i in just the same way as the human body. Concentration should be focused on this life energy flooding in through the planet's "pores" with each inhalation, and then the unwanted waste and toxins flowing back into space with each exhalation.

4. Endeavor to regulate your own breathing so that it is in exact unison with the imagined breathing cycle of Earth; allow the two to become one.

5. You should then imagine that your body has died. Friends place it in a grave and then cover it with soil. Gradually the corpse breaks down, its molecules splitting apart from each other and becoming absorbed as nutritious compost by the soil, thus helping to feed and sustain other organic beings in turn. All that is left of you is a pure awareness without form.

6. Retaining this state of mind, mentally descend to the center of Earth, which should be conceived of as a hollow space like a dark cavern.

7. Within this space, visualize either the Chinese word-character for K'un, or its Trigram or Hexagram.

8. Contemplate that the physical planet is the outer layer, or manifested expression, of the inner spiritual force of K'un. Understand that the natural beginnings and endings of things are in harmony with Earth; generation

arises from decay, life withdraws into putrefaction—all equal and meaningful in the endless cycle of existence. Continue this thought process for as long as you desire.

9. You should then imagine that your consciousness is rising toward the surface of the Earth, gathering your body around you in its recognizable guise once more. As you return to awareness of your temple space, think of yourself as having been born anew, that your life has sprung up from decomposition. Contemplate the new opportunities that await you in the world, the chances to fulfill your Self through the enactment of the Will.

10. Banish by Assuming the Form of Fudo.

Ch'ien Meditation

The following exercise should be carried out as a complement to the previous work with K'un. Both procedures should be given equal attention, in order to encourage balanced development.

PROCEDURE

1. Banish by Assuming the Form of Fudo.

2. Sit in a comfortable asana, or lie in a supine manner on the floor (the former is preferable in order to minimize the risk of falling asleep).

3. Visualize the Trigram, Hexagram, or word-character for Ch'ien in your mind's eye. Let it be the sole focus of your concentration.[1]

4. Project the Hun body, as you learned how to do in the section *Working with the Astral Body*.

5. As soon as you have transferred your center of awareness to the visualized Hun body, rise vertically from your current location and continue this movement until you are in the vault of Space. Earth should be seen as being far below you, directly beneath your feet.

6. Imagine that the Hun is expanding and losing its shape, gradually spreading out across Heaven until it is one with it. Try to feel the sense of vastness of consciousness that is now you.

7. Remaining in this state of mind, turn your attention to the world over which you are arched. Consider how each being who lives upon its surface has a true Path, a destiny that it has an absolute right to fulfill without interference. Reflect on how the Paths of all creatures are individual and sovereign

163

in their outward expressions, requiring the manifestation of circumstances peculiar to each one. Yet, their association with the all-pervasive Tao links all things in a unified whole. Understand that when all beings move in accordance with their own Wills, they are in harmony with the motivating energy of Heaven.

8. Turn your attention to the other planets and stars that have their abodes within your celestial body. Reflect on how each one of these heavenly bodies also has a proper Path, unique and complete to each one, yet all contributing to the overall balance of the universe.

9. Decrease your size and resume the shape of your normal Hun body.

10. Descend vertically to Earth until you return to the location of your physical body.

11. Transfer consciousness back into that body and withdraw the Hun in the usual way.

12. Banish by Assuming the Form of Fudo.

---

1. See Hexagram 1, in part 4.

The Trigram Wheel

This practice is designed to expand the advanced practitioner's understanding of the Trigrams of the I Ching and their virtues. As it is a relatively hard exercise, it is recommended that only those students who have attained a high degree of proficiency in the techniques of visualization, mental concentration, astral projection, and so on, should attempt it.

At first glance, the procedure might seem a little complicated, but regular practice should iron out any difficulties that may be experienced. Although it has been designed as a complete rite, the student may also find it useful, at initial attempts, to split the process into smaller, manageable parts; for instance, you could begin by working with steps 1 through 4, and then gradually adding the remaining stages as confidence and experience increase.

For reasons that will become apparent when reading through the text, this rite is best performed at night, or at least it should be done in a place where you can shut out all exterior light.

PROCEDURE

1. Banish by Assuming the Form of Fudo.

2. Take up your usual asana and relax your body. Allow all tensions, mental and physical, to flow away and quiet your thoughts.

3. Extinguish any candles or lamps upon the altar so that the temple is plunged into darkness. With nothing visible to your eyes, imagine that physical existence itself has ceased to be; all forms have dissolved, all that is left is pure consciousness afloat in Nothingness.

4. Contemplate this infinite Void; understand that it is the primal Wu-wu from which all existence is ultimately spawned.[1] It holds within Itself all

165

the endless possibilities of manifestation that are individually subject to the law of change, but as a state of perfection It remains unaltered and unalterable by the act of Creation. It has neither beginning nor end, no boundaries by which it can be measured or defined. The consciousness of the magician that perceives this is to identify itself with the Hun-tun, the Chaos Center at the heart of Nothingness; it is from this point that the magician will observe and experience all the proceeding steps.

5. The state of Noumena is then to be "broken" by the birth of the Trigrams. Begin to think in terms of compass direction; choose a point of focus and identify this as the south. Visualize a line of light stretching out from your point of consciousness to the south, and see a blazing red Trigram for Ch'ien manifesting at the end of that line. This is the first spoke of your Wheel.

6. Repeat this for all remaining seven spokes, placing the relevant Trigrams, in their appropriate colors, at the ends (these may be found in the Hexagram correspondences in part 4). The order of visualization should be as follows: (1) South/Ch'ien; (2) North/K'un; (3) East/Li; (4) West/K'an; (5) Northeast/Chen; (6) Northwest/Ken; (7) Southwest/Hsuan; (8) Southeast/Tui. Once completed, you should imagine that you are the axle of a Wheel of Trigrams.

7. At this stage, any number of different exercises and practices can be attempted to bring the magician into a dynamic alignment with the Trigrams. For instance, you could meditate on the different colors associated with the symbols. In such a case, you would draw the relevant color down a spoke from one of the Trigrams, and then allow it to swamp your mind, becoming the sole focus of your attention for a time before you send it back up the spoke. Exploration of the individual worlds of the symbols is another possibility. Here, you would move your point of awareness along a chosen spoke, and then pass through the Trigram as if it were a membrane. Once "on the other side," careful attention would then be paid to any visions or sensations that might be experienced. To finish the technique, the consciousness would be drawn back through the Trigram to the Hun-tun center. Alternatively, you might like to meditate on certain gods or beings associated with the Pa Kua, such as the Eight Taoist Immortals; in the latter

case, their symbols alone could be visualized above the relevant Trigrams. Let your imagination create new ideas and opportunities. The method given here is intended to be open-ended, to allow for the student's personal input.

8. The process of "cosmic birth" is then to be reversed, i.e., the spokes and Trigrams must be banished in the order opposite to their creation, leaving the magician's consciousness alone in the Void once more.

9. Light your candles or lanterns, and contemplate your resumed existence in the material world.

10. Banish by Assuming the Form of Fudo.

---

1. See "Yin and Yang: The Eternal Dance" in the section *The Philosophy of the Way*, in part 1.

The I Ching Hexagrams

Hexagram Table

Lower \ Upper	☰	☳	☵	☶	☷	☴	☲	☱
☰	1	34	5	26	11	9	14	43
☳	25	51	3	27	24	42	21	17
☵	6	40	29	4	7	59	64	47
☶	33	62	39	52	15	53	56	31
☷	12	16	8	23	2	20	35	45
☴	44	32	48	18	46	57	50	28
☲	13	55	63	22	36	37	30	49
☱	10	54	60	41	19	61	38	58

Introduction

The following correspondences for the Hexagrams are not exhaustive, nor do I intend them to be so. Each student should endeavor to expand such lists through personal study and practical experience; that which I have given is only a framework upon which to build.

The symbols listed as Archaic Forms are some of the oldest versions of the Chinese characters for the Hexagram titles. They are called Seal Script and they may be used in talismans in just the same way as the usual classical forms.

Designations of Polarity, Compass Direction, and Family Membership primarily follow ancient guidelines that are traditionally attributed to the legendary Fu-hsi. This arrangement is usually called the Primal, or Earlier, Heaven, and traditionally has strong links to occult practices and the spiritual side of life in general. It is based on the fundamental duality of its cosmic aspects. The later alternative listings constructed by the Chou ruler, King Wen, are more commonly used in other books on the I Ching, and go by the term "the Configuration of the Inner World." These are based on ideas concerning the movement of the Trigrams through a yearly cycle—though personally I'm not altogether happy with the sequence—and are particularly concerned with physical matters. There is much that can be said both for and against these two systems, and for the often conflicting commentaries of the ancient Chinese philosophers, but such arguments are for another time and place. Where King Wen's differ from the older version, I have given his attributions, in parentheses (K.W.), alongside those of Fu-hsi, so that the two sets can be compared with each other.

The Guardians of the Quarters are traditional. Though they are generally associated with King Wen's arrangement, I have allocated them to that of Fu-hsi because I believe that they are just as appropriate there as in the former arrangement.

Symbolism finds a place in nearly all aspects of Chinese life, and, consequently, the number of potential correspondences for the Hexagrams is legion. I have restricted myself to giving only an introductory compendium of some of the most well-known emblems. You will see that some of the plants, precious stones, pictorial devices, and so on, appear under a number of different Hexagrams. Firstly, this is due to the fact that certain Hexagrams have very similar natures, and therefore can be associated with the same symbolic items. Also, in Chinese esoteric lore, very few emblems tend to be mutually exclusive. Consequently, a variety of sympathetic attributes are generally ascribed to each item, seemingly blurring their defined parameters to those not familiar with such an arrangement. More confusion can also arise because certain plants may hold differing allegiances depending on their state of maturity. For example, bamboo shoots are generally used as a symbol of the spring and the first flush of youth, whereas the flower of the mature plant is of the nature of winter and old age. I have not tried to artificially tidy this approach to Nature in order to produce a hard and fast Qabalistic-style set of lists, but prefer simply to follow the Chinese example so that I can remain as true to its spirit as possible.

I have one final word on the lists of Magickal Workings. These give a selection of the types of ritual practice, meditation, object of charm-working, and so on, that are appropriate to the nature of each Hexagram. Some are quite straightforward, while others bring in more complex ideas for greater contemplation. This is another area that is ripe for expansion by the imaginative practitioner. The correct time and place for any act or choice of Hexagram, when in doubt, should also be determined by I Ching divination.

Hexagram 1

CH'IEN—HEAVEN

Archaic Form:

Modern Name: Qian.

Esoteric Interpretations: The Great Brilliance that emits the force of the Yang. Warmth. Light. The creative and sexual masculine energy. Primal power and the beginning of things. The Circle of the Firmament. That which has motion. The hidden heart of one's actions. Continuity. Sincerity of thought and action. The aspiration to "do the right thing." The motivation of the Tao. Ascension to the heights of achievement. The Hexagram of the fourth Chinese month (c. May–June) and the beginning of the hot summer season.

Polarity: Yang.

Compass Direction: South (K.W: Northwest).

Guardian of the Quarter: The Red Bird.

Family Member: Father.

Parts of the Body: Head, face, phallus, intestines, thumb.

Colors: Alizarin red, purple, white, reddish yellow, azure blue.

Symbolic Creatures: Dragon, spider, rhinoceros, cicada, partridge, tortoise, eel.

Plants and Perfumes: Pine, aubergine, peony, pomegranate, pear, taro, barley, lotus, ambergris, *ling-chih* ("Fungus of Immortality"), dragon's blood (*Calamus draco*), magnolia, cherry blossom, cedar.

Metals: Iron, copper.

Precious Stones: Jade, amber, malachite.

Emblems: Emperor or king, swastika/fylfot, tripod, circle, "Cloud Scroll" pattern, star, the "Knot of Eternity," tortoise-shell, chariot, wisps of moist vapor that rise upward from the ground, canopy, the two swords of Chao (see Gods).

Ritual Tools: Sword, brush/pen, *shen mien* (a disc, symbolic of heavenly perfection), goad.

Taoist Immortal: Lu T'ung-pin.

Dragon Spirit: T'ien Lung (the Celestial Dragon who holds Heaven aloft and represents its regenerative powers).

Gods: Shang Ti, Yu-ti, T'ien-kuan, Yuan Shih, Fu-hsi, Hu Shen, Chung, Nan-chi Hsien-weng, Mo-li Hung, Chao, Chang Tao-ling, Lao-tzu, Lu Shen, P'an Ku.

Goddesses: T'ien Hou, Pi-hsia-yuan-chun, Ma Ni-li, T'ien Mu.

Magickal Workings: Creativity. Good fortune. Obtaining a better understanding of the True Will/Tao. Ordering events according to the needs of the Will. Increasing personal vital power. Re-energizing male sexual energy.

Hexagram 2

K'un—Earth

Archaic Form:

Modern Name: Kun.

Esoteric Interpretations: The Dark Gateway that opens to the force of the Yin. Cold. Darkness. Mother Goddesses. The womb and tomb of all Creation. Parturition. The origin of female sexuality. That which is at rest. Receptivity. The spirit world. Things supernatural and occult. The mystery of growth from decay. The Underworld. The Hexagram of the tenth Chinese month (c. November–December) and the start of the winter season.

Polarity: Yin.

Compass Direction: North (K.W: Southwest).

Guardian of the Quarter: The Black Tortoise, or the Dark Warrior.

Family Member: Mother.

Parts of the Body: Womb, vagina, stomach, little finger.

Colors: Deep black, rich yellow, light brown.

Symbolic Creatures: Horse (especially a mare), phoenix, ox, cat, pheasant, owl, the *Hsiao* (legendary creature linked to droughts, such as occur in China during winter), fish.

Plants and Perfumes: Paulownia, jujube, plum blossom, bamboo flowers, ivy, pomegranate, peach blossom, azalea, lotus pod, hemerocallis, willow, saffron, gardenia, wintersweet.

Metals: Copper, iron, gold.

Precious Stones: Pearl, mother of pearl, agate.

Emblems: Empress or queen, rhombus, cave, tunnel, conch shell, unicorn horn, egg, the "Plum Blossom" loop, the spiked club of Wen (see Gods), the Barge of Mercy (the boat of Kuan Yin, which transports spirits of the dead to the Otherworld), reed organ, black soil, tree trunk.

Ritual Tools: Cauldron, the *huang* (a half-ring or crescent made from jade or nephrite), the *tsung* (a square-sectioned tube of jade), spirit wand, bottle-gourd, mu-jen, altar, mirror.

Taoist Immortal: Ho Hsien-ku.

Gods: Ti-kuan, Hou Chi, Yen-lo, Pei-ti, Master Stonehead, Ti Ts'ang Wang, T'u-ti, Tzu Wei, Mo-li Shou, Ch'eng-huang, Wen, Chung K'uei, Hu Shen, P'an Kuan, Po-lao.

Goddesses: Nu-kua, Kuan Yin, Ti-ya, Pi-hsia-yuan-chun, Mobo, Hu-tu, Hsuan Nu, Pa, K'eng San Ku-niang, Hsi-wang-mu, Eastern Mother, Tsi-ku, Pai Mu-tan.

Magickal Workings: Fertility. Childbirth (physical and magickal). Contemplating the cycles of generation and decay. Clairvoyance/developing "Yin eyes" (second sight). Underworld journeys. Spiritistic practices. Necromancy and the raising of ghosts. Dreamwork and astral journeying.

Hexagram 3

T'un—Initial Struggle

Archaic Form:

Modern Name: Zhun

Esoteric Interpretations: Spring thunderstorms and rain, which cause dormant seeds to begin their cycle of activity. Commencement. Underground germination. The impetus to move after rest. Simplicity and purity of intention. The energy and fresh confidence of youth, unlimited by restricting fears. New growth, generally.

Opposite Hexagram: 40 Chieh.

Polarity: Yang below Yin (K.W: Yang below Yang).

Trigram Combination: Chen and K'an.

Compass Directions: Northeast and West (K.W: East and North).

Family Members: Eldest son and middle daughter (K.W: eldest and middle sons).

Parts of the Body: Liver, breasts.

Colors: Blue, light green, white.

Symbolic Creatures: Swallow, piglet, ox, boar.

Plants and Perfumes: Willow, peony, ailanthus, olive, wheat.

Metal: Silver.

Precious Stones: Amber, green jasper.

Emblems: Chariot, the Tree of Life, cave, a young plant struggling up through the earth, camps and settlements, flute, vase, sunrise.

Ritual Tool: Axe.

Gods: Mo-li Ch'ing, Kou Mang, Hsien T'ung, Hou Chi, Master Stonehead, No-cha, Shen Nung, Tam Kung.

Goddesses: Ma-ku, K'eng San Ku-niang, Pi-hsia-yuan-chun, Chun T'i, Hsi-ho.

Magickal Workings: Achieving success in new ventures. Easing the transition into new circumstances. Overcoming initial problems and anxieties.

Hexagram 4

MENG—IGNORANCE

Archaic Form:

Modern Name: Meng.

Esoteric Interpretations: A mountain that stands over a dangerous pit. An inability to accept that one does not know everything, and that some goals either cannot or should not be achieved. Problematical, yet solvable, weaknesses that are artificially concealed and exacerbated by outward and false self-assurance. Obstinacy and intellectual arrogance that have no foundation in wisdom. Confusion that arises out of inexperience. That which has much potential, and the inherent capacity to receive nondiscriminatory knowledge, but which is trapped and devoid of onward movement. Obtuseness and stubbornness that must be transcended in order for the truly spontaneous and wise Fool, the possessor of the Tao, to appear. The first creative acts of youthful energy that must be directed toward correct ends.

Opposite Hexagram: 39 Ch'ien.

181

Polarity: Yin below Yin (K.W: Yang below Yang).

Compass Directions: West and Northwest (K.W: North and Northeast).

Trigram Combination: K'an and Ken.

Family Members: Middle and youngest daughters (K.W: middle and youngest sons).

Parts of the Body: Kidneys.

Color: Dull green.

Symbolic Creatures: The young of any animal, gnat, weasel, swallow, donkey, dragon-fly, sturgeon, beetle, pig.

Plants and Perfumes: Bamboo shoots, red rose, wistaria, wild indigo, lemon, fragrant olive, sago tree.

Metal: Tin.

Precious Stone: White cornelian.

Emblems: A wild animal caught in a trap, flute, mist, schools and other places of learning, a spring at the base of a hill.

Ritual Tool: Axe.

Gods: Chu I, Kou Mang, Hsien T'ung, Master Stonehead, Mo-li Ch'ing, No-cha, Wen-ch'ang, Yun-t'ung, Chin Chia, Tam Kung, K'uei Hsing, Man Cheong.

Goddesses: Ma-ku, Pi-hsia-yuan-chun.

Magickal Workings: Arousing genuine and latent talents. Assisting the education of the young or inexperienced. Cultivating a willingness to admit mistakes, and to change course when necessary. Becoming open to the instructive influence of the Tao.

Hexagram 5

Hsu—Necessity

Archaic Form:

Modern Name: Xu.

Esoteric Interpretations: Energy that waits at the threshold, prior to forward projection. Plant shoots that lie still and undeveloped under the soil, until the first rains of spring give them impetus to grow. That which is indispensable for the successful outcome of an event. The necessary period of quiet reflection, rest, and organization of power, before any new action is commenced.

Opposite Hexagram: 6 Sung.

Polarity: Yang below Yin (K.W: Yang below Yang).

Trigram Combination: Ch'ien and K'an.

Compass Directions: South and West (K.W: Northwest and North).

Family Members: Father and middle daughter (K.W: father and middle son).

Parts of the Body: Spleen, liver, forearms.

Color: White.

Symbolic Creatures: Carp, elephant, rat, leopard.

Plants and Perfumes: China-grass, water lily, acanthus, pine, banana.

Metal: Iron.

Emblems: Ruined buildings waiting to be rebuilt, waste lands, wilderness.

Ritual Tool: The *chueh* (a type of chalice).

Dragon Spirit: Suan-ni (rules over rest and relaxation).

Gods: Lei Tsu, Yu-tzu, Tam Kung, Yun-t'ung.

Goddesses: Sao-ts'ing Niang.

Magickal Workings: Restricting action. Successful development of plans. Taming tendencies to move too soon, overreact, or waste energy in fruitless ventures. Clarifying the underlying reasons behind events. Attaining the courage to endure difficulties. Cultivating patience.

Hexagram 6

Sung—Justice

Archaic Form:

Modern Name: Song.

Esoteric Interpretations: The Moon shining under the Firmament, radiating its light upon the world during the Yin hours of darkness. The authority of Heaven/the Divine Will of the Self that is appealed to in times of strife and peril. Equal and fair treatment for all, regardless of status. Words of complaint to officials and spiritual representatives.[1] A child who seeks the advice and assistance of a parent.

Opposite Hexagram: 5 Hsu.

Polarity: Yin below Yang (K.W: Yang below Yang).

Trigram Combination: K'an and Ch'ien.

Compass Directions: West and South (K.W: North and Northwest).

Family Members: Middle daughter and father (K.W: middle son and father).

Parts of the Body: Gall bladder, arms.

Color: Light yellow.

Symbolic Creatures: Cricket, monkey, tiger, leopard, ant, cockerel, Chinese unicorn.

Plants and Perfumes: Pine, pear blossom, coniferous trees in general.

Metal: Iron.

Precious Stone: Pearl.

Emblems: Fiery wheel, rhombus, grain measure, law court, axe.

Ritual Tools: Sword, goad, the *Ju-I* (a type of short sword).

Dragon Spirits: Yai tzu (rules over swords, blood lust, and battle), Pi-han (rules over prisons, quarreling, litigation, and the projection of energy), Chao-feng (associated with danger and the exorcism of evil spirits).

Gods: Kuan Ti, Sun Hou-tzu, No-cha, Ch'ih-yu, Chu Jung, Man Cheong, Pao Kung, Ti-kuan, Shou Shen, Yu Huang.

Goddesses: Kuan Yin, Tou Mu.

Magickal Workings: Gaining assistance to overcome opposition. Self-defense. Obtaining justice. Success in legal action.

---

1. The text of the I Ching oracle for this Hexagram advises the questioner to seek the counsel of "the great man." Nowadays, this might refer to anyone who is relatively advanced in the process of Self-awareness. However, in ancient China, particularly during the time of the Shang-Yin dynasty, the "great man" was the Chief Diviner of the oracle bones and tortoise-shell, who was considered to be the essential mouthpiece of Divine Will.

Hexagram 7

SHIH—THE PEOPLE

Archaic Form:

Modern Name: Shi.

Esoteric Interpretations: Water that flows under Earth, nourishing all organic life. The wisdom of initiates, who freely give of their knowledge to those who seek their guidance, assisting them to evolve. Positions of advantage gained by superior learning or judgment. Social position and status. Life amidst the masses of humanity. The far-reaching influence of a single object, idea, or personality upon a collective.

Opposite Hexagram: 8 Pi.

Polarity: Yin below Yin (K.W: Yang below Yin).

Trigram Combination: K'an and K'un.

Compass Directions: West and North (K.W: North and Southwest).

Family Members: Middle daughter and mother (K.W: middle son and mother).

187

Parts of the Body: Genitals, kidneys, arms.

Colors: Vermilion, yellow, orange, blue.

Symbolic Creatures: Lion, tiger, phoenix, cricket, the *P'eng* (a mythical roc-like bird).

Plants and Perfumes: Yarrow, pear blossom, pine, cypress, saffron, water lily, camphor, water rushes, peony.

Metal: Gold.

Precious Stones: Moss agate, alabaster, topaz, yellow sapphire.

Emblems: Spiral, scholar, book, conch shell, sundial, person with red hair, shepherd, a great city, a sage, soldiers, crowds of people.

Ritual Tools: Yarrow stalks, I Ching coins, fly-whisk, thunderbolt dagger, trident.

Gods: Chu I, Fu-hsi, Kuan Ti, Wen-ch'ang, Kuei Ku-tzu, Lei Hai-ch'ing, Man Cheong, Wong Tai Sin, Ch'eng-huang, Chin Chia, K'uei Hsing, Lao-tzu, Chang Tao-ling, Shang Ti, Yu Huang.

Goddesses: Eastern mother, Hsi-wang-mu, Kuan Yin, Tsi-ku.

Magickal Workings: Bringing forth latent qualities of leadership. Gathering like-minded friends. Directing talents to their proper uses. Authority over spirits. Gathering all necessary powers for the successful manifestation of the Will. Improving teaching skills. Divination.

Hexagram 8

Pi—Union

Archaic Form:

Modern Name: Bi.

Esoteric Interpretations: Streams and rivers that flow upon Earth in regular courses. Water that seeks its own level, following closely to the contours of the land. The mysteries revealed by harmony with the feminine force. Humanity as a collected and united whole.

Opposite Hexagram: 7 Shih.

Polarity: Yin below Yin (K.W: Yin below Yang).

Trigram Combination: K'un and K'an.

Compass Directions: North and West (K.W: Southwest and North).

Family Members: Mother and middle daughter (K.W: mother and middle son).

Parts of the Body: Navel, vagina.

Color: Ochre yellow.

Symbolic Creatures: Goose, mandarin duck, kingfisher, dove, quail, wag-tail, perch.

Plants and Perfumes: Wood oil tree, lotus, pine, vetch, pulses, mugwort, blue mallow.

Metals: Bronze, brass.

Precious Stones: Cornelian, striped gems.

Emblems: Vase, rice cake, royal throne, two people standing together, hair-comb.

Ritual Tool: The Pi (a round disc of jade with a hole in the center).

Gods: Ho-ho, Shang Ti, Yuan Shih.

Goddesses: Nu-kua, Kuan Yin, Mobo, Pi-hsia-yuan-chun.

Magickal Workings: Harmony. Spiritual and mental oneness with all things (Samadhi). Uniting with the True Self/god within, and understanding that this lies at the heart of one's real Path in life. Bringing rebellious egotisms under the control of the Will. Finding sympathetic partners. Inner peace by encouraging Self-acceptance. (Unnecessary conflict, and therefore unhappiness, is the inevitable result of opposition to one's destiny.)

Hexagram 9

HSIAO CHU—MINOR DOMESTICATION

Archaic Form:

Modern Name: Xiao Chu.

Esoteric Interpretations: The Wind blowing above Heaven. Movement that is taking place outside of the directing influence of its proper environment, and is consequently stifled of its original intent and loses its impetus. A society based on conventional "norms" has an inherent tendency to smother or control individual creativity, but is not necessarily all-powerful. Setting out on the road to enlightenment causes initial fears of loss of control and the absence of familiarity; these throw up obstacles in the Way, yet they cannot long withstand the forward momentum and urge for Self-expression of the Will. Short-lived difficulties and setbacks. Petty circumstances in mundane life that temporarily hold back progress, yet present interesting and conquerable challenges to the resourceful.

Opposite Hexagram: 44 Kou.

Polarity: Yang below Yin.

Trigram Combination: Ch'ien and Hsuan.

Compass Directions: South and Southwest (K.W: Northwest and Southeast).

Family Members: Father and eldest daughter.

Part of the Body: Spleen.

Color: Dull green.

Symbolic Creatures: The young of any kind, ox, dragonfly, domesticated cattle.

Plants and Perfumes: Grass/hay, ailanthus, water-pepper.

Metal: Iron.

Precious Stones: Green jasper, smoky quartz.

Emblems: Broom, farms and livestock, pasture land and meadows.

Ritual Tool: Thunderbolt dagger.

Gods: Kuan Ti, No-cha, Shou Shen, Boy of the White Crane, Sun Hou-tzu.

Magickal Workings: Acquiring the strength to overcome successfully minor problems. Cutting the ties that bind. Gaining the confidence to go one's own Way, despite pressure from others who are ignorant of the necessities of one's destiny. Dealing with aspects of the human mind and personality that seek to stand in the way of enlightenment by blocking the smooth Path of the Will.

Hexagram 10

Li—Walking

Archaic Form:

Modern Name: Lu.

Esoteric Interpretations: Treading the Path of the Way. Still water that reflects the light of the starry sky. The adept who is open and receptive to the voice of the god within. The laws of Heaven that are manifested in the lives of creatures. The continual nature of the spiritual journey. The lone hero upon the Warrior's Quest.

Opposite Hexagram: 43 Chueh.

Polarity: Yang below Yang (K.W: Yin below Yang).

Trigram Combination: Tui and Ch'ien.

Compass Directions: Southeast and South (K.W: West and Northwest).

Family Members: Youngest son and father (K.W: youngest daughter and father).

Parts of the Body: Skull, spine, gall bladder, feet, legs.

Color: Black.

Symbolic Creatures: Egret, heron, eagle, donkey, tiger, bear, yak, leopard, monkey, hen, cricket, horse, boar.

Plants and Perfumes: Ailanthus, iris, bitter orange, pomegranate, truffle fungus, mallow, patchouli, peach-wood, willow leaves, calamus, mugwort.

Metals: Iron, silver.

Precious Stones: Jade, amber, diamond.

Emblems: A road, the base of a hill/mountain, shoe, conch shell, the "Knot of Eternity," the *T'ao-tieh* (a mask-like design on early bronzes).

Ritual Tools: Sword, fan, wind chimes, diamond mace, gong, mirror, drum.

Dragon Spirits: Chao-feng (see Hexagram 6), Yai-tzu (see Hexagram 6).

Gods: Ch'ih-yu, Chung K'uei, Erh-lang, Fang-hsiang, Kuan Ti, No-cha, Sun Hou-tzu, Chang Tao-ling, Boy of the White Crane, Ch'I-t'ou, Chu Jung, P'an Kuan, Shou Shen, Wei-t'o, Pa Ch'a, Pi-hsieh.

Goddesses: Kuan Yin, Tou Mu.

Magickal Workings: Exorcism. Protection in dangerous situations. Averting calamity. Gaining the courage to take necessary risks in order to evolve. Adopting the persona of the warrior who is not afraid to walk his or her Way, even in the face of sometimes violent opposition. Stimulating confidence in oneself, even when beset by many problems.

Hexagram 11

T'AI—PEACE

Archaic Form:

Modern Name: Tai.

Esoteric Interpretations: The ecstatic union of Heaven and Earth. The harmonious balance of opposite forces. The equilibration of Yin and Yang, the dynamic polarities of Primal Creation, which leads to a greater understanding and acceptance of the vast varieties of phenomenal life. Mental liberation and movement away from ideological narrow-mindedness. The Hexagram of the first Chinese month (c. February–March), the Festival of the New Year, and the Feast of Lanterns.

Opposite Hexagram: 12 Fao.

Polarity: Yang below Yin.

Trigram Combination: Ch'ien and K'un.

Compass Directions: South and North (K.W: Northwest and Southwest).

Family Members: Father and mother.

Parts of the Body: Phallus, vagina, pregnant womb.

Color: Verdant green.

Symbolic Creatures: Goose, quail, mandarin duck, dove, kingfisher, fox, phoenix, wagtail.

Plants and Perfumes: Apple, pine, moss, peach blossom, plum blossom, orchid, narcissus, lotus, hemp, olive, mugwort, reed, tulip.

Metals: Bronze, brass.

Precious Stone: Cornelian.

Emblems: Vase, bottle, rainbow, the constellation of the Great Bear, pregnant women, jade butterfly, egg, two-headed dragon, a wide-flowing river, rice cake, flute, foetus, saddle.

Ritual Tools: Bottle gourd, axe, firecrackers.

Gods: His Shen, Kou Mang, Ho-ho, Huang Ti, Mo-li Ch'ing, Yao Wang, Fu-hsi, P'an Ku, Shen Nung, Tam Kung, Wong Tai Sin, Wu Kang, Chang Hsien.

Goddesses: Ma-ku, K'eng San Ku-niang, Kuan Yin, Pi-hsia-yuan-chun, Chuang Mu, Ma Ni-li, Nu-kua, T'ien Hou, Tou Mu.

Magickal Workings: Creating peaceful situations and reducing stress. Initiating new beginnings. Fertility. Sexual alchemy. Healing. Rites of purification.[1]

---

1. In shamanistic settings, this is often achieved by fire walking, a spiritual ordeal common to a number of Asian communities at New Year celebrations.

Hexagram 12

FAO—NEGATION

Archaic Form:

Modern Name: Pi.

Esoteric Interpretations: The mouth that says "No!" The first beginnings of movement away from plenty and toward reduction and withdrawal. Division and disharmony. The separation of Heaven and Earth. Yang rises and Yin descends. The harmonious Unity that splits into its constituent parts. Sexual inactivity between partners. The Hexagram of the seventh Chinese month (c. August–September) and the Festival of the Hungry Ghosts. A time to confront personal weaknesses and fears.

Opposite Hexagram: 11 T'ai.

Polarity: Yin below Yang.

Trigram Combination: K'un and Ch'ien.

Compass Directions: North and South (K.W: Southwest and Northwest).

Family Members: Mother and father.

Parts of the Body: Vagina, phallus.

Colors: Black, light brown, dark red.

Symbolic Creatures: Carp, elephant, wild duck, wild goose.

Plants and Perfumes: Lotus blossom, wood anemone, jujube, China-grass, pear blossom, chrysanthemum, banana, cedar.

Metal: Tin.

Emblems: A valley or ravine with a stream running through it, hermit, cave (as a place of seclusion and retreat).

Ritual Tools: Axe, the *T'ien Kan* (the "Heavenly Orange," a spiked sphere used for shamanistic rites of self-mortification).[1]

Gods: Ti Ts'ang Wang, Wang-kung, Yen-lo, Hsu Hao, Mo-li Hai, Lo Hou Hsing, T'ien Kou.

Goddesses: Hsi-wang-mu, Meng, Pa, Tou Mu, Kuan Yin.

Magickal Workings: Cultivating patience during times of decay. Introspection. Frustrating the actions of others. Gaining inner strength to help pass through the psychological process known as "the Dark Night of the Soul."

---

1. A traditional instrument. I don't recommend its use!

Hexagram 13

TUNG JEN—THE UNION OF PEOPLE

Archaic Form:

Modern Name: Tong Ren.

Esoteric Interpretations: The Sun shining under the expanse of the heavenly vault makes no distinction between those on whom it sheds its light. Humankind in fellowship and harmony. Communication between peoples. An appreciation of the different global cultures, with acknowledgement of the factors common to all humans that unite their varied communities in a whole.

Opposite Hexagram: 14 Ta Yu.

Polarity: Yang below Yang (K.W: Yin below Yang).

Trigram Combination: Li and Ch'ien.

Compass Directions: East and South (K.W: South and Northwest).

Family Members: Middle son and father (K.W: middle daughter and father).

Parts of the Body: Eyes, large intestine.

Colors: Red, light yellow.

Symbolic Creatures: Human child, oriole, young ram, phoenix, the P'eng (see Hexagram 7), dove, parrot, swallow, perch.

Plants and Perfumes: Paulownia, wood oil tree, spurge, lotus, pine, cypress, plum, mugwort.

Metals: Brass, bronze, copper.

Precious Stones: Moss agate, cornelian.

Emblems: Rice cake, orchids in a vase, box, basket.

Ritual Tools: Lanterns/candles, bottle gourd.

Gods: Fu-hsi, Ho-ho.

Goddesses: Kuan Yin, Nu-kua, Ti-ya, Tou Mu.

Magickal Workings: Strengthening friendship (especially on a group level). Gaining support from other people for personal ideas. Gaining allies (probably from unexpected sources). Strengthening abilities to communicate successfully with other people.

Hexagram 14

TA YU—GREAT POSSESSION

Archaic Form:

Modern Name: Da You.

Esoteric Interpretations: Solar good fortune directed throughout the world by Divine Will. Personal success achieved through the actuating power of the Self. An independent spirit, allied to a strong and genuine commitment, leads to favorable circumstances. Times of special prosperity. Anything that is done on a grand scale.[1]

Opposite Hexagram: 13 Tung Jen.

Polarity: Yang below Yang (K.W: Yang below Yin).

Trigram Combination: Ch'ien and Li.

Compass Directions: South and East (K.W: Northwest and South).

Family Members: Father and middle son (K.W: father and middle daughter).

Parts of the Body: Intestines.

Colors: Black, gold, red.

Symbolic Creatures: Goldfish, bat, deer, rat, magpie, pheasant.

Plants and Perfumes: Taro, peony, hibiscus, yellow loquat, millet, citron, Buddha's hand, rice.

Metals: Gold, silver.

Precious Stones: Lapis-lazuli, onyx.

Emblems: The *Chu-pao P'en* (the magickal bowl of Yuan-tan; see Gods), scroll, yellow cloud, lunar eclipse, the Money Tree of Ts'ai Shen.

Ritual Tool: Scepter.

Dragon Spirit: Fu-ts'ang Lung (guardian of hidden treasure and deposits of precious metals).

Gods: Yuan-tan, Liu Hai, Lu Shen, Ho-ho, Kuan Ti, Ts'ai Shen, Lo Hou Hsing, Wu Kang.

Magickal Workings: Wealth and prosperity. Accumulation of riches (both physical and spiritual).

---

1. The archaic pictogram for Ta Yu shows a hand, symbolic of purpose and might, concealing the light from the Moon. At one time, *Yu* also meant "an eclipse of the Moon," or "the Dark Moon." In the case of the developed fourteenth Hexagram, this implies a deliberate move to hamper Yin processes of harm and loss, thereby allowing the Yang powers of success and wealth to permeate throughout the land.

Hexagram 15

CH'IEN—MODESTY

Archaic Form:

Modern Name: Qian.

Esoteric Interpretations: A mountain hidden within Earth. Firm, inner resolve within an outwardly calm and passive exterior. People with immense strength of purpose, and the strength to achieve their aims, but who do not make a great spectacle of their skills simply to impress others. Actions that are successfully, and quietly, carried out with sincerity and reverence. Respectful attitudes toward the land and all those that live, and have lived, upon it. The absence of egotism. Nature does not boast about its accomplishments, it just gets on with achieving them as a matter of course!

Opposite Hexagram: 23 Pao.

Polarity: Yin below Yin (K.W: Yang below Yin).

Trigram Combination: Ken and K'un.

Compass Directions: Northwest and North (K.W: Northeast and Southwest).

Family Members: Youngest daughter and mother (K.W: youngest son and mother).

Parts of the Body: Lungs.

Colors: Black, carnation red, white.

Symbolic Creatures: Sparrow, wolf, sheep, Chinese unicorn, earthworm, eel, ant.

Plants and Perfumes: Blue lotus, chestnut, juniper, water lily, bamboo.

Metals: Iron, silver.

Precious Stones: White cornelian, quartz.

Emblems: Bound sheaf of grain, a grassy plain, vase, bell.

Ritual Tools: Moon House (a shrine for ancestor spirits to inhabit), parasol, the *Tung Chueh* (a bronze chalice, connected with ancestor worship).

Dragon Spirit: Cha-yu (a lover of virtue and sincerity).

Gods: Shang Ti, Yuan Shih, Yu Huang, Lao-tzu, P'an Ku.

Goddesses: Kuan Yin, Ti-ya, Eastern Mother.

Magickal Workings: Offerings given to the spirits of the land and to the dead, thereby gaining their favor. Oneness with the numinous current embodied by the ancestors. Strengthening inner emotional strength and quiet exterior dignity. The use of force without aggression (e.g., gently moving aside those who have inadvertently blundered into one's Path).

Hexagram 16

Yu—Cheerfulness

Archaic Form:

Modern Name: Yu.

Esoteric Interpretations: The storm that breaks above the land, causing it to rumble and quake with its thunderous force. The manifestation of energetic activity. Dances and rituals by the Wu that invoke the gods, release thunder, and bring quenching rain to Earth. Festivity without undue restraint, and a time for giving thanks for the pleasures of life. The inwardly strong person who is capable of enjoying light-hearted moments without awkwardness or embarrassment; genuine sincerity does not equal absence of humor, the true adept is one who openly embraces and displays it. The Path is joy. Gatherings that indulge in group acts of pleasure and empowerment. The knowledge of the Hexagrams that enables the initiate to govern his or her existence with gladness.

Opposite Hexagram: 24 Fu.

Polarity: Yin below Yang.

Trigram Combination: K'un and Chen.

Compass Directions: North and Northeast (K.W: Southwest and East).

Family Members: Mother and eldest son.

Parts of the Body: Feet, solar plexus.

Colors: Green, red.

Symbolic Creatures: Dragon, elephant, sandpiper, oriole, magpie, bat, woodpecker, butterfly, fox, fish.

Plants and Perfumes: Bamboo shoots, cypress, hemp, chrysanthemum, persimmon, marsh orchid, thyme, balsam poplar.

Metals: Copper, brass.

Precious Stones: Fine green jade, white jade, cornelian.

Emblems: Basket of flowers, red bat, the "Thunder" pattern (a series of squared spirals), halberd, cloud, leaves, stone chime, dancers, rhinoceros horn, musical instruments.

Ritual Tools: Drum, gong, rattle-drum.

Dragon Spirits: P'u Lao (ruler of gongs and bells), Ch'iu Niu (rules over music), Shen-lung (controller of wind and rain), K'uei (controller of rain), Lung Wang (ruler of rain, storms and oceans).

Gods: Hsi Shen, Lei Hai-ch'ing, Huang Ti, Fu Shen, Mi-lo Fo, Lei Kung, Lei Tsu, Lei Chen-tzu, Fu-hsi, Shen Nung, Tam Kung, T'ien-kuan, Wong Tai Sin, Yu-tzu, Kou Mang.

Goddesses: Kuan Yin, Sao-ts'ing Niang, Ma-ku.

Magickal Workings: Ritual music and drumming. Trance dance. Uniting personal action with movement in Nature as a whole. Rain magick. Healing. Increasing a capacity to enjoy pleasurable things.

Hexagram 17

SUI—FOLLOWING

Archaic Form:

Modern Name: Sui.

Esoteric Interpretations: The waters of a lake that enthusiastically embrace the power of the tempest. Moving power beneath the water that causes ripples on the surface. Active energy that seeks a corresponding receptivity and response from that to which it is given. Magico-spiritual evolution is driven by inner power and its movement. The mind of the adept is like a pool, assimilating and responding to all input from the god within. Adaptation to the varying needs of circumstances and events. Imitation and compliance. Actions determined by advice from wiser minds. Good examples set by others.

Opposite Hexagram: 54 Kuei Mei.

Polarity: Yang below Yang (K.W: Yang below Yin).

Trigram Combination: Chen and Tui.

Compass Directions: Northeast and Southeast (K.W: East and West).

Family Members: Eldest and youngest sons (K.W: eldest son and youngest daughter).

Part of the Body: Stomach.

Colors: Scarlet, light yellow.

Symbolic Creatures: Elephant, sheep, ant, cricket, dog, eel.

Plants and Perfumes: Pear blossom, chestnut, marsh orchid, spikenard.

Metal: Bronze.

Precious Stone: Jasper.

Emblems: Shepherd, bell, basket. A teacher of the lute who plays to his or her student.

Ritual Tools: Broom, yarrow stalks, I Ching coins, parasol.

Gods: Chu I, Kuei Ku-tzu, Lei Hai-ch'ing, Wen-ch'ang, Chih Chia, Fu-hsi.

Goddess: Tsi-ku.

Magickal Workings: Enhancing capacities to work under the direction of others. Seeking a guide or teacher. Gaining advice or information (either from the spirits, another person, or one's own True Self). Divination.

Hexagram 18

Ku—Poison

Archaic Form:

Modern Name: Gu.

Esoteric Interpretations: Air withdrawn from its natural environment and contained within the earth. No movement. Life-giving ch'i that is reabsorbed by the center of the cosmos. Worms ground in a vessel and made into a magickal, death-dealing potion. The reduction of objects to their individual parts. Death and decay. The inner being as distinct from the outer body in the world of appearances. Ancient powers and forces. The breakdown of things prior to regeneration. Destructive feng shui energies and miasmic, unhealthy vapors. Outmoded systems and ideas that are dropped in order to further personal development.

Opposite Hexagram: 53 Chien.

Polarity: Yin below Yin (K.W: Yin below Yang).

Trigram Combination: Hsuan and Ken.

Compass Directions: Southwest and Northwest (K.W: Southeast and Northeast).

Family Members: Eldest and youngest daughters (K.W: eldest daughter and youngest son).

Parts of the Body: Vagina, bones.

Colors: Black, light brown.

Symbolic Creatures: Worm, maggot, the *Ku* (a legendary venomous insect, and a type of spirit evoked by magicians in Hak Tao), blind animals, snake, lizard, reptiles in general, centipede, toad, scorpion, the *Fang-huang* (spirit-creature of waste lands and deserts), the *Hsin* (spirit-creature that lurks near burial mounds).

Plants and Perfumes: Cereals, fungus, poinsettia (poisonous!), gelsemium (poisonous!), wood anemone, camphor, jujube, thistle.

Metal: Copper.

Precious Stone: Smoky quartz.

Emblems: A valley or gorge, desolate landscape, desert, wheel, charnel house, tomb, burial mound, meteor, night sky heavy with clouds, green cloud.

Ritual Tools: Drum, mu-jen, black slippers, water vessel/bowl.

Dragon Spirits: Yai-tzu (see Hexagram 6), Chao-feng (see Hexagram 6).

Gods: Shang Ti, Ti Ts'ang Wang, Wang-kung, Yen-lo, Yuan Shih, Di-jiang, Hsu Hao, Nan-chi Hsien-weng, She-mo Wang, T'ien Kou, Lo Hou Hsing.

Goddesses: Hsi-wang-mu, Meng, Pa.

Magickal Workings: Creating drastic changes that lead to major new situations. Revenge. Malefic magick. Letting go of the past. Finding the possibilities of future growth in the midst of ruin. Turning the worst situations to one's own advantage.

Hexagram 19

LIN—AFFABILITY

Archaic Form:

Modern Name: Lin.

Esoteric Interpretations: The end of wintertime austerity and hardship, and the happy union of people in festivities that mark the turning of the year. The movement of Nature toward the vital promise of spring. Interaction between different levels in human society; no matter what one's social status, all equally anticipate the New Year and join together in welcoming it. Contact and communication with family, friends, and neighbors. Cheerful speech uttered by many mouths. The Hexagram of the twelfth Chinese month (c. January–February).

Opposite Hexagram: 45 Ts'ui.

Polarity: Yang below Yin (K.W: Yin below Yin).

Trigram Combination: Tui and K'un.

Compass Directions: Southeast and North (K.W: West and Southwest).

Family Members: Youngest son and mother (K.W: youngest daughter and mother).

Parts of the Body: Mouth, tongue, womb or belly, vagina, intestines.

Color: Scarlet.

Symbolic Creatures: Chinese unicorn, firefly, pangolin, rat, cockerel, deer, perch, oriole.

Plants and Perfumes: Millet, poppy, pine, cypress, plum blossom, wintersweet, white jasmine.

Metal: Brass.

Precious Stone: Jade.

Emblems: Forest, grove of trees, fish-scales, mandarin, granary, golden pheasant, hat, orchids in a vase.

Ritual Tools: Bottle gourd, lute.

Gods: Kuan Ti, Liu Hai, Man Cheong, Mi-lo Fo, Ho-ho, Fu Shen, Mo-li Shou, T'ien-kuan.

Goddesses: Kuan Yin, Tou Mu.

Magickal Workings: Encouraging openness and friendship between people. Profitable dealings with others. Influential speech.

Hexagram 20

KUAN—MEDITATION

Archaic Form:

Modern Name: Guan.

Esoteric Interpretations: Wind that flows freely over the surface of Earth, discovering all its secrets. A tree that rises upward from the ground, connecting the celestial and chthonic realms. A place to contemplate life and its mysteries. Withdrawal from exterior distractions in order to acquire knowledge. The roving spiritual consciousness of the adept, whose mental state is open and receptive to divine insight. The Hexagram of the eighth Chinese month (c. September–October), the Autumn Equinox, and the Moon Festival.

Opposite Hexagram: 46 Sheng.

Polarity: Yin below Yin.

Trigram Combination: K'un and Hsuan.

213

Compass Directions: North and Southwest (K.W: Southwest and Southeast).

Family Members: Mother and eldest daughter.

Parts of the Body: Eyes, middle of forehead (i.e., the area of the Third Eye), lungs, stomach, cheeks.

Colors: Red, light yellow.

Symbolic Creatures: Owl, heron, elephant, hawk, falcon, crane, cicada, horse.

Plants and Perfumes: Rushes, reeds, cinnamon blossom, willow, pear blossom, tamarisk, camphor, alfalfa, acanthus, mallow, palm leaves.

Metal: Bronze.

Precious Stone: Lapis-lazuli.

Emblems: Taoist temples and monks, bridge, coffin, vase, cave, chariot, the "Knot of Eternity," a sage, hermit, Moon Cakes (round, sweet pastries, eaten during the Moon Festival), watchtower, the World Tree.

Ritual Tools: Cap or other magickal headgear, broom, thighbone trumpet, bell.

Dragon Spirit: Ch'ih Wen (rules over bridges and water).

Gods: Feng Po, Pi-hsieh, Wei-t'o, Lao-tzu, Chang Tao-ling, Fei Lien, Kuei Ku-tzu, Lei Hai-ch'ing, Mo-li Hai.

Goddesses: Kuan Yin, Eastern Mother, Hsi-wang-mu, Tsi-ku, Feng-p'o-p'o, Tou Mu.

Magickal Workings: Gaining esoteric knowledge through meditation. Stimulating intuition. Invocations of god-force (e.g., the magician's deliberate induction of deities into his own psychophysical form, for future projection of their energy and influence into the world). Trance-states and shamanistic projection of consciousness into the realms of the World Tree.

Hexagram 21

SHIH HO—BITING THROUGH

Archaic Form:

Modern Name: Shi Ke.

Esoteric Interpretations: Thunder and lightning, the terrifying voice and authority of divine Will. Absolute power in motion. Force that penetrates. Irresistible momentum. A desperate need to move against suffocation and stagnation. No obstacle is allowed to block the Way. Sudden force that strikes with the devastating impact of a storm. Hard times, but victory is certain.

Opposite Hexagram: 55 Feng.

Polarity: Yang below Yang (K.W: Yang below Yin).

Trigram Combination: Chen and Li.

Compass Directions: Northeast and East (K.W: East and South).

Family Members: Eldest and middle sons (K.W: eldest son and middle daughter).

Parts of the Body: Feet, arms, phallus, teeth, gall bladder, kidneys.

Colors: Vivid red, bright yellow.

Symbolic Creatures: Tiger, ox, leopard, lion, eel, cricket, dog, boar, kite.

Plants and Perfumes: Iris, ailanthus, camphor, truffle fungus, mallow, bamboo, willow, peach-wood, red peas, garlic, areca palm.

Metal: Iron.

Precious Stone: Diamond.

Emblems: Rhombus, lightning, whirling disc, *ignis fatuus* (will-o'-the-wisp).

Ritual Tools: Sword, spear, diamond mace, fan, goad, the Ju-I (see Hexagram 6), drum, black banner.

Dragon Spirits: Pi-han (see Hexagram 6), Chao-feng (see Hexagram 6), Yai-tzu (see Hexagram 6).

Gods: Kuan Ti, T'ien Kou, Ch'ih-yu, Chu Jung, No-cha, Sun Hou-tzu, Chang Tao-ling, Boy of the White Crane, Ch'i-t'ou, Fang-hsiang, P'an Kuan, Pao Kung, Chung K'uei, Erh-lang, Lei Chen-tzu, Lei Kung.

Goddesses: Tien Mu, Hsi-wang-mu.

Magickal Workings: Exorcism. Breaking through barriers and overcoming obstacles (by very active measures). Obtaining justice. Freeing the Path of deep-set problems caused by the ego-consciousness.

Note of caution: By its nature, it should be obvious to anyone that this Hexagram embodies a strong force. Treat it with respect, and be certain that its utilization is right in your own particular circumstances, or you may end up with more than burned fingers! It is often a symbol of last resort, when all other means have failed.

Hexagram 22

FEN—ORNAMENTATION

Archaic Form:

Modern Name: Bei.

Esoteric Interpretations: Fire that is contained within a mountain. The outward image that seeks to complement the inner desire. Concentration on outward appearances and material possessions that can lead to sadness and disappointment if the inner spirit, which makes its possessor truly beautiful, is neglected. The adept who comes to an understanding of the Tao by contemplating the external and personified consequences of its movement. The pleasures that enhance life if enjoyed wisely, but should never be allowed to dictate its value. (Wisdom and personal evolution lie in the journey itself; the importance of things picked up along the Way must be judged in relation to the Path only, and not by society's values.)

Opposite Hexagram: 56 Lu.

Polarity: Yang below Yin (K.W: Yin below Yang).

Trigram Combination: Li and Ken.

Compass Directions: East and Northwest (K.W: South and Northeast).

Family Members: Middle son and youngest daughter (K.W: middle daughter and youngest son).

Part of the Body: Face.

Colors: Red, yellow.

Symbolic Creatures: Shellfish, glowworm, silkworm, pheasant, peacock.

Plants and Perfumes: Grasses, mulberry, ylang-ylang, orchid, hibiscus, henna, saffron.

Metal: Gold.

Precious Stone: Pearl.

Emblems: Cowrie shell, flower basket, bodily embellishments and jewelry, silks and fine clothes.

Ritual Tool: Scepter.

Gods: Fu Shen, Liu Hai, Mi-lo Fo, Wong Tai Sin, T'ien-kuan. Pien Ho.

Goddess: Ma-t'ou Niang.

Magickal Workings: Enhancing pleasure. Casting glamours. The active use of beauty or physical appearance in general. Attraction.

Hexagram 23

PAO—FLAYING

Archaic Form:

Modern Name: Bao.

Esoteric Interpretations: A mountain that rests upon Earth. That which is receptive, united with that which has no movement, results in decreasing circumstances. A time for quiet and stillness, for contemplation upon future projects. Success comes to the one who can wait for the right moment to act. Branches that are cut from a tree and then peeled of their bark, so that their inner cores are revealed. Nature sheds the last of the year's growth before the onset of the dormant wintertime. Getting beyond the outer layer of a thing in order to reveal the potential that lies within. The loss of sexual virginity as an important rite of passage. All births and future movement require something first to yield. The Hexagram of the ninth Chinese month (c. October–November).

Opposite Hexagram: 15 Ch'ien.

Polarity: Yin below Yin (K.W: Yin below Yang).

Trigram Combination: K'un and Ken.

Compass Directions: North and Northwest (K.W: Southwest and Northeast).

Family Members: Mother and youngest daughter (K.W: mother and youngest son).

Parts of the Body: Hymen, skin.

Colors: Black, light brown, dark purple.

Symbolic Creatures: Bustard, leopard, snake, dragonfly, wolf, owl, grebe.

Plants and Perfumes: Chrysanthemum, mallow blossom, wood anemone, water-pepper, thistle, banana, cedar, watermelon.

Metal: Tin.

Precious Stone: Diamond.

Emblems: Cannon, knife, red cloud, tree stump, pestle and mortar, comets, ruined buildings.

Ritual Tools: Thunderbolt dagger, the T'ien Kan (see Hexagram 12), axe.

Dragon Spirits: Chao-feng (see Hexagram 6), Yai-tzu (see Hexagram 6).

Gods: Ti Ts'ang Wang, Wang-kung, Pai Mai Shen, Nan-chi Hsien-weng, T'ien Kou, Wei-t'o, Di-jiang, Hsu Hao, Mo-li Hai, She-mo Wang, Chu Jung, Kuan Ti, Yen-lo.

Goddesses: Chuang Mu, Hsi-wang-mu, Meng, Hsuan-nu, Pai Mu-tan.

Magickal Workings: Cultivating patience during times of crisis. Contemplation upon periods of necessary decay, with increasing understanding and acceptance of their importance to the cycle of life. Introspection and quiet meditation. Assisting vital transition to run its course. Works of destruction.

Hexagram 24

FU—GOING BACK AGAIN

Archaic Form:

Modern Name: Fu.

Esoteric Interpretations: The sound of thunder heard within the still Earth. The old year begins to turn to the prospect of the new, and the coming spring lies as a rich promise in the winter landscape. Moving and creative force exists within all forms, no matter how inert or lifeless such objects may appear to physical sight. Change is a possibility present in all circumstances. That which is about to come again. The reversal of existing conditions. Repetition and habitual actions. The Hexagram of the eleventh Chinese month (c. December–January) and the winter solstice.

Opposite Hexagram: 16 Yu.

Polarity: Yang below Yin.

Trigram Combination: Chen and K'un.

Compass Directions: Northeast and North (K.W: East and Southwest).

Family Members: Eldest son and mother.

Parts of the Body: Abdomen, stomach, liver.

Color: Reddish yellow.

Symbolic Creatures: Bat, cicada, the Hsin (see Hexagram 18), panda, butterfly, magpie, snake, spider, tench, frog.

Plants and Perfumes: Aconite (poisonous!), mangrove, gardenia, bamboo flower, narcissus, evergreen trees, kumquat, poppy, wintersweet, fennel, caraway, fragrant plants in general.

Metal: Gold.

Precious Stone: Agate.

Emblems: Burial mound, serpent-scales, spiral, conch shell, wheel, disc, the Tai-Chi, meander patterns, swastika/fylfot.

Ritual Tools: Finger-ring, drum.

Gods: Pei-ti, Liu Hai, Mo-li Shou, Shang Ti, Yuan Shih, Di-jiang, She-mo Wang, Shou Shen, Lu Shen, Mi-lo Fo, Ti-kuan, Wong Tai Sin, T'ai Sui.

Goddesses: Kuan Yin, Tou Mu, Nu-kua.

Magickal Workings: Increasing optimism. Contact with, and understanding of, the Inner Self. Solving self-created problems. Contemplating the cyclical motion of Nature and the changing seasons. Establishing a return to good fortune after a period of "bad luck." Investigating the connections between seemingly separate events and circumstances (e.g., human incarnations).

Hexagram 25

Wu Wang—Truth

Archaic Form:

Modern Name: Wu Wang.

Esoteric Interpretations: Thunder as the utterance of heavenly command and authority. The Will of the gods in harmony with that of creatures. Movement and projection of energy that is guided by the wisdom of higher powers. Action and ideas that are true because they arise from the purity of the Tao, and not from egotistical pretensions. Spontaneity in events that signifies the eruption of the True Will into matter. All circumstances that arise as a natural course of destiny are correct, whatever their outward form. Sincerity. The possessor of the Tao has the support of the universe behind him.

Opposite Hexagram: 34 Ta Chuang.

Polarity: Yang below Yang.

Trigram Combination: Chen and Ch'ien.

Compass Directions: Northeast and South (K.W: East and Northwest).

Family Members: Eldest son and father.

Parts of the Body: Lungs, stomach, nose.

Colors: White, red, black.

Symbolic Creatures: Dragon, ant, fox, snake, cockerel, Chinese unicorn, heron, eel.

Plants and Perfumes: Cypress, hemp, ginseng, bitter orange.

Metals: Iron, silver.

Precious Stones: Cornelian, amber, quartz.

Emblems: Scroll, vase, bell, head-dress with a cicada motif.

Ritual Tool: Parasol.

Dragon Spirit: Cha-yu (see Hexagram 15).

Gods: Shang Ti, Lao-tzu, She-mo Wang, Shen Nung, Tam Kung, Wong Tai Sin, Yuan Shih, Yu Huang, Di-jiang, Mu Kung, Hsien T'ung, Yao Wang, Chang Tao-ling.

Goddesses: Kuan Yin, Nu-kua, T'ien Hou.

Magickal Workings: Healing by harmonization of the psychophysical body. Flowing in accord with the Will of the True Self. Ascertaining the correct course of action in any state of confusion. Seeing through illusions.

Hexagram 26

TA CHU—GREAT DOMESTICATION

Archaic Form:

Modern Name: Da Chu.

Esoteric Interpretations: Heaven contained within a mountain. The deliberate suffocation of creative action. A block on the ascent of something that naturally rises. Static circumstances caused by energy being unable to express itself. Imaginative genius, put to the temporary use of basic concerns, while its seeks the correct higher road along which it should travel (choosing the wrong Path would be even more disastrous than the temporary withdrawal from activity that is counseled by this Hexagram). Restraints that are placed on the exercising of strength, leading to an increase of internal stress. Avoidance of the loss of vital magickal force in wasteful and unnecessary ventures.

Opposite Hexagram: 33 Tun.

Polarity: Yang below Yin (K.W: Yang below Yang).

Trigram Combination: Ch'ien and Ken.

Compass Directions: South and Northwest (K.W: Northwest and Northeast).

Family Members: Father and youngest daughter (K.W: father and youngest son).

Part of the Body: Spleen.

Colors: Dull green, dark purple.

Symbolic Creatures: Dragonfly, the *Lei-ting* (spirit-creature that lives in dust heaps), rat, wolf, leopard.

Plants and Perfumes: Iris, truffle fungus, rice, sulphur (poisonous!), wistaria.

Metal: Iron.

Precious Stones: Pearl, green jasper.

Emblems: Ash and dust, farmstead and livestock, cattle yoke.

Ritual Tools: Rope (for knot magick), snare, mirror, bottle gourd.

Dragon Spirit: Chao-feng (see Hexagram 6).

Gods: Chung K'uei, Pi-hsieh, Wei-t'o, Chang Tao-ling, P'an Kuan.

Goddesses: Hsi-wang-mu, Kuan Yin.

Magickal Workings: Exorcism (especially through the use of spirit traps and occult ligatures that bind disruptive energies rather than repel them). Accumulating magickal force for future intensive use.

Hexagram 27

I—Nourishment

Archaic Form:

Modern Name: Yi.

Esoteric Interpretations: The arousing force of thunder within a mountain. New and dynamic ideas that are formulated upon a resolute and stable base. The advancement of the human species by the acquisition of knowledge. Personal responsibility for nourishment of the mind. The influential energies/ritually symbolic importance of the constellation of the Great Bear.

Opposite Hexagram: 62 Hsiao Kuo.

Polarity: Yang below Yin (K.W: Yang below Yang).

Trigram Combination: Chen and Ken.

Compass Directions: Northeast and Northwest (K.W: East and Northeast).

Family Members: Eldest son and youngest daughter (K.W: eldest and youngest sons).

Parts of the Body: Jaws, stomach, heart, brain, cheeks.

Colors: Deep purple, blue.

Symbolic Creatures: Porpoise, snake, Chinese unicorn, elephant, sturgeon.

Plants and Perfumes: Onion, palm leaves, fragrant olive, plantain, indigo, woad, acanthus.

Metals: Lead, tin.

Precious Stone: Agate.

Emblems: The Great Bear constellation (known to the Chinese as the Northern Dipper, or Bushel), pair of books, ladle, bridge, rainbow, writing brush and ink stick, chessboard, scholar.

Ritual Tools: Sacred books (such as the *Tao-teh Ching* and I Ching), broom.

Dragon Spirit: Pi-hsi (rules over literature, rivers, and has supernatural strength).

Gods: Wen-ch'ang, K'uei Hsing, Shang Ti, Chu I, Kuan Ti, Chin Chia, Man Cheong, She-mo Wang.

Goddesses: Tou Mu, T'ien Hou, Ma Ni-li.

Magickal Workings: Learning. Developing concentration. Passing tests. Stimulating powers of memory. Assisting fitness of the body in general.

Hexagram 28

TA KUO—GREAT EXCESS

Archaic Form:

Modern Name: Da Guo.

Esoteric Interpretations: A tree that is temporarily drowned by the rising waters of a lake, yet which stands firm. The refusal to be bound by limitations and dangers that are caused by fear. Flexibility in the face of great problems. That aspect of the human spirit that has the courage to act out the role of a hero. Walking forward into the unknown. Striving ever to improve performance and achieve more.

Opposite Hexagram: 61 Chung Fu.

Polarity: Yin below Yang (K.W: Yin below Yin).

Trigram Combination: Hsuan and Tui.

Compass Directions: Southwest and Southeast (K.W: Southeast and West).

Family Members: Eldest daughter and youngest son (K.W: eldest and youngest daughters).

Parts of the Body: Feet, gall bladder, kidneys.

Colors: Red, black.

Symbolic Creatures: Dragon, tiger, cricket, leopard, monkey, lion, glow worm, carp, horse, boar, eagle.

Plants and Perfumes: Ailanthus, ginger, sticky rice.

Metal: Iron.

Precious Stones: Amber, diamond.

Emblems: Crossroads, twin fish, a flooded forest.

Ritual Tools: Diamond mace, sword.

Dragon Spirit: Chao-feng (see Hexagram 6).

Gods: Sun Hou-tzu, Boy of the White Crane, No-cha, Wei-t'o, Chung K'uei, P'an Kuan.

Goddesses: Hsi-wang-mu, Tou Mu, Kuan Yin.

Magickal Workings: Cultivating the strength and courage to go beyond restricting circumstances. Success in perilous ordeals.

Hexagram 29

K'AN—THE PIT

Archaic Form:

Modern Name: Kan.

Esoteric Interpretations: The mysterious power of the Moon and the forces of autumn. Flowing water, as in rivers, streams, rain, and so on. The absence of stable ground and situations that are in a state of flux. Contraction (the natural function of a hole is to draw all outer objects into itself). That which is hidden. Occultism and the paranormal. Concealed risks and dangers. The threshold. The supernatural beings associated with darkness. Death and the spirit world. Yin power in action. Female sexual force.

Polarity: Yin (K.W: Yang).

Compass Direction: West (K.W: North).

Guardian of the Quarter: The White Tiger.

Family Member: Middle daughter (K.W: middle son).

Parts of the Body: Ears, blood, vagina, small intestine, lungs, kidneys, bladder, sweat, ring finger.

Colors: White, blood red.

Symbolic Creatures: Toad, pig, crab, eel, hare, dove, deer, white crane, white tiger, snake, the *K'nei* (a fantastic creature like a one-legged sheep, whose appearance foretells heavy rain), the *Wang-hsiang* (spirit-creature of rivers who devours the brains of the dead), the *Yu-jen* ("winged men"; servitors of the goddess Hsi-wang-mu), the *Shang Yang* (mythical one-legged bird associated with rain), vampire, ghost.

Plants and Perfumes: Paulownia, red amaranth, chrysanthemum, motherwort, cassia, cinnamon, pondweed, narcissus, peach fruit.

Metal: Silver.

Precious Stones: Pearl, coral, white jade (tiger jade).

Emblems: Cloud, wheel, the Moon, ditches and channels, water spring, the Moon Hare with its pestle and mortar, red earth, snare, a hole in the ground, the Sword of Ma (see Gods), empress or queen.

Ritual Tools: Lute, crucible.

Taoist Immortal: Ts'ao Kuo-ch'iu.

Dragon Spirits: Shen Lung (see Hexagram 16), Ti Lung (rules over rivers), Ch'ih Wen (see Hexagram 20), K'uei (see Hexagram 16), Lung Wang (see Hexagram 16), P'an Lung (the "Coiling Dragon of Water"), Huang Lung (spirit of the Yellow River), Pi-hsi (see Hexagram 27), Chao-feng (see Hexagram 6).

Gods: Yu-tzu, Yun-t'ung, Shui Kuan, Ho Ping, Mo-li Hai, P'eng Tsu, Wu Kang, Kung Kung, Chiang Shen, Ma, Hsuan-t'ien Shang-ti, Lei Tsu, Lo Shen.

Goddesses: Ch'ang-o, Sao-ts'ing Niang, Ma Tsu-po, Hsian Fu-jen, Mi Fei.

Magickal Workings: Works of invisibility and concealment. Secretive acts. Menstrual mysteries (e.g., aligning oneself to the spiritual qualities of the menstrual cycle). Lunar invocations. Longevity (specifically through alchemical transmutation involving the menses).[1] Water rituals. Casting glamours and illusions. Creating anxiety and problems for others.

---

1. Hence the Chinese legend of the Moon Hare that prepares an elixir of life in its pestle and mortar—two obvious sexual emblems—from the red bark of cassia.

Hexagram 30

Li—Independence

Archaic Form:

Modern Name: Li.

Esoteric Interpretations: The vitalizing and illuminating energy of the Sun. The stellar manifestation of phallic power. Expansion (heat and light naturally seek to spread out over as wide an area as possible). Separation and departure from the crowd. Living for, and in, the Now. Standing out from the "herd." The courage to act as an individual. Knowledge that is derived from experience rather than study. That which is dry. Fire.

Polarity: Yang (K.W: Yin).

Compass Direction: East (K.W: South).

Guardian of the Quarter: The Blue Dragon.

Family Member: Middle son (K.W: middle daughter).

Parts of the Body: Eyes, heart, middle finger.

Colors: Bright red, rosy pink, bright yellow.

Symbolic Creatures: Raven, crow, cockerel, pheasant, bivalve mollusk (e.g., mussel, oyster, etc.), glowworm, Chinese unicorn, peacock, the *Pi Fang* (a Fire elemental, in the shape of a bird, that is the servitor of the god Hui Lu), kingfisher, goose.

Plants and perfumes: Bamboo shoots, pear, oak, mulberry, onion, iris, magnolia, oleander (poisonous!), barley, aubergine, sarsaparilla, cypress seeds.

Metals: Gold, bronze, iron.

Precious Stones: Malachite, diamond, glass.

Emblems: The Sun, lightning, ploughshare, water dipper made from a bivalve shell, fences and hedges, armor, whirling disc, flames, fiery serpent, the Fu-sang Tree (a mythical giant tree that grows at the place where the Sun rises), hollow tree blasted by lightning, flying bird, fiery wheel, the Pagoda of Li (see Gods), emperor or king.

Ritual Tools: Sword, spear, lantern or candle, mirror.

Taoist Immortal: Li T'ieh-kuai.

Gods: Yi, Chu Jung, Dijun, Kou Mang, Shen Nung, Huo Pu, Mo-li Ch'ing, Mu Kung, Hui Lu, Li, Ch'ih Ching-tzu, Taishan, Sui-zan, Li (different from former), Sun Hou-tzu.

Goddesses: T'ien Mu, Hsi-ho, Chun T'I, Ma Ni-li, Ma-ku.

Magickal Workings: Solar invocations. Cultivating male sexual energy. Helping the inherent beauty of an object show forth. Fire rituals. Gaining knowledge and cultivating discrimination. Movement in other dimensions as a "shining spirit."[1] Initiatory ordeals and rites (e.g., fire walking) that speed up the evolution of human consciousness by testing courage and determination.

---

1. A Chinese shamanist text written c. 500 B.C.E. describes a shaman as one who pours forth a mighty light that stretches out into the distance. This seems to be associated with a certain "bright spirit" that enters the shaman's body, empowering it, and which has links to his "sheng," the state of spiritual perfection or wisdom. There is a strong solar intimation here, and "sheng" can also mean "the splendor of the rising sun." Another character pronounced "sheng" means "to ascend," and appropriately Li's own character is based on a radical that means "a type of short-tailed bird."

Hexagram 31

HSIEN—ALL

Archaic Form:

Modern Name: Xian.

Esoteric Interpretations: A pool of tranquil water upon a mountain. A contemplative adept, abiding in seclusion on a sacred peak, who achieves union with the object of his or her meditation. The actions of advanced spiritual entities, whether incarnate or discarnate. Evolution by contact with nonhuman powers. The harmonious balance of "the ten thousand things."

Opposite Hexagram: 41 Hsun.

Polarity: Yin below Yang (K.W: Yang below Yin).

Trigram Combination: Ken and Tui.

Compass Directions: Northwest and Southeast (K.W: Northeast and West).

Family Members: Youngest daughter and youngest son (K.W: youngest son and youngest daughter).

Parts of the Body: Saliva, stomach.

Colors: White, scarlet, blue.

Symbolic Creatures: Owl, bee, horse, crane, glowworm, stork, nilgai, osprey.

Plants and Perfumes: Cypress, mulberry, lotus, orchid, juniper, spikenard, peony, bamboo, maple.

Metal: Silver.

Precious Stones: Coral, red jade.

Emblems: A tarn, mountain shrine, bridge, winged hat, ladder, the "Knot of Eternity," star, peacock feather, cave, chariot.

Ritual Tools: Bell, gong, spirit wand, mu-jen, thighbone trumpet, lantern or candle.

Dragon Spirit: P'u-lao (see Hexagram 16), Ch'ih Wen (see Hexagram 29).

Gods: An Ch'i, Fu-hsi, Kuei Ku-tzu, Liu Hai, Shang Ti, Tsao-wang, Wong Tai Sin, Yuan Shih, Di-jiang, Lao-tzu, Mu Kung, Chang Tao-ling, Lei Hai-ch'ing.

Goddesses: Eastern Mother, Hsi-wang-mu, Kuan Yin, Tsao-wang Nai-nai, Pi-hsia-yuan-chun, Tou Mu.

Magickal Workings: Communication and contact with the deities and other immortals. Seeking Samadhi (the state of universal oneness). Going beyond the egocentric consciousness to touch the divine inner essence, for the benefit of both oneself and other people. (Just as the initiate seeks wisdom from the gods, so too must that person pass on what is learned, in turn, to other people who seek guidance. The true adept is duty bound to assist his or her fellow beings, in whatever manner is correct for the circumstances.) Contemplation on the individual Paths of beings, which together form the unity of Nature.

Hexagram 32

HENG—CONSTANCY

Archaic Form:

Modern Name: Heng.

Esoteric Interpretations: The dynamic and motivating energy of thunder that incites the free-flowing air into ongoing movement. The eternal cycle of change, which to the adept is stability and permanence. That which is continuous. The lasting nature of the True Self, as compared to the transience of limited bodily incarnations.

Opposite Hexagram: 42 I.

Polarity: Yin below Yang.

Trigram Combination: Hsuan and Chen.

Compass Directions: Southwest and Northeast (K.W: Southeast and East).

Family Members: Eldest daughter and eldest son.

Parts of the Body: Intestines, gall bladder.

Color: Azure blue.

Symbolic Creatures: Dragon, carp, glowworm, cicada, butterfly, horse, tench.

Plants and Perfumes: Chrysanthemum, bitter orange, pomegranate, coriander seeds, lotus, creeping plants.

Metal: Iron.

Precious Stone: Red jade.

Emblems: Wheel, spiral, swastika/fylfot, the Tai-Chi, the "Knot of Eternity," tortoise-shell, conch shell, winding streams and rivers (especially when rendered as a stylized meander pattern).

Ritual Tools: Finger-ring, Tai-Chi amulet.

Gods: Shang Ti, Yuan Shih, Di-jiang, Taishan, Shang Shan, Ling-pao T'ien-tsun, Lao-tzu, T'ai Sui, Chang Tao-ling.

Goddesses: Hsi-wang-mu, Tou Mu.

Magickal Workings: Increasing powers of perseverance and determination. Meditation upon the continuity of the Will in all its manifestations (i.e., understanding that the Path of the Self continues without end through every seemingly separate incarnation). Transcending the human ego and allowing the true Self to govern one's actions.

Hexagram 33

TUN—RETREAT

Archaic Form:

Modern Name: Tui.

Esoteric Interpretations: A mountain under the vast and sweeping sky. The sacred heights to which a hermit retreats in the quiet half of the year, in order to meditate silently and come into closer contact with the Tao and the celestial spirits. Movement toward withdrawal, prior to reprojection in the next Yang period of productivity. The end of the summer's growth, and Nature's announcement that autumn, the season when plant life begins its return journey to the soil, is swiftly approaching. That which ebbs and fades. The gradual sloughing of outer layers. The Hexagram of the sixth Chinese month (c. July–August).

Opposite Hexagram: 26 Ta Chu.

Polarity: Yin below Yang (Yang below Yang).

Trigram Combination: Ken and Ch'ien.

Compass Directions: Northwest and South (K.W: Northeast and Northwest).

Family Members: Youngest daughter and father (K.W: youngest son and father).

Parts of the Body: Bones.

Colors: Black, light brown, dark purple.

Symbolic Creatures: Owl, snake, glowworm, crane, stork, frog, horse, grebe, the Lei-ting (see Hexagram 26).

Plants and Perfumes: Cypress, deciduous trees, lotus, pomegranate blossom, wood anemone, camphor, jujube, hibiscus, watermelon, palm leaves.

Metal: Copper.

Emblems: Mountain shrine, ice and snow, dust, smoke, the Barge of Mercy (see Hexagram 2).

Ritual Tool: The T'ien Kan (see Hexagram 12).

Gods: Nan-chi Hsien-weng, Ti Ts'ang Wang, Yen-lo, Hsu Hao, Hu Shen, P'an Kuan, She-mo Wang, Lao-tzu, T'ien Kou.

Goddesses: Hsi-wang-mu, Meng, Hsuan-nu.

Magickal Workings: Escaping from calamities. Safe retreat. Initiation and metamorphosis. Withdrawal from a situation in order to instigate change. Easing the transition into death. Contemplation upon the process of decay. Hiding things by occult means. Increasing one's understanding that at certain times fighting is not productive and will just lead to disaster. (Sometimes, circumstances are such that one must simply give way to another force, either because one is personally in the wrong, or in order to fight better on another day. Loss is a spur to progress and new growth.)

Hexagram 34

Ta Chuang—Great Strength

Archaic Form:

Modern Name: Da Zhuang.

Esoteric Interpretations: The might of Heaven that regulates a storm (even a great, driving force like Thunder cannot act without the agreement of divine Will). That which can contain enormous pressure without breaking. The active and stimulating movement of power under the guidance of spiritual laws. The Hexagram of the second Chinese month (c. March–April) and the festival of the spring equinox. The season of bursting growth.

Opposite Hexagram: 25 Wu Wang.

Polarity: Yang below Yang.

Trigram Combination: Ch'ien and Chen.

Compass Directions: South and Northeast (K.W: Northwest and East).

Family Members: Father and eldest son.

Parts of the Body: Arms, shoulders, muscles, heart, kidneys, spine.

Color: Bright red.

Symbolic Creatures: Dragon, eagle, ram, elephant, leopard, bear, tiger, lion, tortoise.

Plants and Perfumes: Ginseng, ephedra, oak, camphor, apricot flowers, peony, dragon's blood (*Calamus draco*), areca palm, wild apple blossom.

Metal: Iron.

Precious Stones: Malachite, diamond.

Emblems: Large people and animals, the "Thunder" pattern, warrior, thunderball.

Ritual Tools: Diamond mace, goad, thunderbolt dagger, trident, drum.

Dragon Spirits: Pi-hsi (see Hexagram 27), Pa-hsia (a dragon who supports heavy weights), Pi-han (see Hexagram 6).

Gods: Boy of the White Crane, Ch'ih-yu, Lei Kung, Lei Chen-tzu, Sun Hou-tzu, Yuan Shih, Yu Huang, No-cha, Kuan Ti.

Magickal Workings: Health matters. Stimulating vigorous life force/ch'i. Controlling emotional forces and directing them to worthwhile ends. Meeting and defeating opposition head-on.

Hexagram 35

CHIN—GROWTH

Archaic Form:

Modern Name: Jin.

Esoteric Interpretations: The vitalizing rays of the Sun that shine upon the face of Earth, causing all things to flourish. Light that illuminates the dark land. Activity that begins with the dawn and continues until sunset. Creatures occupied in the daily tasks that are most fitting to their true natures. Forms that are invested with the fire and spirit of life.

Opposite Hexagram: 36 Ming I.

Polarity: Yin below Yang (K.W: Yin below Yin).

Trigram Combination: K'un and Li.

Compass Directions: North and East (K.W: Southwest and South).

243

Family Members: Mother and middle son (K.W: mother and middle daughter).

Parts of the Body: Intestines, seminal fluid.

Colors: Carnation red, scarlet, rosy pink, bright yellow.

Symbolic Creatures: Bat, bee, deer, rat, silkworm, spider, glowworm, goose.

Plants and Perfumes: Cypress, yellow loquat, hibiscus, taro, Buddha's hand, mulberry, fragrant olive, sarsaparilla, narcissus, calamus, white jasmine, maple.

Metal: Gold.

Precious Stones: Coral, onyx.

Emblems: Winged hat, peacock feather, the Fu-sang Tree (see Hexagram 30), sunrise, granary, child holding a lotus pod, birds feeding upon the ground.

Ritual Tool: Scepter.

Gods: Lu Shen, Dijun, Kuan Ti, Liu Hai, Yi, Yuan-tan, Taishan, Hou Chi, Ts'ai Shen, Wong Tai Sin.

Goddesses: Chun T'i, Hsi-ho, Ma Ni-li, Ma-t'ou Niang.

Magickal Workings: Drawing on the inner *ching* (the sexual essence in the body) for empowerment. Advancement and success in one's proper daily work. Contemplation on the idea that each day should be a joyous opportunity to manifest the desires and needs of the Self.

Hexagram 36

MING I—DEATH OF LIGHT

Archaic Form:

Modern Name: Ming Yi.

Esoteric Interpretations: The descent of the Sun into the Underworld, prior to rebirth the following dawn. The dominance of lunar power and darkness. The activities of nocturnal creatures and beings associated with the forces of the Yin. Intelligence and charisma, possessed by an evolved individual, which are attacked by those with a "herd" mentality who dislike uniqueness and difference. Talents that are deliberately shrouded, for a time, in order to protect their possessor from persecution.

Opposite Hexagram: 35 Chin.

Polarity: Yang below Yin (K.W: Yin below Yin).

Trigram Combination: Li and K'un.

Compass Directions: East and North (K.W: South and Southwest).

Family Members: Middle son and mother (K.W: middle daughter and mother).

Part of the Body: Womb.

Colors: Black, silver.

Symbolic Creatures: Crab, toad, hare, cat, kuei (ghosts).

Plants and Perfumes: Bamboo, peach petals, wistaria, watermelon.

Metals: Copper, silver.

Precious Stones: Coral, moonstone.

Emblems: Sunset, the Barge of Mercy (see Hexagram 2), albino animals, the Moon shining through a window.

Ritual Tool: Parasol.

Gods: Ti Ts'ang Wang, Yen-lo, Wu Kang, Lo Hou Hsing, T'ien Kou.

Goddesses: Ch'ang-o, Hsi-wang-mu, Meng.

Magickal Workings: Underworld pathworkings and meditations. Black Sun rituals (invocations of the solar power in its Underworld phase). Operations of concealment and secrecy. Invisibility. Lunar invocations.

Hexagram 37

CHIA JEN—THE FAMILY OF HUMANKIND

Archaic Form:

Modern Name: Jia Ren.

Esoteric Interpretations: Fire beneath wood. The warmth of a communal hearth, around which a family gathers. A place where people come together in a sense of community and common good. Group soul. Kinship and fellow feeling. The cultural heritage, handed down from ancestors, that gives societies a sense of their place in the world. Ethnic roots. Concern for the welfare of others. Humanity dwelling together in one home (Earth), but with no attempts to subdue individual expressions of thought or personality. Loss of racial, cultural, gender, and social caste barriers between people.[1] A universal energizing source; the actuating fire of godhead is the birthright of all, and not the few. A group is strong if it supports the individuality of its members.

Opposite Hexagram: 50 Ting.

Polarity: Yang below Yin (K.W: Yin below Yin).

Trigram Combination: Li and Hsuan.

Compass Directions: East and Southwest (K.W: South and Southeast).

Family Members: Middle son and eldest daughter (K.W: middle and eldest daughters).

Parts of the Body: Eyes, large intestine.

Color: Light yellow.

Symbolic Creatures: Phoenix, the P'eng (see Hexagram 7), dove, parrot, ant, quail, horse, dog, perch, oriole.

Plants and Perfumes: Apple, lotus, chestnut, plum.

Metals: Bronze, brass.

Precious Stones: Cornelian, alabaster, striped gems.

Emblems: Vase, house or dwelling, family group, animal shelter, barn, gateway, box, kitchen hearth.

Ritual Tools: Parasol, bottle gourd.

Gods: Ho-ho, Fu-hsi, Sui-zan, Yu Huang, T'ien-kuan, Shang Ti, Tsao-wang.

Goddesses: Eastern Mother, Nu-kua, Tsao-wang Nai-nai.

Magickal Workings: Attaining a sense of oneness with humanity. Strengthening cohesion in groups. Peace in families. Contemplating the proper position of things (i.e., every object in Nature should be allowed to exist in its own space and carry out its own function, without undue interference from others or attempts to create a "norm"). Tolerance for different viewpoints. (This does not mean that you have to agree with those views or avoid arguing opposite opinions. It is simply an acknowledgement that another person is entitled to hold a idea contrary to you. However, the action that follows from that may be another matter altogether; for example, one can disagree with the tenets of a certain religion, but it is not acceptable to act violently toward its practitioners if they haven't persecuted others themselves.)

---

1. In its nature, Chia Jen is perhaps closer to its opposite Hexagram, Ting, than to any other pairing in the I Ching.

Hexagram 38

K'ui—Opposition

Archaic Form:

Modern Name: Kui.

Esoteric Interpretations: The Sun burning over a marsh or lake, each power staying on its own level without mingling. The heat of a fire that has unstoppable upward motion, and still water that seeks all opportunities to drain itself away downward. Seeming discord in opposing elements. The astronomical opposition of celestial bodies. Polarization that gives the chance for future productive union, resulting in change. Two poles of energy must split apart before they can unite. Division is the necessary precursor to the birth of new life. All the aspects of existence can only be known because they have an opposite against which they can be contrasted.

Opposite Hexagram: 49 Ko.

Polarity: Yang below Yang (K.W: Yin below Yin).

Trigram Combination: Tui and Li.

Compass Directions: Southeast and East (K.W: West and South).

Family Members: Youngest and middle sons (K.W: youngest and middle daughters).

Part of the Body: The breast.

Color: Dull green.

Symbolic Creatures: Dragonfly, mosquito, owl, partridge.

Plants and Perfumes: Thistle, wild rose.

Metal: Tin.

Precious Stone: Green jasper.

Emblems: A valley or ravine with a stream, people standing back-to-back, pairs of creatures moving in opposite directions, piebald horse.

Ritual Tool: Axe.

Dragon Spirits: Pi-han (see Hexagram 6), Yai-tzu (see Hexagram 6).

Gods: T'ien Kou, Sun Hou-tzu.

Magickal Workings: The creation of discord. Contemplating the need for diversity. Breaking stagnant situations by the formation of multiple choices.

Hexagram 39

CH'IEN—MISFORTUNE

Archaic Form:

Modern Name: Qian.

Esoteric Interpretations: An impassable river that is met with at the top of a grueling mountain climb. Difficult journeys that cause a traveler to stumble and falter. Pits and traps that lie in the path ahead. Perilous situations that are often encountered when attempting to move forward. Temporary withdrawal from dangerous circumstances, in order to obtain advice as to the best way to deal with the problem. Seeking safer ground.

Opposite Hexagram: 4 Meng.

Polarity: Yin below Yin (K.W: Yang below Yang).

Trigram Combination: Ken and K'an.

Compass Directions: Northwest and West (K.W: Northeast and North).

Family Members: Youngest and middle daughters (K.W: youngest and middle sons).

Part of the Body: Saliva (as used in ritualistic spitting to avert troubles).

Colors: Dull green, dark purple.

Symbolic Creatures: Dragonfly, owl, wolf.

Plants and Perfumes: Patchouli, waterpepper, China-grass, plum fruit.

Metal: Iron.

Emblems: Barriers and walls, pit, red cloud, traveler in a winter landscape, a lame person or animal, snow-bound dwelling, Shadow Wall (a false wall in a house, used to stop ghosts from entering).[1]

Ritual Tool: The protective circle or *fang-sheng*.

Dragon Spirit: Chao-feng (see Hexagram 6).

Gods: Ch'i-t'ou, Erh-lang, No-cha, Fang-hsiang, Pi-hsieh, Shou Shen, Tai Shan.

Goddesses: Kuan Yin, Tou Mu.

Magickal Workings: Defensive blocks. Instigating sudden, evasive action to avoid hazards. Intensive introspection. Pulling back from the brink of disaster. Successfully avoiding conflicts that cannot be won.

---

1. This symbolic shield is traditionally placed behind the main entrance to Chinese homes, the theory being that ghosts can only travel in straight lines and will be confounded by such an obstacle placed in their path. There is obviously an element of feng shui philosophy in this practice.

Hexagram 40

CHIEH—LOOSENING KNOTS

Archaic Form:

Modern name: Jie.

Esoteric Interpretations: Thunderstorms that bring forth longed-for rain. The movement of masculine force that encourages an equivalent response in its feminine partner. Violent and thrusting force that has the power to break through traps and other problems. A piercing intellect that solves mental conundrums. The explanation of mysteries and secrets. The removal of bonds that bind people's ideas or their actions.

Opposite Hexagram: 3 T'un.

Polarity: Yin below Yang (K.W: Yang below Yang).

Trigram Combination: K'an and Chen.

Compass Directions: West and Northeast (K.W: North and East).

Family Members: Middle daughter and eldest son (K.W: middle and eldest sons).

Parts of the Body: Phallus, heart, kidneys.

Colors: Vibrant red, light brown.

Symbolic Creatures: Tiger, hawk, falcon, sturgeon, cricket, fox, snake, horse, ox, boar.

Plants and Perfumes: Peony, camphor, wood anemone, acanthus, water chestnut, lichee fruit.

Metal: Iron.

Precious Stones: Diamond, soapstone.

Emblems: Ox horn, bodkin, awl, book, lightning.

Ritual Tools: Sword, broom, the Ju-I (see Hexagram 6).

Dragon Spirits: Pi-han (see Hexagram 6), Yai-tzu (see Hexagram 6).

Gods: Chu I, Kou Mang, Kuan Ti, Kuei Ku-tzu, Mo-li Ching, Nan-chi Hsien-weng, Wen-ch'ang, Wong Tai Sin, Lei Kung, Lei Tsu, Lei Chen-tzu, She-mo Wang, No-cha, Yu-tzu.

Goddesses: Ma-ku, Kuan Yin, Tsi-ku, T'ien Mu, Sa-ts'ing Niang.

Magickal Workings: Solving problems. Lifting curses or removing binding spells. Success in tests and exams. Acquiring esoteric knowledge. Springtime rituals. Operations involving the forceful projection of energy. Breaking alliances. Rites of transition for the dying.

Hexagram 41

H SUN—D ECREASE

Archaic Form:

Modern Name: Sun.

Esoteric Interpretations: The waters of a lake that evaporate and decrease at the foot of a mountain, in the future becoming rain-bearing clouds that refresh the vegetation on its slopes. Losing something in order to gain another and better thing, for the benefit of all (like the lake that willingly gives up its life-force for the good of the mountain's environment and its own future increase). Willingness to surrender prized possessions (physical and magico-spiritual) in order to achieve initiation into a more evolved state of being. Acts of "self-sacrifice." The transient nature of officialdom and all its short-term rewards.[1] Some aspects of the old order must die in order for desired transformation to take place. Creation arises from destruction.

Opposite Hexagram: 31 Hsien.

Polarity: Yang below Yin (K.W: Yin below Yang).

Trigram Combination: Tui and Ken.

Compass Directions: Southeast and Northwest (K.W: West and Northeast).

Family Members: Youngest son and youngest daughter (K.W: youngest daughter and youngest son).

Parts of the Body: Bones.

Color: Black.

Symbolic Creatures: Falcon, glowworm, crane, stork, owl.

Plants and Perfumes: Willow, water-pepper, palm leaves, thistle.

Metal: Copper.

Emblems: Chrysalis, ice and snow, dust, smoke, comet.

Ritual Tools: T'ien Kan (see Hexagram 12), the Hsien (ancient cult object, used to hold sacrificial offerings to the spirits).

God: Hu Shen.

Goddesses: Kuan Yin, Eastern Mother, Pa, Hsi-wang-mu, Hsuan-nu.

Magickal Workings: Shamanistic ordeals that lead to increased knowledge and power. Reducing the tendency to overaccumulate objects or people. Transcending the limitations of the embodied human consciousness. Malefic magick against another person's property. Instigating the process of change.

---

1. Lu T'ung-pin, one of the Eight Taoist Immortals, gave up a prosperous career as a mandarin in favor of immersion into the Way of the Tao.

Hexagram 42

I—Increase

Archaic Form:

Modern Name: Yi.

Esoteric Interpretations: Wind that brings in rain clouds. Atmospheric conditions that generate abundant growth in the world. Excess and surplus. Personal advantage gained by improved circumstances.

Opposite Hexagram: 32 Heng.

Polarity: Yang below Yin.

Trigram Combination: Chen and Hsuan.

Compass Directions: Northeast and Southwest (K.W: East and Southeast).

Family Members: Eldest son and eldest daughter.

Parts of the Body: Intestines.

Colors: Bright red, carnation red, verdant green.

Symbolic Creatures: Dove, bat, deer, dragon, rat, pig, goldfish, ox, pheasant.

Plants and Perfumes: Tangerine, orange, loquat, hibiscus, taro, millet, Buddha's hand, cubeb berries, lotus pod, narcissus, pomegranate, rape flowers.

Metal: Gold.

Precious Stones: Coral, blood amber, onyx, lapis-lazuli.

Emblems: Money, gold and silver bars, the *Chu-pao P'en* (the magick bowl of Yuan-tan; see Gods), a boy flying a kite in a cloudy sky, the Money Tree of Ts'ai-shen (see Gods), egg, a dish that fills with water to the point of overflowing, yellow cloud, bell, red ball.

Ritual Tool: Scepter.

Dragon Spirit: Fu-ts'ang Lung (see Hexagram 14).

Gods: Yuan-tan, Lu Shen, Chang Hsien, Ho-ho, Kuan Ti, Liu Hai, Master Stonehead, Ts'ai Shen, Wu Kang, Hsi Shen, Hou Chi, Wong Tai Sin, Shou Shen, Tam Kung, T'u-ti.

Goddesses: Kuan Yin, Hu-tu, Pai Mu-tan, K'eng San Ku-niang, Pi-hsia-yuan-chun.

Magickal Workings: Wealth. The accomplishment of desires. Multiplication of existing situations. Fertility. Gaining friends. Love rites. Obtaining help from those outside one's immediate circle of contacts. Assisting the fortunes of other people.

Hexagram 43

CHUEH—DECISION

Archaic Form:

Modern Name: Jue.

Esoteric Interpretations: The rule of Heaven/the Will, which is brought to bear upon problem matters. The operation of creative movement in stagnant circumstances. Confusion allayed by appeal to "higher powers." Choosing between two options. Oracular rhymes and verses. Solutions that get right to the heart of difficulties. The Hexagram of the third Chinese month (c. April–May). The last of the mild days of spring before the onset of the summer's heat.

Opposite Hexagram: 10 Li.

Polarity: Yang below Yang (K.W: Yang below Yin).

Trigram Combination: Ch'ien and Tui.

Compass Directions: South and Southeast (K.W: Northwest and West).

Family Members: Father and youngest son (K.W: father and youngest daughter).

Parts of the Body: Mouth, tongue, throat, liver.

Colors: Red, scarlet, light yellow.

Symbolic Creatures: Shrike, ant, fox, Chinese unicorn, snow goose.

Plants and Perfumes: Peach blossom, peony, pear blossom, cassia, bamboo, juniper, sticky rice, vetch, pulses, spikenard, cherry.

Metal: Iron.

Precious Stones: Pearl, mother of pearl, quartz, soapstone.

Emblems: Archery target, bow and arrows, official seal of government or authority, axe, law court.

Ritual Tools: Yarrow stalks, I Ching coins, spirit wand, the *Luan* (a type of planchette), mirror.

Dragon Spirit: Pi-han (see Hexagram 6).

Gods: Kuan Ti, Kuei Ku-tzu, Lei Hai-ch'ing, Wong Tai Sin, Chang Tao-ling, Pao Kung, Ti-kuan, Hu.

Goddesses: Hsi-wang-mu, Kuan Yin, Tsi-ku, Tou Mu.

Magickal Workings: Divination. Invocatory formulae or mantras. Awakening the astral senses. Obtaining justice and success in legal cases.

Hexagram 44

Kou—Sexual Union

Archaic Form:

Modern Name: Gou.

Esoteric Interpretations: The air that rises to mingle with the Firmament, or a tree that grows to unite the land with the sky symbolically. The freedom of the wind to move everywhere, without obstruction, under the vast expanse of Heaven. The mysterious force inherent in female sexuality. Joy, pleasure, and the easing of tension by sexual encounters. Freedom of the individual to "love as he Will." Loss of the restrictions caused by arbitrary and unjustifiable social morality. The Hexagram of the fifth Chinese month (c. June–July), the festival of the summer solstice, and the rise to dominance of the Yin in the second half of the year.

Opposite Hexagram: 9 Hsiao Chu.

Polarity: Yin below Yang.

Trigram Combination: Hsuan and Ch'ien.

Compass Directions: Southwest and South (K.W: Southeast and Northwest).

Family Members: Eldest daughter and father.

Parts of the Body: Female genitalia, thighs, mouth, spleen.

Colors: Pink, red, purple.

Symbolic Creatures: Sparrow, mussel, kingfisher, otter, butterfly, fox, the Phoenix of the Cinnabar Mountain (a legendary bird of the South Pole, linked to sexual alchemy, the vulva, etc.), dog.

Plants and Perfumes: Red peony, willow, aloes wood, cardamom seeds, azalea, cubeb berries, apple blossom, cherry, magnolia, jasmine, pomegranate, walnut, hibiscus.

Metals: Silver, copper.

Precious Stones: Lodestone (magnetite), blood amber.

Emblems: Rainbow, twin fish, fire pit, honeycomb, conch shell, two-headed dragon, empress or queen, reed organ, green lamp.

Ritual Tools: Aphrodisiacs and love philters, altar.

Gods: Wu Kang, Pai Mai Shen, Chang Tao-ling.

Goddesses: Chuang Mu, Hsi-wang-mu, Kuan Yin, Pai Mu-tan, Hsuan-nu, P'an Chin-lien.

Magickal Workings: Sex magick and alchemy. Attracting partners. Empowering the vital energy of the warrior woman/female adept. Creating "chance encounters." Increasing magickal force by the utilization of lust.

Hexagram 45

Ts'ui—Coming Together

Archaic Form:

Modern Name: Cui.

Esoteric Interpretations: Water that gathers itself together in one place upon the earth. Collections or groupings of any kind. Like-mindedness. Any group of people that holds a consensus view. Ancestral numinous force that filters down through the generations, uniting people in a shared culture. The power of individuals, marshaled and projected toward a common end.

Opposite Hexagram: 19 Lin.

Polarity: Yin below Yang (K.W: Yin below Yin).

Trigram Combination: K'un and Tui.

Compass Directions: North and Southeast (K.W: Southwest and West).

Family Members: Mother and youngest son (K.W: mother and youngest daughter).

Parts of the Body: Spleen, large intestine.

Colors: Emerald green, light yellow.

Symbolic Creatures: Owl, kingfisher, phoenix, the P'eng (see Hexagram 7), dove, wolf, horse, perch.

Plants and Perfumes: Lotus, pine, cypress, plum, mugwort.

Metals: Bronze, brass.

Precious Stones: Jadeite, alabaster.

Emblems: Soul Tablets (plaques that list a family's ancestors), jungle and dense forest, bundles of grass, orchids in a vase, basket, shaman, priest or priestess.

Ritual Tools: The combined Will of a group, the Tung Chueh (see Hexagram 15), Moon House (see Hexagram 15).

Gods: Shang Ti, Ho-ho, Mu Kung.

Goddesses: Eastern Mother, Ti-ya, Nu-kua, Hsi-wang-mu.

Magickal Workings: Group rituals. Empowering occult societies. Contact with energy and knowledge embodied in the ancestral substrata. Drawing in magickal force for future use.

Hexagram 46

Sheng—Ascent

Archaic Form:

Modern Name: Sheng.

Esoteric Interpretations: Trees that grow up through the soil. Irresistible upward momentum. The symbolic ascent of the seeker after magico-spiritual wisdom. The flight of consciousness to other planes of being, and the personal magickal evolution that such journeys proffer to the magician by reason of contact with the inhabitants of those realms. Promotion and advancement.

Opposite Hexagram: 20 Kuan.

Polarity: Yin below Yin.

Trigram Combination: Hsuan and K'un.

Compass Directions: Southwest and North (K.W: Southeast and Southwest).

Family Members: Eldest daughter and mother.

Parts of the Body: Throat, top of the head (fontanelle area).

Color: Blue.

Symbolic Creatures: Grasshopper, bat, bee, crane, stork, frog, horse, deer.

Plants and Perfumes: Loquat, ailanthus, Buddha's hand, palm leaves, orange tree, maple, cypress.

Metal: Gold.

Precious Stones: Coral, jade.

Emblems: Pilgrim on a sacred mountain, winged hat, ladder, peacock feather, the rising Sun, the Barge of Mercy (see Hexagram 2), stirrup, child holding a lotus pod, monkey riding on a horse, chariot, flute, the World Tree.

Ritual Tools: Mirror, fly-whisk, ritual cap or headgear.

Gods: Lu Shen, Pa Ch'a, Liu Hai, Chang Tao-ling, P'an Kuan, Sun Hou-tzu, An Ch'i.

Goddesses: Kuan Yin, Hsi-wang-mu, Eastern Mother, Tsi-ku.

Magickal Workings: Astral projection ("rising on the planes"). Shamanistic rites of ecstasy. Self-development through occult exercises. Elevating consciousness through the use of mantra. General success and advancement in one's endeavors.

Hexagram 47

K'un—Exhaustion

Archaic Form:

Modern Name: Kun.

Esoteric Interpretations: The waters of a lake that are drained away by ditches and channels. Energy that is gradually debilitated by attrition. Growth restrained by artificial borders. An object that is sapped of its strength and so begins to wither. Situations of siege. The reduction of outward expression, with concentration centered on inner certainty. The sage who retains confidence in the Tao, even when in the midst of very hard times, and does not give in to feelings of oppression. Silence.

Opposite Hexagram: 60 Chieh.

Polarity: Yin below Yang (K.W: Yang below Yin).

Trigram Combination: K'an and Tui.

Compass Directions: West and Southeast (North and West).

Family Members: Middle daughter and youngest son (K.W: middle son and youngest daughter).

Parts of the Body: Bones.

Colors: Dull green, dark blue.

Symbolic Creatures: Chiang shih (vampire), kuei (ghost), cat, dragonfly, fox, the Wang-hsiang (see Hexagram 29), the Ku (see Hexagram 18), weasel, stoat, owl, leopard.

Plants and Perfumes: Vines, iris, truffle fungus, mallow, bamboo, rice, garlic, red peas, willow leaves, ginger, calamus.

Metal: Copper.

Precious Stone: Pearl.

Emblems: Enclosure, wall, prison, ashes, a man sleeping under a tree, the T'ao-t'ieh (see Hexagram 10), a stunted or wilting tree hemmed in by walls, a man with a blue face, Shadow Wall (see Hexagram 39).

Ritual Tools: Bottle gourd, rope, mu-jen, snare.

Dragon Spirits: Chao-feng (see Hexagram 6), Pi-han (see Hexagram).

Gods: Chung K'uei, erh-lang, Fang-hsiang, Kuan Ti, No-cha, Pi-hsieh, Wei-t'o, Chang Tao-ling, Fu-hsi, Hsu Hao, Ch'i-t'ou, P'an Kuan Wang-kung.

Goddesses: Hsi-wang-mu, Meng, Pa.

Magickal Workings: Defensive exorcism. Occult bindings. Esoteric vampirism (i.e., the deliberate siphoning of vital force or activating power that enables the victim or circumstance to be affected, to operate successfully). Restraining actions when they would be self-defeating. Control of the thought processes/concentration exercises.

Hexagram 48

Ching—A Well

Archaic Form:

Modern Name: Jing.

Esoteric Interpretations: Springs of water that nourish the roots of plants. The communal water source for a community. An area retained for public use in the midst of private property. A communal well in the middle of private fields. The fountainhead of magico-religious philosophy by which a culture is energized and empowered. Individual diversity built upon a common middle ground. The wellspring from which flow all motivations and desires. The Hexagram of the sacred temple prostitute, the sex initiatrix who conducts candidates into the mysteries of sexual alchemy. Celibacy as a way of life is a fruitless exercise; a well is only of use if water is actually drawn from it! The regulation of life's activities as timed by the "menstrual calendar." The essence or spirit of a thing.

Opposite Hexagram: 59 Huan.

Polarity: Yin below Yin (K.W: Yin below Yang).

Trigram Combination: Hsuan and K'an.

Compass Directions: Southwest and West (K.W: Southeast and North).

Family Members: Eldest and middle daughters (K.W: eldest daughter and middle son).

Parts of the Body: Vagina, neck, throat, solar plexus.

Colors: Pink, dark red, yellow.

Symbolic Creatures: Crab, whale, hare, cicada, fox, silverfish, stag.

Plants and Perfumes: Ephedra, motherwort, azalea, apricot, *Ling-chih* ("the Fungus of Immortality"), aloes wood, ylang-ylang, gotu kola, peach, pear.

Metals: Silver, bronze.

Precious Stones: Moonstone, pearl, red jade.

Emblems: Twin fish, fire pit, wells and springs, honeycomb, conch shell, red earth, jade crab, shaman, priestess.

Ritual Tools: Mirror, the Chien (see p. 67), crucible.

Gods: Pai Mai Shen, Mo-li Shou, Nan-chi Hsien-weng, P'eng Tsu, Wu Kang, Yuan Shih, Shang Ti, Hu, Shou Shen, Di-jiang.

Goddesses: Chuang Mu, Ch'ang-o, Kuan Yin, Pai Mu-tan, P'an Chin-lien, Hsuan-nu, Hsi-wang-mu, Eastern Mother.

Magickal Workings: Feminine sexual and menstrual mysteries. Works to improve the communal good. Rousing group action. Occult utilization of the *Yin Shui* ("Yin Water"; a Taoist term for female sexual secretions, associated with longevity and sexual potency). Channeling and drawing upon ch'i energy. Rites of passage. Contact with ancestral forces.

Hexagram 49

KO—CHANGE

Archaic Form:

Modern Name: Ge.

Esoteric Interpretations: Fire in the midst of a marsh. The process of transition from one state to another. The plastic nature of appearances. Constant change as the Way of the Universe. New situations caused by the union of opposites. Diametrically opposed elements that cancel each other out, leading to the birth of a new state of being. The action of magickal force.

Opposite Hexagram: 38 K'ui.

Polarity: Yang below Yang (K.W: Yin below Yin).

Trigram Combination: Li and Tui.

Compass Directions: East and Southeast (K.W: South and West).

Family Members: Middle and youngest sons (K.W: middle and youngest daughters).

Parts of the Body: Skin, face.

Color: White.

Symbolic Creatures: Dragon, owl, fox, otter, tiger, were-animals in general, snake, clam, mosquito, chameleon.

Plants and Perfumes: Hibiscus, peach blossom, hallucinogenic fungi, mandrake, ginseng, willow, paulownia, yarrow.

Metal: Silver.

Precious Stone: Mother of pearl.

Emblems: The flayed hide of an animal,[1] leather, whirligig pattern, spiral, the Tai-Chi, the World Tree, *Ko* (a type of ancient halberd), cinnabar refined in an alchemical crucible, chrysalis, wheel, swastika/fylfot, check patterns.

Ritual Tools: Mask, feng shui compass, crucible.

Gods: Chang Tao-ling, T'ai Sui, Ling-pao T'ien-tsun, Hu, She-mo Wang, Wei-t'o, Lao-tzu.

Goddesses: Hsi-wang-mu, Kuan Yin, Eastern Mother, Ti-ya.

Magickal Workings: Transformation and illusion. Shapeshifting (i.e., of the astral form). Alchemy. Contact with power-animal spirit allies. Atavistic resurgence of ancestral powers (human and otherwise). Assisting the overthrow of outmoded ways and theories. Contemplation on the change of Ages/Aeons. Rituals tied to astrological times. Use of the kujikiri.[2] Occult workings, generally.

---

1. The skin of the "dragon-horse" of the Yellow River, which was supposed to have displayed upon its back designs that led Fu-hsi to develop the Trigrams, was said to have been preserved at the Shang imperial court for many years until its destruction or loss (the details of which are unknown). It would seem that there are undeniable and deliberate connections between the traits of this forty-ninth Hexagram, the I Ching as a treatise on Transformation, and the nature of the legendary hide.

2. See the section *In O Musubi*, in part 3.

Hexagram 50

TING—THE TRIPOD

Archaic Form:

Modern Name: Ding.

Esoteric Interpretations: Fire from wood. The communal ritual cooking and libation vessel, used to accept a community's collective offering to the spirits. The Womb of the Tao, from which all life's bounties and creatures have arisen. The nurturing power of mother goddesses.

Opposite Hexagram: 37 Chia Jen.

Polarity: Yin below Yang (K.W: Yin below Yin).

Trigram Combination: Hsuan and Li.

Compass Directions: Southwest and East (K.W: Southeast and South).

Family Members: Eldest daughter and middle son (K.W: eldest and middle daughters).

Parts of the Body: Buttocks, vagina, womb, belly, breasts.

Colors: Deep red, reddish yellow.

Symbolic Creatures: Bat, woman, pig, hawk, falcon, panda, cockerel, spider.

Plants and Perfumes: Orange, rice, tangerine, ivy, yellow loquat, apricot, willow, hemerocallis, cypress seeds, narcissus, alfalfa, evergreen trees, mugwort.

Metal: Gold.

Precious Stones: Lapis-lazuli, agate, turquoise.

Emblems: Rhombus, egg, Soul Tablet (see Hexagram 45), vase.

Ritual Tools: Tripod/cauldron, the Tung Chueh (see Hexagram 15), Moon House (see Hexagram 15), the Hsien (see Hexagram 41).

Gods: Lu Shen, Shang Ti, Liu Hai, Shou Shen, Ti Ts'ang Wang.

Goddesses: Kuan Yin, Mobo, Ti-ya, Pi-hsia-yuan-chun, Nu-kua, Tou Mu, Eastern Mother, Hsi-wang-mu, Hu-tu, Ma Ni-li, T'ien Mu.

Magickal Workings: Receiving empowerment and knowledge from numinous ancestral heritage. Good fortune. Improving powers of concentration (especially in situations that involve sight or hearing).

Hexagram 51

CHEN—SHAKING FORCE

Archaic Form:

Modern Name: Zhen.

Esoteric Interpretations: Flames flickering upon a hearth. The mirth of Heaven and the voice of the storm. The sudden, moving, and actuating power of thunder. Impetus applied to still conditions, such as the vibrant spring's upheaval of quiet winter. The excitation of new and fervent growth. The irresistible surge of life. Energy in motion. Fighting and strength. Anger. Decision-making undertaken with vehemence of mind. Development. The time for rain. Measuring the seasons.[1]

Polarity: Yang.

Compass Direction: Northeast (K.W: East).

Family Member: Eldest son.

Parts of the Body: Feet, gall bladder, liver, legs, kidneys, middle finger.

Colors: Azure blue, yellow, verdant green, fiery red.

Symbolic Creatures: Dragon, dove, ox, pig, the K'nei (see Hexagram 29), leopard, the *Pei-a* and the *Wa-lung* (spirit-creatures of the Northeast), cricket, quail, kite, monkey.

Plants and Perfumes: Fragrant olive, wheat, sedges and rushes, bamboo shoots, hazel, willow, calamus, balsam poplar, rape flowers.

Metals: Iron, lead.

Precious Stones: Amber, pearl, diamond, mother of pearl.

Emblems: Flaming thunderball, hammer, chisel, anvil, the "Thunder" pattern (a series of linked, squared spirals), warrior, thunder clouds and rain, large road, boggy land, lush landscapes.

Ritual Tools: Drum, firecrackers, diamond mace, gong, thunderbolt dagger, trident, sword.

Taoist Immortal: Chang-kuo Lao.

Dragon Spirits: K'uei (see Hexagram 16), Lung Wang (see Hexagram 16), Shen Lung (see Hexagram 29), Pi-han (see Hexagram 6), Yai-tzu (see Hexagram 6), P'u-lao (see Hexagram 16).

Gods: Lei Kung, Tsao-wang, Chu Jung, Kou Mang, Shen Nung, Huo Pu, Lei Chen-tzu, Lei Tsu, Hui Lu, Mo-li Ch'ing, Ch'ih Ching-tzu, Li, Sui-zan, Chang Tao-ling, Ch'ih-yu, Hou Chi, No-cha, Yu-tzu, Sun Hou-tzu.

Goddesses: Tsao-wang Nai-nai, Ma-ku, Eastern Mother, Sao-ts'ing Niang.

Magickal Workings: Stimulating occult power. Fire rituals. Revenge. The use of force to stimulate growth. Fertility. Ritual drumming. Ecstatic states attained through wild trance-dance. Strengthening courage. Rain magick. Stimulating movement in any stagnant situation.

---

1. The Chinese word-character for Chen may originally have been intended to refer to a woman in the midst of menses; hence, periods of the year as marked out by the menstrual calendar. Also, the menses is thereby likened to the downpour of the springtime tempest, which signals the ending of the old season and the beginning of a new period of creative action and fertility.

Hexagram 52

KEN—RESISTANCE

Archaic Form:

Modern Name: Gen.

Esoteric Interpretations: The solidity and steadfastness of a mountain. Massive strength within an outwardly passive exterior. Forthrightness and defiance. A place to which one flees as a strong bastion of defense. The immovability of rock. A quiet refusal to surrender. Power that does not need to boast of its abilities. Stubbornness. The foundation of things. The place where Yin and Yang alternate eternally. The concept of Center.

Polarity: Yin (K.W: Yang).

Compass Direction: Northwest (K.W: Northeast).

Family Member: Youngest daughter (K.W: youngest son).

Parts of the Body: Buttocks, stomach, spleen, hands, fingers (especially the little finger), joints, gall bladder, spine.

Colors: Dark yellow, black, reddish yellow.

Symbolic Creatures: Dog, rat, elephant, butterfly, tortoise, the *K'ui* (spirit-creature of mountains and hills), the *Yi-yang* (spirit-creature associated with the Northwest), the *Shan-hsiao* (spirit-creature of mountains), the *Ti-chiang* (a fabulous bird that lives in the Celestial Mountain).

Plants and Perfumes: Creepers, pine, pomegranate, upright meadow crowfoot, lotus.

Metals: Iron, silver.

Precious Stone: Diamond.

Emblems: Gateway, door, mountains and hills, rocks and stones, pathway, eunuch, many-branched tree, the *Hsu-mi Shan* (Chinese version of mythic Mount Sumeru, symbol of the Heart of the Universe), flute, Shadow Wall (see Hexagram 39).

Ritual Tools: Finger-ring, *shih kan t'ang* stones.

Taoist Immortal: Han Hsiang-tzu.

Dragon Spirits: Pa-hsia (see Hexagram 34), Suan-ni (see Hexagram 5), Chiao (a dragon of mountains and marshes), Chiao-t'u (spirit who guards doorways).

Gods: Ti-kuan, Shang Shan, Tai Shan, Ch'eng-huang, T'u-ti, Di-jiang, Chung K'uei, Ch'i-t'ou, Erh-lang, Fang-hsiang, Pi-hsieh, Wei-t'o, Ts'ui Yang, Shang Ti, Yuan Shih.

Goddesses: Hsi-wang-mu, Hu-tu. Ch'i ku-tzu.

Magickal Workings: The cultivation of unmoving resistance and defiance. Strengthening self-confidence. Meditation on the source of being, and rituals involving the symbolic use of the omphalic mountain. Formulating a firm foundation at the beginning of any new venture. Passive meditation. Rest and recuperation. Earth rituals. Blocking movement. Bringing order to chaotic situations. Warding off malice.

Hexagram 53

CHIEN—ADVANCING BY DEGREES

Archaic Form:

Modern Name: Jian.

Esoteric Interpretations: The patient growth of a tree upon a mountain. The slow but steady progress of a pilgrim climbing a sacred mountain to its windswept heights. Gradual movement up the mountain's path that symbolizes the personal journey along the Way. Evolution of the human consciousness that results from the progressive and disciplined practice of occult exercises. The training of initiates.

Opposite Hexagram: 18 Ku.

Polarity: Yin below Yin (K.W: Yang below Yin).

Trigram Combination: Ken and Hsuan.

Compass Directions: Northwest and Southwest (K.W: Northeast and Southeast).

Family Members: Youngest and eldest daughters (K.W: youngest son and eldest daughter).

Parts of the Body: Thighs, heart, stomach.

Color: Light yellow.

Symbolic Creatures: Carp, goose, glowworm, horse, elephant.

Plants and Perfumes: China-grass, plantain, orange tree.

Metal: Iron.

Emblems: Pilgrim on a sacred mountain, arrow, chessboard, lute, unicorn horn, book, a gently flowing river.

Ritual Tools: Mirror, the Chien (see p. 57).

Dragon Spirit: Pi-hsi (see Hexagram 27).

Gods: Chu I, Kuan Ti, K'uei Hsing, Wen-ch'ang, Chin Chia, Lao-tzu, Chang Tao-ling.

Goddesses: Kuan Yin, Hsi-wang-mu, Tsi-ku.

Magickal Workings: Stimulating and enhancing personal evolution. Taming tendencies to "run before you can walk." Matters of education. The gradual acquisition of knowledge through occult practices such as skrying.

Hexagram 54

KUEI MEI—THE MARRIAGE OF THE YOUNGER SISTER

Archaic Form:

Modern Name: Gui Mei.

Esoteric Interpretations: Thunder over a lake. The union of a young woman, full of self-confidence, with an older man of great power and prestige. A partnership of mature energy and imaginative spirit. Deliberate movements toward youthfulness and the attitudes and values of the young. The importance of youth to society. Vital, creative force that has become somewhat jaded and requires a fresh influx of new inspiration in order to remain effective.[1] Promotion of the young to positions of influence.

Opposite Hexagram: 17 Sui.

Polarity: Yang below Yang (K.W: Yin below Yang).

Trigram Combination: Tui and Chen.

Compass Directions: Southeast and Northeast (K.W: West and East).

Family Members: Youngest and eldest sons (K.W: youngest daughter and eldest son).

Parts of the Body: Face, hair.

Color: Vivid purple.

Symbolic Creatures: Parrot, kingfisher, fox, glowworm, pheasant, swallow, peacock.

Plants and Perfumes: Azalea, white peony, apricot, apple blossom, magnolia, camellia, orchid, licorice, plum blossom, reeds, saffron, hibiscus.

Metal: Silver.

Precious Stones: Jade, pearl.

Emblems: Honeycomb, young people (especially women), belt/girdle, red ball.

Ritual Tool: Hair (e.g., as used in spells involving the ritual binding/unbinding of tresses in order to seduce).

Gods: Fu-hsi, Hsien T'ung, No-cha, Yun-t'ung, Boy of the White Crane, Wu Kang.

Goddesses: Nu-kua, Hsuan-nu.

Magickal Workings: The active use of beauty. Seduction and enchantment. Initiation into the mysteries of the *Hieros Gamos* (Sacred Marriage between two initiates, who then work together toward common ends). Encouraging the transformation of old, redundant ways by the introduction of new ideas. Enhancing feelings of "second youth." Arousing fresh enthusiasm.

---

1. In the traditional I Ching, this Hexagram is not generally regarded as being fortunate. This is due to the fact that it is the young woman who instigates the marriage, and to the patriarchal Confucian mind that is an unacceptable breach of propriety. Strip away such restricting protocol and you are left with a much more interesting and useful character.

Hexagram 55

FENG—PROSPERITY

Archaic Form:

Modern Name: Feng.

Esoteric Interpretations: A tempest that brings forth lightning upon the world; rousing and moving power that willfully displays its strength in a spectacular burst of energy. The manifestation of occult desire and divine force. Great multitudes of things. Mountains of grain. The growth-inducing ability of rain-bringing thunder combined with the nurturing warmth of the Sun results in an abundant harvest for all. Anything that multiplies on a grand level. Justified success for work well done.

Opposite Hexagram: 21 Shih Ho.

Polarity: Yang below Yang (K.W: Yin below Yang).

Trigram Combination: Li and Chen.

Compass Directions: East and Northeast (K.W: South and East).

Family Members: Middle and eldest sons (K.W: middle daughter and eldest son).

Parts of the Body: Intestines, spleen, face.

Colors: Vibrant red, gold.

Symbolic Creatures: Phoenix, bee, bat, deer, rat, goldfish, ox, pheasant.

Plants and Perfumes: Yellow loquat, tangerine, taro, hibiscus, storax, citron, millet, Buddha's hand, mulberry, pomegranate, rice.

Metal: Gold.

Precious Stones: Coral, onyx, lapis-lazuli.

Emblems: The Chu-pao P'en (see Hexagram 42), corn sheaf, basket filled with grain, the Money Tree of Ts'ai Shen (see Gods), bough of a tree, granary, yellow cloud, crowing cockerel, divine beings.

Ritual Tools: The sacred Fire, scepter.

Dragon Spirit: Fu-ts'ang Lung (see Hexagram 14).

Gods: Lu Shen, Yuan-tan, Ho-ho, Kuan Ti, Liu Hai, Ts'ai Shen, Hou Chi, Wong Tai Sin, Shou Shen.

Goddess: Kuan Yin.

Magickal Workings: Prosperity and general good fortune. Alleviating conditions of hardship (physical, mental, and spiritual). Increasing abilities to gather and direct occult force to the attainment of personal goals. Successful execution of plans, carried out under Will. Achieving renown through the enthusiastic action of one's proper work.

Hexagram 56

Lu—Travel

Archaic Form:

Modern Name: Lu.

Esoteric Interpretations: The Sun that travels over a mountain, indicating both its Yin (shady) and Yang (sunny) sides. Motion along a particular Path, with acceptance of all its events and all that such occurrences imply. Seeing each step along the Way as being necessary and avoiding stagnation in any single aspect once its time has passed. Knowing when to move onto the next stage, and removing attachments to particular circumstances or items. A life's worth should be judged by its deeds, and not by its accumulation of ephemeral things. Following the road of destiny that has been marked out for an individual since birth. The journey in search of the Self.

Opposite Hexagram: 22 Fen.

Polarity: Yin below Yang (K.W: Yang below Yin).

Trigram Combination: Ken and Li.

Compass Directions: Northwest and East (K.W: Northeast and South).

Family Members: Youngest daughter and middle son (K.W: youngest son and middle daughter).

Parts of the Body: Feet, spine, gall bladder.

Color: Red.

Symbolic Creatures: Bear, tiger, donkey/ass, leopard, heron, quail, boar.

Plants and Perfumes: Bitter orange, pomegranate, patchouli.

Metal: Iron.

Precious Stone: Amber.

Emblems: Shoe, conch shell, troops on the march, a traveler walking many miles.

Ritual Tools: Conch shell trumpet, the Ju I (see Hexagram 6).

Gods: Ch'ih-yu, Boy of the White Crane, P'an Kuan, Wei-t'o, An Ch'i, Lao-tzu.

Goddess: Tsi-ku.

Magickal Workings: Strengthening the courage to move into unfamiliar zones. Assisting the discovery of one's Path, and then gaining the confidence to walk it. Safety when traveling. Contemplating the necessity for all beings to travel their own Way without interference from others.

Hexagram 57

HSUAN—YIELDING

Archaic Form:

Modern Name: Xuan.

Esoteric Interpretations: The changeable wind moving under Heaven. Mutability. That which advances and recedes continuously. Selection and choice. That which comes round full circle. A Yin attitude of flexibility influencing the Yang power of motion, reacts successfully to all situations. The inability to be grasped. Adepts may choose their outward mask to fit each situation, yet never lose sight of their essential Tao. Air penetrates all nooks and crannies, and touches every aspect of life; so the spiritual consciousness is also free to roam where it will and have influence in every situation. The avoidance of direct conflict. Cunning. Wood is shaped according to a carver's desire, yielding to his or her tools as the carver tries to bring out a depiction of the true nature of the material; so, too, should human intelligence give way to the motivating impulse and higher wisdom of the divine Self that cannot itself be captured, but only experienced.

Polarity: Yin.

Compass Direction: Southwest (K.W: Southeast).

Family Member: Eldest daughter.

Parts of the Body: Thighs, whites of the eyes, forehead, lungs, nose, liver, solar plexus, index finger.

Colors: White, light blue.

Symbolic Creatures: Monkey, fowl, hawk, falcon, fox, tench, partridge.

Plants and Perfumes: Ephedra, sandalwood, wheat, orchid, hibiscus, lotus, water chestnut, lichee fruit.

Metal: Silver.

Precious Stones: Lapis-lazuli, jasper.

Emblems: A bald person, carpenter's tools, plumbline, tall tower, wheel, disc, spiral, circle, axe, swastika/fylfot.

Ritual Tools: Censer, incense, finger-ring, I Ching coins, yarrow stalks, mask.

Taoist Immortal: Lan Ts'ai-ho.

Dragon Spirit: Shen-lung (see Hexagram 16).

Gods: Feng Po, Lu-pan, Juang K'un, Mu Kung, Lei Hai-ch'ing, Fei Lien, Kuei Ku-tzu, Hu, Wong Tai Sin, Sun Hou-tzu.

Goddesses: Feng-p'o-p'o, Tsi-ku.

Magickal Workings: Air rituals. The magick of perfumes and incense. Becoming uncatchable like the wind. Defense by evasion. Selecting the right choice when there are a number of equal-seeming options (e.g., by the use of divination). Cultivating greater flexibility. Penetrating obstacles unseen and by gentle methods.

Hexagram 58

TUI—REJOICING

Archaic Form:

Modern Name: Dui.

Esoteric Interpretations: A collected body of water (ponds, marshes, lakes, seas, etc.) that rests upon firm ground. Exchanging grief and sadness for joy and amusement by the use of appropriate words. A happy gathering of friends who lose all emotional restriction in each other's company. A time to relax and enjoy pleasant things. The mysterious and magickal forces of the twilight. That which forms a spiritual crossing point between two states of being. (Tui, representing still water, combines within itself the fluidic nature of liquid and the stillness of the land in which it lies; hence, it is a traditionally potent threshold, a place of power where the dimensions of humankind and gods intersect—recognized in many world cultures—and consequently where greater awareness of spiritual levels of consciousness can be attained.) Bodily pleasures. Carefree delight. Words that have the power to spellbind listeners. Mysteriousness.

Polarity: Yang (K.W: Yin).

Compass Direction: Southeast (K.W: West).

Family Member: Youngest son (K.W: youngest daughter).

Parts of the Body: Mouth, tongue, solar plexus, pericardium, ring finger, vagina.

Colors: White, pink, red.

Symbolic Creatures: Sheep, goat, shark, fox, otter, bat, oriole, kingfisher, butterfly, badger, the *Wei-to*[1] (spirit-creature of marshes, whose appearance foreshadows for-tuitous times), stoat, weasel, sparrow, oyster.

Plants and Perfumes: Willow, pondweeds and watergrasses, azalea, chrysanthemum, mugwort, jasmine, aloes wood, hemerocallis, persimmon, narcissus, peach blossom and fruit, sticky rice.

Metal: Silver.

Precious Stones: Lodestone, moss agate, blood amber, pearl.

Emblems: Cloud, mist, rainbow, wave, red bat, twin fish, halberd, honeycomb, leaves, sorcerer/sorceress, rhinoceros horn, rice cake, salt, crossroads, green lamp.

Ritual Tools: Bell, gong, scepter, bottle gourd, thighbone trumpet.

Taoist Immortal: Chung-li Ch'uan.

Dragon Spirits: Li (rules over seas), Kien (rules over marshes), Lung Wang (see Hexagram 16), Chih-wen (see Hexagram 20), Chiao (see Hexagram 52), P'an Lung (see Hexagram 29), P'u-lao (see Hexagram 16), Ch'iu Niu (see Hexagram 16).

Gods: Shui Kuan, Hsuan-t'ien Shang-ti, Hsi Shen, Kung Kung, Mi-lo Fo, Pai Mai Shen, Chang Tao-ling, An-kung, Fu Shen, Hu, T'ien-kuan, Yang Hou, Wei-t'o.

Goddesses: T'ien Hou, Kuan Yin, P'an Chin-lien, Chuang Mu, Pai Mu-tan, Ma Tsu-po, Hsian Fu-jen, Mi Fei, Shui-mu Niang-niang, A-ma, Hsi-wang-mu.

Magickal Workings: Increasing joy and happiness. Sexual magick and alchemy. Con-templating the fact that pleasure is a vital part of the Tao. Sorcery and the evoca-tion of spirits. Seduction and enchantment. Water rituals. Magickal phenomena in general. Helping to dispel sorrow.

---

1. Not to be confused with the god Wei-t'o.

Hexagram 59

HUAN—VANISHING

Archaic Form:

Modern Name: Huan.

Esoteric Interpretations: Wind and water flowing away from each other, with no stable middle ground. A piece of wood that floats downstream, out of sight of the viewer. Gusting wind that scatters rivulets of water. Dispersion and dissipation. Illusions. The metaphysical journey of the initiate who moves his or her attention from the world of appearances toward the things of the spirit.

Opposite Hexagram: 48 Ching.

Polarity: Yin below Yin (K.W: Yang below Yin).

Trigram Combination: K'an and Hsuan.

Compass Directions: West and Southwest (K.W: North and Southeast).

Family Members: Middle and eldest daughters (K.W: middle son and eldest daughter).

Part of the Body: Crown of the head (at the area of the fontanelle).

Colors: Light brown, white.

Symbolic Creatures: Ibis, crane, stork, frog, snake, horse, fox.

Plants and Perfumes: Cypress, hibiscus, peach petals, wistaria, watermelon.

Metals: Silver, tin.

Emblems: Ice and snow, smoke, dust, a boat upon a river, temple, hermit.

Ritual Tools: Mask, lantern/candle.

Gods: Shang Ti, Yuan Shih, Yu Huang, Hsu Hao, Feng Po, Hu Shen, Lao-tzu, Chang Tao-ling, An Ch'i, Hu.

Goddesses: Hsi-wang-mu, Ch'ang-o, Kuan Yin, Tsi-ku, Hsuan-nu, Feng-p'o-p'o, Eastern Mother.

Magickal Workings: Works of invisibility. Casting illusions and glamours. Meditation that leads to transcendence from physical matters. Elevating the human consciousness to higher levels. Escape from peril.

Hexagram 60

CHIEH—TIME[1]

Archaic Form:

Modern Name: Jie.

Esoteric Interpretations: Running water that flows into a lake. A body of water that can contain only a limited amount of additional fluid before it bursts its banks. Regulation and temperance. Time measured by the periodic cycle of the Moon and by the ebb and flow of the seas. The movement of time is like the ceaseless flow of rivers into oceans. The division of the year into specific periods. Regular festivals and holidays. Events that conform to unchanging and precise schedules. Zodiacal signs allotted to the years.

Opposite Hexagram: 47 K'un.

Polarity: Yang below Yin (K.W: Yin below Yang).

Trigram Combination: Tui and K'an.

Compass Directions: Southeast and West (K.W: West and North).

Family Members: Youngest son and middle daughter (K.W: youngest daughter and middle son).

Part of the Body: Face.

Color: Red.

Symbolic Creatures: Snake, tench.

Plants and Perfumes: Bamboo, pomegranate, lotus, red rose.

Metal: Iron.

Emblems: Clock, joints on a bamboo stick, signs of the zodiac, calendar, wheel, disc, swastika/fylfot.

Ritual Tools: Zodiacal almanac/ephemeris, feng shui compass.

Gods: Tsao-wang, Fu-hsi, T'ai Sui, Ling-pao T'ien-tsun, She-mo Wang.

Goddesses: Tsao-wang Nai-nai, Tou Mu.

Magickal Workings: Contemplating the mysteries of time. Invoking the energies associated with sacred festivals. Seasonal rites. Zodiacal rituals.

---

1. In China, there exists a traditionally important system of time measurement called *Chia-tzu,* "the Cycle of Sixty," that combines the chronological arrangements of the Ten Celestial Stems and the Twelve Earthly Branches. Each one of the twelve signs of the Chinese Zodiac rules over one year. Beginning with the Rat, and finishing with the Pig, a cycle of twelve years is completed. Five such complete periods form the Chia-tzu. Each year of the entire Cycle of Sixty is ruled over by a different deity.

Hexagram 61

CHUNG FU—INNER CONFIDENCE

Archaic Form:

Modern Name: Zhong Fu.

Esoteric Interpretations: Wind that plays over water, stirring it into activity. The action of invisible powers upon the visible world. The authority and wisdom of the center of one's being that guides all lesser actions in the course of the Will. The heart of oneself that is beyond all failings of the human personality. Fortunate circumstances that arise from actions carried out with unshakable self-confidence. The inner pride and self-esteem that is necessary for people to realize their full potentials. Learning to rely upon one's own abilities, rather than always expecting other people to solve one's problems.

Opposite Hexagram: 28 Ta Kuo.

Polarity: Yang below Yin (K.W: Yin below Yin).

Trigram Combination: Tui and Hsuan.

Compass Directions: Southeast and Southwest (K.W: West and Southeast).

Family Members: Youngest son and eldest daughter (K.W: youngest and eldest daughters).

Parts of the Body: Heart, solar plexus, navel, kidneys, nose.

Colors: Reddish yellow, green.

Symbolic Creatures: Bat, hen, Chinese unicorn, dragon, ant, snow-goose.

Plants and Perfumes: Ginseng, bitter orange, camphor, pine, sago-tree.

Metals: Iron, gold.

Precious Stones: Amber, white cornelian.

Emblems: An arrow that hits the center of a target, tortoise-shell, the Hsu-mi Shan (see Hexagram 52), rocks and stones, animal nurturing and protecting its young, a hen with its chicks.

Ritual Tools: Broom, parasol, goad.

Dragon Spirit: Cha-yu (see Hexagram 15).

Gods: Shang Ti, Yuan Shih, Lao-tzu, Di-jiang.

Magickal Workings: Strengthening self-confidence. Increasing respect for others. Drawing upon and utilizing the ch'i energy. Meditating on the deity within/the True Self. Introspection. Stimulating and altering one's persona through contact with the central point of consciousness (i.e., allowing the Self to influence outer conduct).

Hexagram 62

Hsiao Kuo—Minor Excess

Archaic Form:

Modern Name: Xiao Guo.

Esoteric Interpretations: Thunder that rumbles above a mountain. The power of the storm gods, displayed upon the sacred peak but kept separate from the rest of the earth. A mountain's summit is exposed and has little soil, so trees that grow there are stunted in spite of the fructifying storms that regularly break overhead, yet still they attempt slowly to forge their way toward the sky. Fertility and abundance reduced in scope. Caution and minor blocks applied to the projection of force. Power curtailed to a large degree, but not completely. Actions that are carried out without undue ceremony or boasting. Quiet and unassuming behavior that achieves its modest ends and stolidly works through difficulties. Success in small matters.

Opposite Hexagram: 27 I.

Polarity: Yin below Yang (K.W: Yang below Yang).

Trigram Combination: Ken and Chen.

Compass Directions: Northwest and Northeast (K.W: Northeast and East).

Family Members: Youngest daughter and eldest son (K.W: youngest and eldest sons).

Parts of the Body: Spleen, stomach.

Color: Light yellow.

Symbolic Creatures: Carp, elephant, leopard, rat.

Plants and Perfumes: Radish, ailanthus, ginger, willow.

Metal: Iron.

Precious Stones: Green jasper, pearl.

Emblems: Dwarf trees (bonsai), a bird's nest or perch placed near the ground.

Ritual Tool: The Chueh (see Hexagram 5).

Gods: Boy of the White Crane, Lao-tzu.

Goddesses: Kuan Yin, Tou Mu.

Magickal Workings: Overcoming minor obstacles. Acquiring a small amount of assistance for problems (but only the minimum that is needed and only for minor concerns). Placing constraints upon action when necessary. Promoting caution in the use of force. Small changes of fortune.

Hexagram 63

CHI CHI—THE ATTAINMENT OF RELIEF

Archaic Form:

Modern Name: Ji Ji.

Esoteric Interpretations: A cycle of events that has reached its completion. The harmony of the Sun and Moon. The dynamic and ecstatic union of opposites. Sexual conjunction, resulting in an androgynous whole. Equilibrium achieved at the point of orgasm. Perfect balance between the negative and positive forces of Nature (thereby depicting the occult sum $-1 + (+1) = 0$). The Dyad that becomes the Monad. Harmony that yet contains within itself the seeds of disorder/division (i.e., a new cycle of separation/creation must immediately begin again after the state of equilibrium is achieved). The mysteries of the *Yab-Yum* (Tibetan term meaning "Father and Mother") as expressed in sexual alchemy.

Opposite Hexagram: 64 Wei Chi.

Polarity: Yang below Yin (K.W: Yin below Yang).

Trigram Combination: Li and K'an.

Compass Directions: East and West (K.W: South and North).

Family Members: Middle son and middle daughter (K.W: middle daughter and middle son).

Parts of the Body: Phallus, vagina, eyes.

Colors: Pink, red, reddish yellow.

Symbolic Creatures: Mandarin duck, snake, men and women, goose, kingfisher, quail, dove.

Plants and Perfumes: Wood oil tree, ginseng, cubeb berries, apple, lotus, orchid, cherry, mugwort, reeds, jasmine, mandrake.

Metals: Gold, silver, bronze, brass.

Precious Stones: Blood amber, cornelian.

Emblems: Entwined serpents, shoe, rainbow, basket, twin creatures, two fish united yet swimming in opposite directions (as in the zodiacal symbol for Pisces), the Tai-Chi, jade butterfly, vase, cinnabar refined in the alchemical crucible, chrysalis, two-headed dragon, weighing scales, crossroads.

Ritual Tools: Crucible, sexual postures, finger-ring, Tai-Chi amulet.

Dragon Spirit: Suan-ni (see Hexagram 5).

Gods: Hsi Shen, Ho-ho, Wu Kang, Fu-hsi, P'an Ku, She-mo Wang, Wei-t'o, Pai Mai Shen.

Goddesses: Nu-kua, Pai Mu-tan, Chuang Mu, P'an Chin-lien.

Magickal Workings: Sexual union and the channeling of combined energies. Creating harmonious situations. Pacifying anger. Invocations of the Divine Hermaphrodite. Transcending the sense of separateness from other things. Foretelling actions that should be done or are to come. Uniting with the object of one's meditation (i.e., the oneness of subject and object).

Hexagram 64

Wei Chi—No Relief

Archaic Form:

Modern Name: Wei Ji.

Esoteric Interpretations: The Sun and Moon departing from one another. Separation of opposites prior to future reunion. The concept of division as being synonymous with that of creation. The Monad splits to become the Dyad. Male and female as quantifiable genders. Movement toward manifestation that begins again after the state of withdrawal. Preparation to start a new cycle of activity.

Opposite Hexagram: 63 Chi Chi.

Polarity: Yin below Yang (K.W: Yang below Yin).

Trigram Combination: K'an and Li.

Compass Directions: West and Li (K.W: North and South).

Family Members: Middle daughter and middle son (K.W: middle son and middle daughter).

Part of the Body: Womb.

Color: Vibrant green.

Symbolic Creatures: Snake, cicada, butterfly, chameleon, wild goose, wild duck, fish.

Plants and Perfumes: Fragrant olive, iris, magnolia, tree peony, plum blossom.

Metal: Tin.

Emblems: Egg, valley or ravine with a stream running through it, an embryo, flute.

Ritual Tools: Axe, sword.

Gods: P'an Ku, Chang Hsien, Kou Mang, Mo-li Ch'ing, Master Stonehead.

Goddesses: Ma-ku, Pi-hsia-yuan-chun.

Magickal Workings: Contemplating the need for division and diversity. Sorting out "the wheat from the chaff." Learning to "recognize the planes" and to avoid confusing them (i.e., acquiring the ability to view objects, entities, and circumstances in their proper perspective and in the light of their individual requirements). Avoiding troublesome situations. Cultivating the patience to wait for the right opposite to come along with which one should unite. (The state of disorder should not always be dealt with as if it were a problem needing to be solved quickly by sheer brute force. Harmony should come about at the right time, place, and by union with the correct object. Love—the action of the magickally dynamic union of opposites—should be enacted according to the genuine needs of the Tao/Will, and not dictated by wholly egotistical desires.)

Appendices

Appendix A
The Eight Taoist Immortals

The Eight Taoist Immortals are some of the best-known and most widely used images in Chinese art, popping up on any number of different items from the most beautiful ceramics to simple blocks of ink. They are also popular subjects in Chinese opera. But who are they, and why are they so important to Chinese legend and Taoist philosophy?

Basically, they represent a group of eight humans who have attained immortality by the use of Taoist magick and meditation. Each one has a history and, usually, many stories of their exploits on Earth among lesser mortals. Although separate individuals, they are said, nonetheless, to meet occasionally to discuss the state of humankind.

Each Immortal acts as a patron for a particular human endeavor or profession. Together, they also represent the dualistic "Eight Conditions of Life": male/female, noble/peasant, old age/youth, and poverty/prosperity. These evolved beings should not be confused with other Taoist immortals, of whom there are said to be quite a number, as they form a very distinct group. Nor should they be placed in the same category as deified humans such as Kuan Ti; the use of Taoist methods by the Eight is very specific to their immortality.

All the Eight Immortals (Chin. *Pa-hsien*) carry totem items by which they may be identified in artwork. Sometimes the totems alone may be used to represent them. As such, these items form the sacred Eight Taoist Emblems, which act as a rival grouping to the well-known Eight Buddhist Emblems.

Being a sacred ogdoad—a ritualistic and formal grouping of eight beings—they can be seen to have a certain relationship to the Eight Trigrams of the I Ching. My suggestions for the individual associations between Trigram and Immortal can be found in the relevant Hexagram listings in part 4.

Below are listed the various personalities, together with a brief description of their legends and supernatural qualities, totem emblems, and areas of influence.

Figure 15. The sword of Lu T'ung-pin.

Lu T'ung-pin. "Lu, the cave visitor"; also known as Shun Yang Tzu. The most influential of the Eight, Lu was variously said to have been born during the time of the T'ang dynasty or the later Sung dynasty. At one time a successful mandarin, he then became a sage and recluse who learned alchemical skills under the tutelage of a fellow Immortal, Chung-li Chuan. He is also said to have had an intimate relationship with Ho Hsien-ku that resulted in her own elevation to the group.[1]

Lu is associated with healing, medicine, and the exorcism of spirits and demons. His main symbol is a sword, called *Chan-yao Kuei*, "the Sword that Destroys Ghosts" (see figure 15). He obtained this useful occult weapon from a dragon spirit, whereupon he discovered that it had the magickal ability to fly around by itself and seek out his enemies. It also gave him the curious power to conceal himself from the sight of other people by cloaking his form with the darkness of Space. He is also sometimes depicted with a fly-whisk, the so-called *Yun-chou*, "Cloud-sweeper," that enables him to fly by magickal means.[2]

In addition to these attributions, this Immortal is also the patron of barbers.

Figure 16. The bottle gourd of Li T'ieh-kuai.

Li T'ieh-kuai. "Li of the iron crutch"; also known as Li K'ung Mu, "Li of the hollow eyes." He is said to have been taught the secrets of Taoism by the goddess Hsi-wang-mu, who rules over the western paradise of the immortals. Once upon a time, Li was a man without physical problems. However, during a long period in which he went astral traveling, one of his disciples cremated Li's material body because he thought his master was dead. When the Immortal returned from his trip, he found that there was nothing but ashes left for his spirit to re-enter. Having only limited time left in which to find a replacement, before his P'o spirit also died, he was only able to find the body of a recently deceased and rather physically disadvantaged beggar; hence his usual crippled form and the need for his iron crutch.[3]

Li takes a particular interest in medicine and poverty, and his major symbol is the bottle gourd, or calabash (see figure 16). Legends tell that Li hangs this upon a wall each night, shrinks himself to a miniature size, and then jumps into it, using it as his earthly abode; this is an obvious reference to the Taoist use of gourds as spirit-traps. Not surprisingly, then, this Immortal is also revered as the patron of magicians and astrologers.

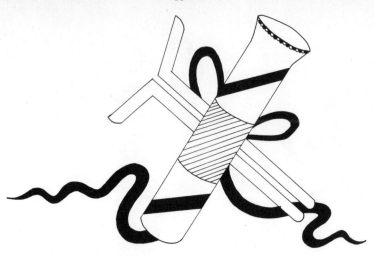

Figure 17. The fish drum of Chang-kuo Lao.

Chang-kuo Lao. "Old Chang-kuo"; a magician who is generally regarded as having lived sometime in the seventh to eighth centuries C.E. He lived on the slopes of Chung-t'iao Mountain, and is probably best known for the magickal white donkey on which he rides. This useful creature can carry Chang-kuo one thousand miles every day, and when not required, he folds it up like a piece of paper and packs it away.[4] To reuse it, he merely has to spit water upon it, whereupon it resumes its full donkey shape.

Another Taoist magician, by the name of Yeh Fa-shan, once declared that Chang-kuo was not actually a man, but a supernatural white bat that had come forth from the Primal Chaos of Hun-tun. Known for his necromantic skills and similar occult prowess, Chang-kuo himself also stated that he had, in a previous incarnation, been Grand Minister to the semimythical emperor Yao (c. 2357–2255 B.C.E.).

Some say that Chang-kuo acquired his eternal life by swallowing a Pill of Immortality, given to him by Li T'ieh-kuai. He is influential in the realm of childbirth, and his symbols are the *Yu-ku* ("fish drum") and two drumsticks (see figure 17). He is also the patron of artists and writers.

Figure 18. The castanets of Ts'ao Kuo-chiu.

Ts'ao Kuo-chiu. "Ts'ao, the country's maternal uncle." This Immortal was originally the son of a military leader and was the elder brother of an empress of China, sometime in the tenth century C.E. during the Sung dynasty. Ts'ao has something of an ambiguous reputation. Some accounts say that he was enamored of the Way from a very young age, and loved it above all mundane accomplishments. However, other less sympathetic stories declare that his devotion to Taoism only came about due to remorse over his previous acts of brutality against a certain woman.

His emblem is a pair of castanets (see figure 18), and he is considered to be the patron of all actors and actresses.

Figure 19. The flute of Han Hsiang-tzu.

Han Hsiang-tzu. "Han, the boy from the Hsiang River"; also known as Ch'ing Fu. Probably the most historically verifiable of all the Eight, Han was the nephew of a famous ninth-century scholar called Han Yu, and he chose to study the Way under the tutelage of Lu T'ung-pin. Always depicted playing a flute (see figure 19), his music has the power to cause flowers to bloom instantaneously; accordingly, he is the patron of musicians. Han is also a giver of divinatory oracles.

Figure 20. The fan of Chung-li Ch'uan.

Chung-li Ch'uan. "Powerful Chung-li"; also known as Han Chung-li. A complex character, he was born in Shensi Province, either during the time of the Chou dynasty or the later Han dynasty (hence his alternative name). Chung-li was an accomplished alchemist who discovered the secret of the Philosopher's Stone. His subsequent control of the generative forces in Nature led him to be titled "King-emperor of the True Active Principle" (i.e., the Yang polarity). He is closely linked to Lu T'ung-pin; the two even fought against each other in one of the internal Chinese conflicts between the Sung rulers and the Liao minority of Northern China (Chung-li supported the Sung, while Lu sided with the Liao).

Chung-li has the ability to fly and can resurrect the dead by using his magickal fan, his totem emblem (see figure 20). His areas of influence are, naturally enough, alchemy and immortality, yet he is also said to have special interest in matters of the sea (probably due to a belief that his fan can create favorable winds for boats and ships).

311

Figure 21. The basket of flowers of Lan Ts'ai-ho.

Lan Ts'ai-ho. "Lan, who is in harmony with all things." Probably the most enigmatic and abstruse of all the Eight, this character is very reminiscent of certain types of shaman. He or she is a youthful cross-dresser of indeterminate sex, possibly a hermaphrodite. Originally a poor street-singer, Lan is sometimes depicted wearing a tattered blue robe and only one shoe. The name *Lan* means "blue, indigo," and this color is often associated with Otherworld beings; interestingly, the tattered garment can also be seen as an indication of a supernatural nature, because Chinese ghosts traditionally wear ragged gowns with no hems. In this Immortal, a picture is shown of a person who, from the very start of life, was half in and half out of the worlds of the spirits. This may account for the absence of one shoe; i.e., Lan only lived part of his or her life in the mundane society of human beings.

This Immortal is something of an esoteric fool, whose songs carry portents of the future.[5] Somewhat prosaically, Lan is the patron of minstrels, gardeners, and those who deal with the arrangement of flowers. The totem that Lan carries is a brimming basket of flowers (see figure 21).[6]

Figure 22. The lotus of Ho Hsien-ku.

Ho Hsien-ku. "Ho, the immortal maiden." The only true woman among the Eight, Ho was initiated into the Way of the Tao by Lu T'ung-pin. He saved her from the double dangers of a demon and a life of banality in the domestic home. Ho became Lu's sexual partner in Taoist practices. Other tales assert that a supernatural being came to her in a dream and told her to consume a powdered jewel that was called *Yun-mu Shih.* By doing this, she was elevated to the status of a Hsien.

Originally, Ho was the daughter of a shopkeeper in the seventh century C.E., and was famed for her heroic stamina in traveling long distances on foot to collect bamboo shoots to make into medicine for her sick mother.

Due to her relationship with Lu T'ung-pin, Ho may be viewed as an archetypal image of a Taoist sexual priestess, and could be profitably invoked in matters relating to such a role. Her sacred emblem is a lotus flower (symbolic of the vulva) on a long stem (see figure 22). Another, and rather more prosaic and contradictory role, is to be the patron of housewives, though this bears all the hallmarks of a Confucian or Buddhist interpolation, as does the rather prudish claim that when Ho became an Immortal, she vowed to remain a virgin henceforth!

1. Thereby indicating the mysteries of empowerment and longevity that are present in Taoist sexual practices.
2. The Ching Chung Koon temple, in the New Territories of Hong Kong, claims to have this actual instrument, as well as Lu's demon-slaying sword. They are revered sacred relics to the incumbent priests and the temple's worshippers.
3. It is possible that this particular story contains mythicized elements that show the ancient link between Taoist magick and the practices of Siberian shamanism. As ritual props during the process of soul-flight, certain Tungusian shamans made use of symbolic crutches that were intended to assist their journeys in the spirit-worlds. Such esoteric symbolism also has a partial reflection in the traditional Western wizard's staff, as used by pagan figures such as the Scandinavian god Odin in his guise of Wanderer.
4. Compare this with the paper spirit horses discussed in the section *The Gate of Dreams*, in part 3.
5. This echoes the global idea that prophesying songs and other powerful utterances burst forth from shamanistic magicians when they are in the midst of their ecstatic trances.
6. This is possibly due to *Lan* being phonetically identical to another word-character meaning "a basket."

Appendix B

I Ching, Tarot, and the Qabalah

The Yi King is mathematical and philosophical in form. Its structure is cognate with that of the Qabalah; the identity is so intimate that the existence of two such superficially different systems is transcendent testimony to the truth of both.

Aleister Crowley, *Magick*.[1]

As with the Qabalah, the I Ching lays out a system of cosmic correspondences, by the use of which all types of manifestation may be organized into various "compartments" according to their individual natures. The enquiring student will see that there are many interesting comparisons that can be drawn between these two magickal systems, and that such investigation will do much to expand the potentials inherent in both.

The lists given below, which follow the general guidelines suggested by Aleister Crowley, show the possible connections between some of the Chinese Hexagrams and the Sephirothic/Tarot correspondences of the Qabalah. For more information regarding specific links to the Tarot, the student would do well to study Crowley's *The Book of Thoth*.

PRIMARY HEXAGRAMS		SEPHIROTH
Ch'ien	(1)	Da'ath
K'un	(2)	Malkuth
K'an	(29)	Yesod
Li	(30)	Tiphareth

315

PRIMARY HEXAGRAMS		SEPHIROTH
Chen	(51)	Geburah
Ken	(52)	Netzach
Hsuan	(57)	Hod
Tui	(58)	Chesed

HEXAGRAMS		MAJOR ARCANA	COURT CARDS
Meng	(4)	The Star	
Shih	(7)	The Universe	
Pi	(8)	The Universe	
Tung Jen	(13)	The Priestess	
Ta Yu	(14)	The Priestess	
Ch'ien	(15)	The Moon	
Sui	(17)	Lust	Queen of Wands
Ku	(18)	The Tower	Princess of Swords
Kuan	(20)	The Aeon	
Shih Ho	(21)	Adjustment	
Fen	(22)	Death	
Pao	(23)	The Moon	
I	(27)		Princess of Wands
Ta Kuo	(28)		Queen of Swords
Hsien	(31)	Fortune	Queen of Disks
Heng	(32)	The Hanged Man	Knight of Swords
Chia Jen	(37)	The Devil	
K'ui	(38)	The Hermit	
Ch'ien	(39)	The Star	
Hsun	(41)	Fortune	Princess of Cups

HEXAGRAMS		MAJOR ARCANA	COURT CARDS
I	(42)	The Hanged Man	Prince of Wands
Sheng	(46)	The Aeon	
Ching	(48)	The Sun	
Ko	(49)	The Hermit	
Ting	(50)	The Devil	
Chen	(51)		Knight of Wands
Ken	(52)		Princess of Disks
Chien	(53)	The Tower	Prince of Disks
Kuei Mei	(54)	Lust	Knight of Cups
Feng	(55)	Adjustment	
Lu	(56)	Death	
Hsuan	(57)		Prince of Swords
Tui	(58)		Queen of Cups
Huan	(59)	The Sun	
Chung Fu	(61)		Prince of Cups
Hsiao Kuo	(62)		Knight of Disks
Chi Chi	(63)	Art	
Wei Chi	(64)	Art	

---

1. See Aleister Crowley, *Magick* (London: Routledge & Kegan Paul, 1984), 270.

Appendix C

Pronunciation of Chinese

Chinese is a tonal language; in other words, the tone in which the words are pronounced helps to determine the meaning that the speaker is trying to convey. This can be better appreciated by perusing a Chinese dictionary, where it will be seen that many words have the same Romanized form, only their tone marks and their individual word-characters serve to differentiate them. The four basic tones in Mandarin Chinese (the dominant and standard Chinese dialect) are level intonation; rising intonation; falling then rising intonation; and falling intonation. However, in order to avoid confusing the general reader who is unfamiliar with Chinese, accent marks determining tone have been omitted from this book.

As a basic and very rough guide to pronunciation of some of the more difficult letters and diphthongs, both in Wade-Giles Romanization and modern Pinyin phonetics, study the following list.

ts/c	=	ts (as in "lets")
ch/q	=	ch; sometimes dj (as for "James")
hs/x	=	sh
zh	=	j (as in "June")
a	=	long vowel (as in "father)
ai	=	eye
ao	=	ow (as for "cow")
e	=	short vowel (as in "her")
ei	=	ay (as in "freight")

eng	=	ung (with the *e* as in "h*er*")
i	=	ee (or as in "sir" if after c, ch, r, s, sh, z, zh)
ia	=	ya
ie	=	ye (as for "yelp")
iu	=	yo
o	=	short vowel (as in "pot")
ou	=	long vowel sound (as in "though")
ong	=	oong
u	=	oo (but like the German ü if after j, q, x)
ua	=	wah
ui	=	way
uo	=	a short sound that rhymes with "war"
g	=	always hard (as in "get")
ow	=	rhymes with "cow"
un	=	as the *an* in "sembl*an*ce"
ur	=	rhymes with "fur"
y	=	always consonantal (as in "yet")

Many other letters approximate, roughly, to their English equivalents. So, as examples, feng shui is pronounced *fung shway*, I Ching sounds like *ee djing*, and Chou is pronounced like the name *Joe*.

Appendix D

A List of Gods, Goddesses, and Spirits

The following list comprises brief details on each Chinese deity mentioned in the correspondences in part 4. Dragon spirits are not included here, but may be found listed under the relevant Hexagrams. Chinese mythology contains many hundreds of different spiritual beings, and those that are given here provide but a sample selection of the gods and goddesses that are available to be invoked by the interested practitioner. The student should always feel free to add to the list and develop appropriate Hexagram correspondences.

A-ma. Goddess of sailors.

An Ch'i. God who leads mortals to P'eng-lai (Home of the Immortals in the Eastern Seas).

An-kung. God of sailors.

Boy of the White Crane. Youthful god who assists heroes in their work.

Chang Hsien. God of bows and archery, and bringer of children to childless couples.

Ch'ang-o. Also known as Heng-o. Goddess of the Moon.

Chang Tao-ling. Also known as T'ien Shih, "the Heavenly Master." God of exorcism, magick, and Taoist meditation; the deified founder of the structured magico-religious system of Taoism.

Chao. Guardian of the southern quarter.

Ch'eng-huang. Also known as Cheng Huang Shen. God of cities; an earth deity.

Chiang Shen. God of the Yangtze River.

Ch'ih Ching-tzu. Spirit of Fire.

Ch'ih-yu. Bear spirit, associated with bravery and military pursuits.

Ch'i ku-tzu. The Seven Young Ladies. A group of demi-goddesses, though some say they are just kuei, associated with mountains.

Chin Chia. God and protector of scholars.

Ch'i-t'ou. Also known as Ch'u-k'uang. A spirit who repels the ghosts of the wandering dead.

Chuang Mu. Goddess of bedrooms and the activities that go on in them!

Chu I. God of examinations and scholars.

Chu Jung. God of fire, forging, and metalwork; also known as the Celestial Executioner.

Chung. God of the South.

Chung K'uei. Protector against evil spirits and defender of travelers. Also called the Recorder of Hell, because he makes lists of all the dead who enter the Underworld.

Chun T'i. Goddess of the dawn.

Di-jiang. God of sacks. A personification of the Primal Chaos who is associated with the concept of "center."

Dijun. God of the Sun and the East.

Eastern Mother. Ancient goddess associated with shamanism.

Erh-lang. God who repels demons.

Fang-hsiang. Spirit who repels sickness and evil spirits. Sometimes he is depicted as a quartet of pottery figures, and is used to defend the cardinal compass points.

Fei Lien. Spirit of the Wind.

Feng Po. The Earl of Wind.

Feng-p'o-p'o. "Mrs. Wind." Goddess of the Wind and consort of Feng Po.

Fu-hsi. The legendary first earthly emperor. Revealer of the knowledge of the Trigrams, bringer of civilization to the Middle Kingdom, and brother-lover of Nu-kua.

Fu Shen. The spirit of happiness.

Ho-ho. The Divine Twins. Gods of harmony, concord, and riches.

Ho Ping. Also known as Ping I. God of the Yellow River.

Hou Chi. God of cereals.

Hsian Fu-jen. Goddess of water.

Hsien T'ung. The Immortal Youth. A servitor of Mu-kung.

Hsi-ho. Mother of the Suns. Goddess of sunrise.

Hsi Shen. God of joy and love.

Hsi-wang-mu. Sometimes just known as Wang. Queen of the Western Paradise of the Immortals, goddess of magick and sorcery, plague and pestilence; also guardian of the Peach of Immortality.

Hsuan-nu. Dark Girl. Goddess of frost and snow, and the sexual initiator of the legendary Yellow Emperor, Huang Ti. Possibly just a variant form of Hsi-wang-mu.

Hsuan-t'ien Shang-ti. Supreme Lord of the Dark Heaven. The Regent of Water.

Hsu Hao. Spirit of emptiness and devastation.

Hu. Chief of the magickal and shape-shifting fox spirits. Finder of lost things and lord of all cunning.

Huang K'un. God and patron of incense makers.

Huang Ti. The Yellow Emperor. Patron of doctors.

Hui Lu. Spirit of Fire and a legendary magician.

Huo Pu. God of fire.

Hu Shen. God of hail.

Hu-tu. Empress Earth. Goddess of earth and fertility.

K'eng San Ku-niang. Three goddesses of childbirth.

Kou Mang. God of seed-time, sowing, and the spring.

Kuan Ti. Otherwise called Kuan Kung, and Kuan Yu. God of war, justice, the police, divination, riches, and literature.

Kuan Yin. "She who pays attention to sound" (i.e., the cries of suffering humanity, but possibly also having a veiled reference to the use of vocal tones and mantra in meditation); also known as Sung-tzu Niang-niang, and to the Japanese as Kwan-non. Goddess of fecundity, healing, magick, prostitution, childbearing, compassion, and mercy; the most popular and diverse of the Chinese goddesses, and linked to the Tibetan deity Avalokitesvara (from whom the Chinese name of the goddess is a direct translation).

K'uei Hsing. God of literature and the Great Bear constellation.

Kuei Ku-tzu. Patron of fortunetellers and diviners.

Kung Kung. God of water.

Lao-tzu. The apotheosized author of the *Tao-teh Ching*. The quintessential personification of the enlightened Taoist sage, also known as the Supreme Patriarch of the Tao.

Lei Chen-tzu. The Son of Thunder.

Lei Hai-ch'ing. God and patron of musicians and diviners.

Lei Kung. Lord Thunder; god of thunderstorms.

Lei Tsu. God of thunder, clouds, and rain.

Li. God of fire.

Li. Guardian of the eastern quarter.

Ling-pao. T'ien-tsun. Spiritual Heavenly Worthy; god of the Taoist Second Heaven. A guardian of spiritual texts (especially the *Tao-teh Ching*), a regulator of Time (particularly of the Present) and the yearly fluctuations of Yin and Yang.

Liu Hai. God of benevolence and money.

Lo Hou Hsing. The spirit of eclipses.

Lu-pan. God of carpenters and builders.

Lo Shen. God of rivers.

Lu Shen. God of good luck and fortunate circumstances.

Ma. Guardian of the western quarter.

Ma-ku. Goddess of springtime.

Man Cheong. Cantonese god of literature and guardian of civil servants and officials.

Ma Ni-li. The Queen of Heaven, Mother of the Dipper. Goddess of the Sun and the Great Bear constellation. Probably identical to Tou Mu.

Master Stonehead. God of children and fertility.

Ma-t'ou Niang. Goddess of silkworms and mulberry trees.

Ma Tsu-po. Goddess of waters.

Meng. Also known as Meng-po Niang Niang. Goddess of Hell and maker of the Broth of Oblivion that makes the dead forget their former lives.

Mi Fei. Goddess of Water.

Mi-lo Fo. Fat-belly Buddha. God of laughter and pleasure. In Mahayana Buddhism, he is "the salvationary Buddha who is to come," better known as Maitreya.

Mobo. Goddess of maternal kindness.

Mo-li Ch'ing. Otherwise called Ch'ih Kuo, "Green Spirit." God of the East and the spring.

Mo-li Hai. Otherwise called Kuang Mu. God of the sea, the West, and autumn.

Mo-li Hung. Also known as Tseng Chang; "the Red Spirit." God of the South and summer.

Mo-li Shou. Otherwise called To Wen. God of longevity, the North, and winter.

Mu Kung. Also known as Tung Wang Kung. God of the East and Wind/Wood. A leader of the immortals and consort of the goddess Hsi-wang-mu.

Nan-chi Hsien-weng. God of the South Pole who decides who should die at a normal age, and which few may achieve longevity.

No-cha. Also known as Li No-cha. Youthful and spirited hero-god of combat, and protector against oppressors and evil spirits.

Nu-kua. Ancient creator goddess, restorer of cosmic harmony, and sister-lover of Fu-hsi.

Pa. Goddess of drought.

Pa Ch'a. God of grasshoppers who protects crops against damaging insects.

Pai Mei Shen. God with the White Eyebrows. God of sex and prostitutes.

Pai Mu-tan. White Peony. Goddess of love and sexuality.

P'an Chin-lien. Goddess of sex, prostitutes, and brothels.

P'an Ku. The Primal Being. Certain legends state that his body was divided into numerous pieces to form the world and its creatures.

P'an Kuan. God of exorcism, guardian of the deceased in the Otherworld and of those that travel there during life.

Pao Kung. God of justice.

Pei-ti. Emperor of the North.

P'eng Tsu. God of longevity.

Pien Ho. God of jewelers and maker of beautiful things.

Pi-hsia-yuan-chun. Also known as Sheng Mu, "Holy Mother," and Yu-nu, "Jade Maiden." Princess of Streaky Clouds; goddess of childbirth, women, children, and an associate of Mu Kung.

Pi-hsieh. Guardian deities, protectors of temples and tombs.

Po-lao. Ancient god of horses.

Sao-ts'ing Niang. Goddess of rain and clouds.

Shang Shan. God of mountains and Earth.

Shang Ti. Otherwise called Tien. Supreme god of Heaven/the sky; the divine ancestor, the First Principle. He is linked to the spiritual essence or True Self present in every living thing.

She-mo Wang. Patron gods of serpents.

Shen Nung. Also known as Ti Huang Shih. God of fire, agriculture, and medicine.

Shou Shen. A god of longevity, bringer of good fortune to the destitute, and a guardian against malicious forces.

Shui Kuan. The Agent of Water.

Shui-mu Niang-niang. The Water Mother.

Sui-zan. The Bringer of Fire; a Chinese Prometheus.

Sun Hou-tzu. Otherwise called Sun Wu-k'ung. Great Sage Equal of Heaven, better known as the Monkey King from the ancient story *Journey to the West*. God of victorious battle, and an emblem of striving force that battles against the odds.

Tai Shan. Otherwise called Chin Hung. Personification of the sacred Tai Mountain; god of the East and the Sun, and a guard against destructive force and malicious spirits.

T'ai Sui. God of Jupiter, time, and the general yearly cycle.

Tam Kung. Cantonese child-god; healer of the sick and controller of the weather.

T'ien Hou. The Empress of Heaven. Goddess of the Great Bear constellation and sailors.

T'ien Kou. The Celestial Dog. God of Sirius, storms, catastrophe and destruction, etc.

T'ien-kuan. God known as The Agent of Heaven. A dispenser of happiness according to the orders of divine Will.

T'ien Mu. Mother of Heaven. Goddess of lightning.

Ti-kuan. The Agent of Earth. He gives forgiveness for worldly crimes and other actions that transgress divine law.

Ti Ts'ang Wang. King of Earth's Womb. Ruler of the Underworld and the dead.

Ti-ya. Also known as Ti-mu, "Earth Mother." Divine ancestor of living creatures.

Tou Mu. Goddess of the Great Bear constellation and the Pole Star, longevity, and compassion. Similar in nature to Kuan Yin.

Ts'ai Shen. God of wealth.

Tsao-wang. Otherwise called Tsao Chun Shen. God of the kitchen hearth (now rarely seen in Chinese homes) who reports on human actions to Heaven at the end of each year.

Tsao-wang Nai-nai. Goddess of the kitchen hearth and consort of Tsao-wang.

Tsi-ku. The Purple Lady, also known as Tsi-ku Niang and San-ku. Goddess of divination, mediumship, fortunetelling, clairvoyance, etc.

Ts'ui Yang. God of the sacred mountain of Heng Shan.

T'u-ti. Earth gods.

Tzu Wei. Also known as Po I-k'ao. God of the North Polar Star.

Wang-kung. God of plagues.

Wei-t'o. God of crossroads and a guardian of temples.

Wen. Guardian of the northern quarter.

Wen-ch'ang. God of scholars, literature, and examinations; he also has associations with the Great Bear constellation.

Wong Tai Sin. Cantonese god of divination, the granting of wishes, and a healer of the sick.

Wu Kang. God of the Moon, love, and marriage.

Yang Hou. God of the sea.

Yao Wang. God and patron of doctors and medicine.

Yen-lo. God and ruler of the dead and the Underworld.

Yi. The Archer. God of the Sun.

Yuan Shih. God who personifies the First Principle of Creation, the highest Taoist deity. He is associated with the arousal of the Kundalini or bodily ch'i force.

Yuan-tan. Otherwise called Hsuan Tan. God of wealth.

Yu Huang. The Jade Emperor of Heaven.

Yun-t'ung. God known as the Little Boy of the Clouds.

Yu-tzu. The Master of Rain.

Chronology of the Chinese Dynasties

Shang-Yin	c. 1600–1027 (B.C.E.)
Western Chou	1027–771
Eastern Chou	770–481
Warring States (Chan Kuo)	480–222
Ch'in	221–207
Han	202–220 (C.E.)
Three Kingdoms	221–265
Six Dynasties	265–580
Sui	581–618
T'ang	618–906
Five Dynasties	907–960
Sung	960–1279
Yuan (Mongols)	1280–1368
Ming	1368–1644
Ch'ing (Manchus)	1644–1912
Republic	1912–1949
People's Republic	1949–

Glossary

Chin. Chinese   J. Japanese

Skt. Sanskrit   Tib. Tibetan

Russ. Russian   Gk. Greek

Animism. A spiritual view of life that regards all objects within Nature, including so-called inanimate things such as rocks and trees, as being invested with integral and subtle spirit-force.

Asana (Skt.). A specific bodily posture adopted for the purposes of meditation, concentration, etc.

Bon (Tib.). The original pre-Buddhist and shamanistic tradition of Tibet, which has been partially absorbed into Tibetan Buddhism in the guise of the Black Hat sect.

Chan-meng (Chin.). Divination by the interpretation of dreams.

Ch'i (Chin.). "Vital breath"; the subtle, energizing force, emanated from the Tao, that invests all organic matter with life.

Chiang-shih (Chin.). A resurrected corpse that has become a vampire; it also refers to a living person, in a cataleptic trance, who roams abroad in an astral state, sucking energy from others.

Chien (Chin.). The ritual sword. See *Ta-tao.*

Chi-kung (Chin.). Techniques that utilize breath control and bodily postures in order to increase ch'i in the psychophysical body. Also known as Qigong.

Ching (Chin.). The magick mirror, used for skrying, astral projection, psychic defense, etc.

Chuang-tai (Chin.). Occult hand gestures; the phrase literally means "the outward form of an inner attitude." See *Kettsuin* and *Mudra.*

Chung (Chin.). The ritual bell; used to summon divine beings, mark specific points in rituals, etc.

Da Siu Yan (Chin.). In Cantonese dialect, this means "Little People Hitters"; practitioners of *Hak Tao*, who punish others (the so-called "little people") on behalf of their clients. The phrase probably refers, as well, to the use of *mu-jen* in destructive image magick.

Fang-sheng (Chin.). The symbol of the double rhombus. It is used as a protective device and, in a modified form in this book, as a substitute for the ritual circle.

Fang-shih (Chin.). "Formula scholar," or "method master." One who is an adept in magick, alchemy, astrology, divination, etc.

Feng shui (Chin.). "Wind and water." A Chinese form of geomancy that seeks to enhance the constructive effects of natural earth energies, or minimize their destructive qualities, when considering the style and location of buildings, tombs, and so on. The phrase can also be loosely translated as "the custom of water," which relates to the stress-free harmony with the flow of the environment that the art seeks to achieve. Genuine, traditional feng shui is a great skill and should not be confused with the modern occidental variety, which often amounts to little more than interior design with a bit of hollow esoteric theory sprinkled on top.

Fudo (J.). Otherwise known as Dainichi Nyorai; a deity of Wisdom and Fire who is invoked in rites of banishment and exorcism. See *Shugendo*.

Hak Tao (Chin.). Cantonese term for the "Black Path." It specifically refers to magickal practices that are intended to bring harm to other people, by the medium of cursing, etc.

Hsien (Chin.). "Immortal beings," both human and otherwise. Sometimes hsien may also be very magickally advanced people who are not necessarily immortal in a bodily sense, but who may be somewhat long-lived nonetheless.

Huang-tao (Chin.). "The Imperial Way." The Chinese Zodiac, used by Taoist magicians to calculate the most auspicious times to construct and consecrate talismans.

Hufu (Chin.). An amulet or magickal talisman. The Chinese word literally means "a spell that guards," or "an agreement (i.e., with the spirits) for protection."

Hun (Chin.). One of a person's two spirit-bodies, sometimes called the "higher soul." It is linked to the Yang polarity. See *P'o*.

332

Hun-tun (Chin.). The original and primal Chaos, existing at the heart of the Void, out of which were born the conditions required for manifested existence.

Immortal. In this book, the term is generally used to mean a person who has obtained eternal existence in an individual and particular form, whether spiritual or physical, by the performance of Taoist magickal and meditative techniques. See *Hsien* and *Pa-hsien*.

In (J.). The Japanese version of *Yang*. See *Yo*.

In O Musubi (J.). "Making the Sign"; a technique for the casting of spells and for stimulating deep meditation, that utilizes a grid of nine lines, traced with a hand mudra, upon which a further character or sigil may be visualized.

Jinja (J.). "Kami Place"; a shrine dedicated to Shinto gods and spirits.

Kami (J.). The spirits that inhabit and have influence over every aspect of Nature.

Kami-no-Michi (J.). The true Japanese version of the Chinese-derived word *Shinto*.

Ku (Chin.). The ritual drum, used for empowerment purposes and in trance work.

Kuei (Chin.). A troublesome ghost.

Ling (Chin.). "Magickal power," or "spiritual essence."

Middle Kingdom. The land of China, so-called from the traditional view that human beings hold the central, balancing position between the dual powers of Heaven and Earth. It is essentially a shamanistic phrase, cognate in meaning with the Norse *Midgard*.

Ming (Chin.). "Fate," or "destiny." An individual's true Path in life.

Mudra (Skt.). Hand gestures that are used to assist contemplation, or to channel specific magickal energies in order to fulfill certain goals.

Mu-jen (Chin.). "Wooden people"; carved dolls used in Chinese magick to house spirits or other magickal energies.

Musubi (J.). The inherent Will of a being's True Self to express its nature in the phenomenal worlds.

Nagare (J.). "Flow"; the Shinto equivalent of the current of the Tao, which expresses itself in and through Nature via the process of change, and with which all things should move in harmony.

Neidan (Chin.). "Interior alchemy"; the attainment of inner balance and perfection by the sublimation of sexual energy, ch'i, etc. See *Waidan*.

Pa-hsien (Chin.). "The Eight Immortals"; a collection of individual immortals who play a unique, guiding role in Taoist philosophy, and who act as patrons for various human endeavors and careers.

Pa Kua (Chin.). "Eight Diagrams"; the Trigrams of the I Ching.

P'o (Chin.). The "lower soul" of a person, linked to the polarity of Yin. See *Hun*.

Sennin (J.). Mountain recluses and magicians who have attained bodily immortality by occult methods, and who have general mastery of magickal practices. These characters figure in many Japanese legends. See *Hsien*.

Shaman (Russ.). From the Tungusian term *saman*; one who carries out the practices of shamanism.

Shamanism. Practices that involve the shaman acting as intermediary between the gods and his or her community for the benefit of all. These acts usually involve methods of healing, soul-flight (astral projection), trance (often by active methods such as dance), the use of animal-spirit allies, or the assistance of discarnate shamanistic predecessors, magickal combat and sorcery, etc. The shaman is also the human repository of his or her tribe's cultural heritage and its dynamic link to ancestral force. Contrary to many modern ideas, shamans are not those who merely work as solo practitioners or are concerned purely with healing as that term is commonly understood. Nor is shamanism a religion in the sense that it has a formalized priesthood, doctrines, or dogma, established acts of orthodox worship for devotees, converts, and so on. Instead, it represents various esoteric ways of dealing with life by communicating with, and in most instances seeking to control, the spirits held to be responsible for all aspects of the tribe's physical world and cultural viewpoint. In this, shamans specifically take upon themselves the burden of the community's welfare. Many people may utilize shamanistic techniques or ideas, but are not shamans merely by association with such things. The "job description" must involve acts of direct mediation or struggle for the specific good of others, as well as for oneself. Such action can sometimes place the shaman's own life in danger.

Shan (Chin.). The ritual fan, used in necromantic rites, exorcisms, etc.

Shintai (J.). "God-body"; any physical object that is regarded as sacred and is revered because it is deemed to hold within itself the spiritual power of a deity. Such an object can be an actual image of the divinity concerned, or a symbolic amulet such as a sword, mirror, jewels, etc.

Shinto (J.). "The Way of the Gods"; the animistic and indigenous religion of the Japanese state.

Shugendo (J.). An eclectic and magickal sect that combines elements of Tantric Buddhism, Shinto, Taoism, etc. Its adherents are known as *Yamabushi*, and they are devotees of the god Fudo. The school was officially banned by a Japanese emperor in the nineteenth century C.E.

Tai-Chi (Chin.). The Divine Monad, or state of Primal Unity. It is represented by the symbol of the Yin and Yang conjoined, which is thought by some to be an emblem of the Cosmic Egg, divided into its component parts of albumen and yolk. The symbol illustrates the spiral and continuous cyclical movement of creation and destruction, gain and loss, action and rest, etc.; it is the condition of cosmic perfection brought about by the harmonious interaction and balance of the Positive and Negative.

Tao (Chin.). "Way, path, road"; the underlying cause behind all phenomena that manifests itself in individual expressions according to the correct nature and function of an object through which it moves. It is the universal and abstract force that is the source of spiritual and magickal energy.

Taoist. A person who is committed to obtaining union with the Tao by finding out how it desires to manifest specifically and uniquely in his or her life, and then living according to such knowledge. Magickal methods and mystical practices are used to stimulate personal awareness of Tao. However, the term is often linked purely to ordained priests and priestesses within the organized Taoist religion, and to the worshippers who belong to one of its various sects.

Tao-jen (Chin.). "Tao person"; in this book, the term is used to designate anyone who uses Taoist methods, and is generally in alignment with the overall philosophy of the Tao, yet is not necessarily an official priest or priestess, initiate of a Taoist school, or member of the formal Taoist religion.

Ta-tao (Chin.). The ritual sword, used by the magician as a symbol of his Will and authority over spiritual beings and magickal forces. See *Chien*.

Teh (Chin.). "Power, qualities, virtues"; the nature and form of the flow of Tao, as it is expressed in the phenomenal universe.

Thelema (Gk.). "Will, desire, wish"; the magickal, neopagan, and philosophical system espoused by Aleister Crowley. Like esoteric Taoism, it considers the main objective in an individual's life to be the discovery, and subsequent enactment, of the True Will, i.e., the specific manner in which a person's True Self (as opposed to the limited ego-self of the human personality) wishes to manifest in the cosmos. By being true to one's Will, harmony with the flow of the universe is achieved. Magickal development and practice is viewed as being a primary way by which the human consciousness may go beyond self-created barriers and become united with inner spiritual source.

Yamabushi (J.). "Mountain warriors"; reclusive adepts of the Shugendo sect who incorporate many magickal techniques into their religious practices.

Yang (Chin.). The positive aspect of existence that links to the sunny side, warmth, light, the Sun, that which gives, Heaven, the sexual function of the male of a species, that which is outside, etc.

Yin (Chin.). The negative aspect of existence, linking to shade, cold, darkness, the Moon, that which receives, the Earth, the sexual function of the female of a species, that which is inside, etc.

Yo (J.). The Japanese version of Yin. See *In*.

Waidan (Chin.). "Exterior alchemy"; that which is practiced in alchemical rooms or laboratories, utilizing substances such as herbs, minerals, metals, etc. See *Neidan*.

Wu (Chin.). "Sorcerer, magician (male and female), witch; magick." The term properly refers to a practitioner of Chinese magick who utilizes pronounced shamanistic methods, and who often takes on the shaman's tribal role.

Wu-wei (Chin.). "Not doing, no action"; the mode and law of life that is followed by a Taoist, whose spontaneous deeds are in accordance with the flow of Tao as it chooses to express itself through that person.

Selected Bibliography
and Further Reading

Unfortunately, most books on Chinese magick and the history and practices of Taoism are unavailable in English translations. Some Chinese temples house several thousand such books, most of which will never be seen by Westerners. However, the following list includes a sample selection available in English that express Taoist views, as well as some comparative tomes on related matters. It is intended to be generally wide-ranging in scope, but should not be looked upon as being in any way exhaustive; the chosen titles are merely examples of their various types.

All dates mentioned refer to the edition of the work consulted, not necessarily to the first date of publication.

Ashe, Geoffrey. *The Ancient Wisdom*. London: Sphere Books Ltd., 1979.

Barber, Richard, and Anne Riches. *A Dictionary of Fabulous Beasts*. Ipswich: The Boydell Press, 1975.

Bardon, Franz. *Initiation into Hermetics*. Wuppertal, Germany: Dieter Ruggeberg, 1981.

Blofeld, John. *Beyond the Gods*. London: George Allen & Unwin, 1974.

Bloomfield, Frena. *The Book of Chinese Beliefs*. London: Arrow Books Ltd., 1985.

Budge, E. A. Wallis. *The Egyptian Book of the Dead*. New York: Dover, 1967.

Bunson, Matthew. *Vampire: The Encyclopedia*. London: Thames & Hudson, 1993.

Campbell, Joseph. *The Masks of God*. Vol. 2 of *Oriental Mythology*. London: Penguin, 1988.

Cavendish, Richard (ed.). *Mythology: An Illustrated Encyclopedia*. London: Orbis, 1980.

Chia, Mantak, and Michael Winn. *Taoist Secrets of Love*. New York: Aurora Press, 1984.

Chia, Mantak, and Maneewan Chia. *Healing Love through the Tao: Cultivating Female Sexual Energy*. New York: Healing Tao Books, 1986.

Chinese-English Dictionary. Beijing, 1985.

Clayre, Alasdair. *The Heart of the Dragon*. London: Channel 4, 1984.

Clemen, Carl, et al. *Religions of the World: Their Nature and their History*. London: Harrap, 1931.

Cosgrove, Maynard G. *The Enamels of China and Japan: Champleve and Cloisonne*. London: Robert Hale, 1974.

Cotterell, Arthur. *The First Emperor of China*. London: Macmillan, 1981.

———. *China: A Concise Cultural History*. London: John Murray Publishers Ltd., 1988.

Crowley, Aleister. *Magick*. London: Routledge & Kegan Paul, 1984.

———. *Magick Without Tears*. Phoenix: Falcon Press, 1986.

———. *The Confessions of Aleister Crowley*. London: Arkana, 1989.

———. *The Book of Thoth*. York Beach: Weiser, 1985.

———. *777 and other Qabalistic Writings of Aleister Crowley*. York Beach: Weiser, 1987.

———. *The Magical Record of the Beast 666*. London: Duckworth, 1972.

———. *The Magical Diaries of Aleister Crowley*. St. Helier: Neville Spearman, 1979.

———. *The Holy Books of Thelema*. York Beach: Weiser, 1983.

———. *Liber Aleph*. York Beach: Weiser, 1991.

———. *Tao Te Ching*. York Beach: Weiser, 1995.

Cunningham, Scott. *Cunningham's Encyclopedia of Magical Herbs*. St. Paul: Llewellyn, 1988.

David-Neel, Alexandra. *Magic and Mystery in Tibet*. London: Corgi, 1971.

Davis, F. Hadland. *Myths and Legends of Japan*. Singapore: Graham Brash Ltd., 1989.

Deng, Ming-Dao. *Chronicles of Tao*. San Francisco: HarperCollins, 1993.

De Groot, J. J. M. *Religious System of China*. Leyden, 1892.

De Visser, W. M. W. *The Dragon in China and Japan*. Amsterdam, 1913.

Dore, Henri. *Researches into Chinese Superstitions*. Shanghai: Tusewei Printing Press, 1917.

Douglas, Nik, and Penny Slinger. *Sexual Secrets*. Rochester: Destiny Books, 1979.

Eberhard, Wolfram. *A Dictionary of Chinese Symbols*. London: Routledge, 1986.

Eliade, Mircea. *Shamanism: Archaic Techniques of Ecstasy*. New York: Pantheon, 1964.

Farrar, Janet, and Stewart Farrar. *The Witches' Goddess*. London: Robert Hale, 1987.

Faulkner, R. O. *The Ancient Egyptian Book of the Dead*. London: British Museum Publications, 1989.

Fisher, Robert E. *Buddhist Art and Architecture*. London: Thames & Hudson, 1993.

Gernet, Jacques. *A History of Chinese Civilization*. Cambridge: Cambridge University Press, 1996.

Grant, Kenneth. *Aleister Crowley and the Hidden God*. London: Muller, 1973.

———. *Cults of the Shadow*. London: Muller, 1975.

———. *Hecate's Fountain*. London: Skoob Books, 1992.

———. *Images & Oracles of Austin Osman Spare*. London: Muller, 1975.

Graves, Robert (ed.). *New Larousse Encyclopedia of Mythology*. Feltham: Hamlyn, 1975.

Hatsumi, Masaaki. *Ninjutsu History & Tradition*. USA: Unique Publications, 1995.

Henricks, Robert G. *Te-Tao Ching*. London: Bodley Head, 1990.

Herne, Richard. *The Whispering Signs*.

Huson, Paul. *Mastering Herbalism*. London: Abacus, 1977.

Johnson, Buffie. *Lady of the Beasts*. Vermont: Inner Traditions International, 1994.

Legeza, Laszlo. *Tao Magic: The Secret Language of Diagrams and Calligraphy*. London: Thames & Hudson, 1987.

Legge, James. *I Ching*. New York: Mentor, 1971.

———. *The Texts of Taoism*. Vols. 1 & 2. New York: Dover, 1962.

Mackenzie, Donald A. *China and Japan: Myths and Legends*. London: Senate, 1994.

McNamara, Sheila, and Xuan Ke Song. *Traditional Chinese Medicine*. London: Hamish Hamilton, 1997.

Miller, Richard Alan. *The Magical & Ritual Use of Herbs*. New York: Destiny, 1983.

Monaghan, Patricia. *The Book of Goddesses & Heroines*. St. Paul: Llewellyn Publications, 1990.

Mookerjee, Ajit, and Madhu Khanna. *The Tantric Way*. London: Thames & Hudson, 1977.

Palmer, Martin. *Travels through Sacred China*. London: Thorsons, 1996.

Palmer, Martin; Jay Ramsay; and Xiaomin Zhao. *I Ching: Shamanic Oracle of Change*. London: Thorsons, 1995.

Palmer, Martin; Man Ho Kwok; and Joanne O'Brien. *The Contemporary I Ching*. London: Rider, 1989.

Picken, Stuart D. B. *Shinto: Japan's Spiritual Roots*. Tokyo: Kodansha International Ltd., 1984.

Polo, Marco. *The Travels of Marco Polo*. Translated by Teresa Waugh, from the Italian adaptation by Maria Bellonci. London: Sigwick & Jackson, 1984.

Rafferty, Kevin. *City on the Rocks: Hong Kong's Uncertain Future*. London: Viking, 1989.

Shah, Idries. *Oriental Magic*. St. Albans: Paladin, 1973.

——. *The Secret Lore of Magic*. London: Abacus, 1972.

Shrine of Wisdom. *The Simple Way of Lao Tsze*. Brook: Shrine of Wisdom Publications, 1951.

Sullivan, Michael. *The Arts of China*. London: Cardinal, 1973.

Temple, Robert K. G. *Conversations with Eternity: Ancient Man's Attempts to Know the Future*. London: Rider, 1984.

Turnbull, Stephen. *Samurai Warlords*. London: Blandford, 1992.

Vitebsky, Piers. *The Shaman*. London: Macmillan/Duncan Baird Publishers, 1995.

Walker, Barbara G. *The Woman's Dictionary of Symbols and Sacred Objects*. San Francisco: Harper & Row, 1988.

Walters, Derek. *Chinese Mythology*. London: Aquarian, 1992.

Watson, William. *The Genius of China*. London: Times Newspapers Ltd., 1973.

Wei Wu Wei. *Ask the Awakened*. London: Routledge & Kegan Paul, 1963.

Werner, Edward T. C. *Ancient Tales and Folklore of China*. London: Senate, 1995.

Whittaker, Clio. *An Introduction to Oriental Mythology*. The Apple Press, 1989.

Wieger, S. L. *Chinese Characters*. New York: Dover, 1965.

Wilhelm, Richard. *I Ching or Book of Changes*. London: Arkana, 1989.

Williams, C. A. S. *Outlines of Chinese Symbolism & Art Motives*. New York: Dover, 1976.

Wood, Frances. *Did Marco Polo Go to China?* London: Secker & Warburg, 1995.

Wu, Ch'eng-en. *Monkey/The Journey to the West*. Translated by Arthur Waley. London: Unwin, 1979.

Yee, Chang. *Chinese Calligraphy*. London: Methuen & Co. Ltd., 1938.

Index

A

Acupuncture, 78, 113
Ainu, 23
Alchemy, 28, 40, 50–51, 73, 78, 142, 148, 196,
    262, 269, 272, 290, 299, 310
Altar, 39–40, 70–71, 101, 121, 134–135, 144,
    151–152, 165, 178, 262
Amaterasu, 7, 55, 66
Ancestors, 6, 14, 17, 61, 69, 133, 135, 204,
    247, 264
Animism, 23
Asana, 77, 112, 132, 144–145, 149–151, 163,
    165

B

Bardon, Franz, 56, 79, 84, 127
Bell, 53–54, 70, 91, 142, 144, 204, 208, 214,
    224, 236, 258, 290
Bloomfield, Frena, 25
Bon, 37
Book of Changes, The, 3, 15, 17–18, 26
Book of the Dead, The, 7, 26, 67, 127
Book of the Law, The, 29
Buddhism, 21, 24, 41, 325

C

Censer, 75, 119, 288
Ch'i, 13, 46, 50, 65–66, 74, 109–113,
    125–127, 138–140, 160, 209, 236,
    242, 266, 270, 278, 286, 292, 296,
    321–322, 328
Ch'in Shih-huang-ti, 14
Chang Tao-ling, 18–20, 102, 115, 176, 188,
    194, 214, 216, 224, 226, 236, 238, 260,

262, 266, 268, 272, 276, 280, 290, 292,
    321
Chaos, 27, 59, 126, 166, 308, 322
Chi-kung, 13–14, 21, 50, 109–110, 112–113,
    148, 153
Chiang Tzu-ya, 124
Chou, 9, 11–12, 17, 124, 129, 137, 173, 310,
    320
Chuang-tzu, 8, 12–14, 26
Chung-li Ch'uan, 65, 290,
    310–311
Cinnabar, 50, 113, 262, 272, 300
Confucians, 9, 11–12, 17, 22–23, 282,
    312
Cotterell, Arthur, 4, 25
Crowley, Aleister, 26, 29, 32–33, 83–84, 87,
    159, 315, 317

D

Da Siu Yan, 25, 127
Dee, Dr. John, 84, 121
Destiny, 30, 32, 126, 153, 155, 163, 190, 192,
    223, 285
Divination, 3, 15–17, 23, 84, 86, 103–104,
    129, 134–135, 174, 188, 208, 260, 288,
    323, 327–328
Dragon, 20, 46, 141–146, 176, 184, 186,
    194, 196, 202, 204, 206, 210, 214, 216,
    220, 224, 226, 228, 230, 232–233, 236,
    238, 242, 250, 252, 254, 258, 260, 262,
    268, 272, 276, 278, 280, 284, 288, 290,
    296, 300, 306, 321
Drum, 59–60, 131–132, 143, 145, 194, 206,
    210, 216, 222, 242, 276, 308
Duke of Chou, The, 17, 129

E

Earth, 5, 7, 9–10, 16, 18, 28, 40, 42, 44,
  50–51, 55–56, 78–79, 97, 99, 109,
  119–120, 130, 132, 147, 160–161,
  163–164, 177, 180, 187, 189, 195, 197,
  203, 205, 209, 213, 219, 221, 232, 243,
  247, 263, 270, 278, 297, 305, 321, 323,
  326–327
Egypt, 7, 125
Eight Taoist Immortals, 10, 67, 166, 256, 305
Enochian, 84, 121
Ephedra, 110–111, 113, 242, 270, 288
Epona, 130
Exorcism, 6, 19–20, 43, 65, 78, 102, 186, 194,
  216, 226, 268, 306, 321, 326

F

Fan, 65–66, 111, 194, 216, 310–311
Fang-sheng, 41–42, 97, 99, 104, 132, 252
Feng shui, 22–23, 25, 56, 66, 69, 97, 160, 209,
  252, 272, 294, 320
Festival of Lanterns, 69
Fire, 16, 59, 74, 78–79, 83, 89–90, 92, 101,
  112, 119–120, 131, 142, 196, 217,
  233–234, 243, 247, 249, 262, 270–271,
  273, 276, 284, 322–324, 326
First Emperor, The, 14–15, 2
Five Elements, 20, 24, 102
Fu-hsi, 15, 173, 176, 188, 196, 200, 206, 208,
  236, 248, 268, 272, 282, 294, 300, 322,
  325
Fudo, 24, 89–92, 95, 98–99, 101–102,
  104–105, 111–112, 119–120, 126–127,
  132–133, 135, 138–139, 144, 146,
  151–152, 155, 157, 160–161, 163–165,
  167

G

Ghost Writing, 61, 117–118
Ghosts, 6, 24, 65–66, 69, 178, 197, 246, 252,
  306, 311, 322
Ginseng, 110–111, 123, 224, 242, 272, 296,
  300
Grant, Kenneth, 6, 25, 33

H

Heaven, 4–5, 7–10, 16, 18, 28, 39, 44, 50–51,
  109, 121, 130, 141, 148, 163–164, 173,
  175–176, 185, 191, 193, 195, 197, 225,
  241, 259, 261, 275, 287, 323–328
Henna, 51, 74, 218
Heru-Ur, 7
Hexagrams, 16–18, 37, 44, 46, 60, 71, 95,
  97–98, 103–105, 107, 111–112, 130, 132,
  136, 140, 151, 155–157, 160, 163–164,
  166, 169, 171, 173–175, 177, 179, 181,
  183, 185–187, 189, 191–195, 197,
  199–203, 205, 207, 209–211, 213,
  215–217, 219–227, 229–233, 235–237,
  239–261, 263–291, 293, 295–301, 305,
  315–317, 321
Ho Hsien-ku, 178, 306, 312–313
Hong Kong, 25, 75, 313
Horse, 129–133, 136, 178, 194, 214, 230, 236,
  238, 240, 248, 250, 254, 264, 266, 280,
  292
Hsi-wang-mu, 9, 14, 62, 148, 178, 188, 198,
  210, 214, 216, 220, 226, 230, 232, 236,
  238, 240, 246, 256, 260, 262, 264, 266,
  268, 270, 272, 274, 278, 280, 290, 292,
  307, 323, 325
Hsien, 4, 9–10, 180, 182, 196, 224, 235, 256,
  258, 274, 282, 302, 312, 316, 321, 323
Hun, 135, 148–152, 163–164

I

I Ching, 3, 15–18, 23, 25–26, 56, 60, 71, 83,
  95, 103–105, 109, 129–130, 140, 155, 165,
  169, 173–174, 186, 188, 208, 228, 248,
  260, 272, 282, 288, 305, 315, 320
Immortals, 4, 9–10, 14–15, 20, 65, 67,
  101–102, 109, 131, 166, 176, 178, 232,
  234, 236, 256, 270, 276, 278, 288, 290,
  305–312, 321, 323, 325
Incense, 10, 73–75, 101, 119, 124, 130, 135,
  151, 288, 323

J

Japan, 7, 10, 14, 23–26, 46, 53, 55, 70, 124,
  137–138, 140, 159

Jinja, 53, 130
Journey to the West, The, 41, 326
Jung, Carl, xii–xiii

K

Kakuzo, Okakura, 142
Kami, 23, 49, 53, 130
Kelly, Sir Edward, 84, 121
Kettsuin, 77, 140
Khan, Kublai, 21–22
Ko Hsuan, 20, 26, 118
Ko Hung, 118
Kojiki, 7, 26
Korea, 23–24
Ku, 6, 59, 176, 196, 204, 209–210, 268, 279,
    300, 302, 316, 326
Kuei, 6, 24–25, 66, 69, 148, 188, 207–208,
    214, 236, 246, 254, 260, 268, 281, 288,
    306, 317, 322, 324
Kujikiri, 138–139, 272
Kundalini, 15, 79, 142, 328
Kung fu, 109, 159

L

Lanterns, 69–71, 119, 144, 167, 195, 200,
    234, 236, 292
Lao-tzu, 8–12, 20, 27, 74, 115–116, 176, 188,
    204, 214, 224, 236, 238, 240, 272, 280,
    286, 292, 296, 298, 324
Legge, James, xiii, 26, 33, 121, 339
Li, 9–10, 15, 26, 46, 110, 113, 166, 193, 199,
    201, 215, 218, 233–234, 243, 245, 248,
    250, 259, 271, 273, 276, 283, 286, 290,
    300–301, 307–308, 315, 324–325
Longevity, 10, 13–14, 20, 50, 117, 232, 270,
    313, 325–327
Lu T'ung-pin, 102, 176, 256, 306, 309–310,
    312

M

Magickal record, 85
Manchu, 22, 44
Mandrake, 123, 272, 300
Martial arts, 13, 45, 67, 139
Metal, 23, 45, 54–55, 78, 120, 180, 182, 184,
    186, 188, 192, 198, 208, 210, 212, 214,
    216, 218, 220, 222, 226, 230, 232, 236,
    238, 240, 242, 244, 250, 252, 254, 256,
    258, 260, 266, 268, 272, 274, 280, 282,
    284, 286, 288, 290, 294, 298, 302
Ming-ch'i, 6
Mirror, 55–57, 149, 151–152, 178, 194, 226,
    234, 260, 266, 270, 280
Mongols, 21–22
Moon, 5, 7, 16, 26, 28, 66, 185, 202, 204,
    213–214, 231–232, 246, 264, 274, 293,
    299, 301, 316, 321, 328
Mu-jen, 123–127, 133–135, 178, 210, 236,
    268
Mudra, 24, 46, 77–79, 89, 91–95, 98, 101,
    118–119, 138–139, 144, 155–156
Mugwort, 57, 74, 101, 190, 194, 196, 200,
    264, 274, 290, 300
Musha shugyo, 25, 30
Musubi, 28, 137–138, 272

N

Nagare, 24
Ninja, 10, 24–25, 30, 138
Nishina, Daisuke, 24
Nu-kua, 15, 178, 190, 196, 200, 222, 224,
    248, 264, 274, 282, 300, 322, 325

O

Odin, 130, 313
Oracle bones, 16, 186
Osiris, 7

P

P'o, 66, 147–149, 151, 307
Pa Kua, 15, 18, 48, 56, 166
Pao-P'o-Tzu, 118
Peach of Immortality, The, 10, 323
Peng-lai, 14
Polo, Marco, 21, 26
Pranayama, 13, 79, 110

Q

Qabalah, 142, 315

R

Robe, 47–48, 53, 311
Runes, 121, 136

S

Sahaja, 32
Self, 31–32, 39–40, 43, 45, 56, 70, 101–102,
    131, 161, 185, 190, 201, 208, 222, 224,
    237–238, 244, 285, 287–288, 296, 326
Sennin, 10
Set, 7, 11, 21, 25–26, 29, 39, 49, 54, 56, 66,
    84, 101, 104, 110, 112, 121, 132, 134,
    159–160, 174, 207
Shaman, 4–5, 123–124, 129–130, 234, 264,
    270, 311
Shamanism, 4, 6, 8, 10, 12–14, 16, 18, 20–24,
    26, 28, 30, 32, 40, 42, 44, 46, 48, 50, 52,
    54, 56, 60, 62, 66, 70, 74, 78, 84, 86, 90,
    92, 94, 98, 102, 104, 110, 112, 116, 118,
    120, 124, 126, 130, 132, 134, 138, 140,
    142, 144, 146, 148, 150, 152, 156, 160,
    164, 166, 174, 176, 178, 180, 182, 184,
    186, 188, 190, 192, 194, 196, 198, 200,
    202, 204, 206, 208, 210, 212, 214, 216,
    218, 220, 222, 224, 226, 228, 230, 232,
    234, 236, 238, 240, 242, 244, 246, 248,
    250, 252, 254, 256, 258, 260, 262, 264,
    266, 268, 270, 272, 274, 276, 278, 280,
    282, 284, 286, 288, 290, 292, 294, 296,
    298, 300, 302, 313, 322
Shang, 17, 124, 176, 188, 190, 204, 210, 222,
    224, 228, 232, 236, 238, 248, 264, 270,
    272, 274, 278, 292, 296, 326
Shen, 5, 10, 23, 124, 148, 176, 178, 180, 186,
    192, 194, 196, 202, 206, 212, 218, 220,
    222, 224, 232, 234, 240, 244, 252, 256,
    258, 262, 266, 270, 274, 276, 284, 290,
    292, 300, 321, 323–327
Shinto, 23–24, 26, 28, 49, 53, 55, 130, 159
Shugendo, 24–25
Siberia, 4
Skrying, 55–57, 103, 105, 152, 280
Spare, Austin Osman, 29, 33, 63
Spirit ladder, 6–7
Ssu-ma Ch'ien, 9

Stone warriors, 97, 99, 101, 104
Sun, 5, 7, 16, 26, 28, 40, 55, 62, 66, 70, 89,
    120, 132, 138, 186, 192, 194, 199, 216,
    230, 233–234, 242–243, 245–246,
    249–250, 255, 266, 276, 283, 285, 288,
    299, 301, 317, 322, 325–328
Sung, 10, 21, 74, 183, 185, 306, 309–310
Sword, 6, 43–46, 55, 61–62, 65, 78, 89,
    92–95, 98–99, 101–102, 111, 118–119,
    138–139, 142, 145, 176, 186, 194, 216,
    230, 232, 234, 254, 276, 302, 306, 313

T

T'ang, 21, 24, 97–99, 278, 306
Tai-Chi Chuan, 45–46
Tai-Chi, 21, 24, 27–29, 41, 44, 46, 48, 222,
    238, 272, 300
Taiwan, 20, 25–26
Talismans, 6–7, 18–21, 23–24, 39, 46, 49–51,
    57, 61–63, 98, 109, 115–121, 125–126,
    130, 135, 137–138, 142–144, 146, 155,
    157, 173
Tantra, 150
Tao, 3–4, 8–9, 11–15, 17–19, 23, 25–32,
    40–41, 43, 48, 65, 70, 77–78, 83, 101–102,
    113, 117, 120, 124, 141–143, 159, 164,
    175–176, 181–182, 210, 217, 223, 239,
    256, 267, 273, 287, 290, 302, 312, 324
Tao-teh Ching, 8–9, 11, 27, 141, 146, 228, 324
Tao-tsang, 21, 115
Taoism, 3–4, 6, 8, 10, 12, 14, 16–24, 26–30,
    32–33, 37, 40, 42, 44, 46, 48, 50, 52, 54,
    56, 60, 62, 66, 70, 74, 78, 84, 86, 90, 92,
    94, 98, 102, 104, 110, 112, 115–116, 118,
    120–121, 124, 126, 130, 132, 134, 138,
    140–142, 144, 146, 148, 150, 152, 156,
    160, 164, 166, 174, 176, 178, 180, 182,
    184, 186, 188, 190, 192, 194, 196, 198,
    200, 202, 204, 206, 208, 210, 212, 214,
    216, 218, 220, 222, 224, 226, 228, 230,
    232, 234, 236, 238, 240, 242, 244, 246,
    248, 250, 252, 254, 256, 258, 260, 262,
    264, 266, 268, 270, 272, 274, 276, 278,
    280, 282, 284, 286, 288, 290, 292, 294,
    296, 298, 300, 302, 307, 309, 321

Tarot, 33, 120, 315
Temple, Robert, 16, 26
Temple, 35, 39–42, 47, 53, 56, 70–71, 73–74,
84, 89, 91, 93, 97–98, 126, 132, 151–152,
161, 165, 269, 292, 313
Ten Celestial Stems, The, 74
Thelema, 29, 32–33, 95
Thunder, 48, 57, 59–61, 75, 107, 117,
205–206, 215, 221, 223, 227, 237,
241–242, 275–276, 281, 283, 297, 324
Tortoise-shell, 16–17, 176, 186, 238, 296
Trigrams, 15, 17–18, 26, 41, 56, 71, 109–111,
132, 151–152, 155–156, 160, 163,
165–167, 173, 179, 182–183, 185, 187,
189, 192–193, 195, 197, 199, 201, 203,
206–207, 210–211, 213, 215, 218, 220,
222, 224, 226–227, 229, 235, 237, 239,
241, 243, 245, 248, 250–251, 253,
256–257, 259, 262–263, 265, 267,
270–273, 279, 281, 283, 286, 291, 293,
296, 298, 300–301, 305, 322
True Will, 32, 176, 223
Ts'ai Shen, 124, 202, 244, 258, 284, 327
Tsi-ku, 133–135, 178, 188, 208, 214, 254,
260, 266, 280, 286, 288, 292, 327
Tsuki-yumi, 7
Tumo, 113

V

Vampire, 67, 232, 268
Void, The, 27, 59, 167
Voodoo, 60, 136, 153

W

Water, 9–10, 16, 21, 31, 50, 57, 62, 74, 78–79,
110, 112, 120–121, 123, 143, 146, 159,
184, 187–189, 193, 204, 207, 210, 214,
231–232, 234–235, 249, 254, 258, 263,
269–270, 288–291, 293, 295, 308, 323–326
Wen, King, 17, 173

Wilhelm, Richard, xiii, 113
Wind/Wood, 74, 78, 119–120, 325
World Tree, 5, 214, 266, 272
Wu, 4–7, 13, 16, 22, 24–25, 27, 48, 57, 61, 74,
78, 110, 129, 196, 202, 205, 223, 232, 241,
246, 258, 262, 270, 282, 300, 328
Wu-wei, 27, 29–32, 70

Y

Yamabushi, 24–25
Yang, 3, 8, 11, 13, 16, 18, 24, 26–29, 40, 43,
48, 51, 70, 78, 103, 113, 135, 137,
140–141, 148, 167, 175, 179, 182–183,
185, 187, 189, 192–193, 195, 197, 199,
201–203, 206–207, 209, 211, 215, 218,
220–221, 223, 226–227, 229, 231–233,
235, 237, 239, 241, 243, 245, 247, 249,
251, 253, 256–257, 259, 261, 263, 267,
270–271, 273, 275, 277–279, 281, 283,
285–287, 290–291, 293, 295, 298–299,
301, 306, 310, 324, 327–328
Yarrow, 16, 103, 188, 208, 260, 272, 288
Yin Fu Ching, 121
Yin, 3, 8–9, 11, 13, 16, 18, 24, 26–29, 40, 43,
48, 51, 66–67, 78, 103, 113, 130, 133, 135,
140, 142, 147–148, 167, 177–179,
182–183, 185–190, 192–204, 206–207,
209, 211–215, 218, 220–222, 224,
226–227, 229–231, 233, 235–237, 239,
243, 245, 247, 249, 251–254, 256–263,
265–267, 270–274, 277, 279–281,
283–288, 290–293, 295, 298–299, 301,
323–324, 327
Yoga, 15, 84, 112, 150
Yu, 13, 186, 188, 199, 201–202, 204–205,
221, 224, 242, 248, 292, 309, 316, 323,
328

Z

Zodiac, 56, 120, 294

*Llewellyn publishes hundreds of books
on your favorite subjects.*

LOOK FOR THE CRESCENT MOON

to find the one you've been searching for!

To find the book you've been searching for, just call or write for a FREE copy of our full-color catalog, *New Worlds of Mind & Spirit. New Worlds* is brimming with books and other resources to help you develop your magical and spiritual potential to the fullest! Explore over 80 exciting pages that include:

- Exclusive interviews, articles and "how-tos" by Llewellyn's expert authors

- Features on classic Llewellyn books

- Tasty previews of Llewellyn's latest books on astrology, Tarot, Wicca, shamanism, magick, the paranormal, spirituality, mythology, alternative health and healing, and more

- Monthly horoscopes by Gloria Star

- Plus special offers available only to *New Worlds* readers

To get your free *New Worlds* catalog, call 1-800-THE MOON

or send your name and address to

Llewellyn, P.O. Box 64383, St. Paul, MN 55164–0383

Many bookstores carry New Worlds— ask for it! Visit our web site at www.llewellyn.com.